Measuring Efficiency in Health Care

With the health care sector accounting for a sizeable proportion of national expenditures, the pursuit of efficiency has become a central objective of policy makers within most health systems. However, the analysis and measurement of efficiency is a complex undertaking, not least because of the multiple objectives of health care organisations and the many gaps in information systems. In response to this complexity, research in organisational efficiency analysis has flourished. This book examines some of the most important techniques currently available to measure the efficiency of systems and organisations, including data envelopment analysis and stochastic frontier analysis, and also presents some promising new methodological approaches. Such techniques offer the prospect of many new and fruitful insights into health care performance. Nevertheless, they also pose many practical and methodological challenges. This is a timely critical assessment of the strengths and limitations of efficiency analysis applied to health and health care.

ROWENA JACOBS is a Research Fellow at the Centre for Health Economics, University of York.

PETER C. SMITH is Professor of Economics at the University of York.

ANDREW STREET is Senior Research Fellow at the Centre for Health Economics, University of York.

Measuring Efficiency in Health Care

Analytic Techniques and Health Policy

ROWENA JACOBS, PETER C. SMITH AND
ANDREW STREET

CAMBRIDGE
UNIVERSITY PRESS

CAMBRIDGE UNIVERSITY PRESS
Cambridge, New York, Melbourne, Madrid, Cape Town, Singapore, São Paulo

Cambridge University Press
The Edinburgh Building, Cambridge CB2 2RU, UK

Published in the United States of America by Cambridge University Press, New York

www.cambridge.org
Information on this title: www.cambridge.org/9780521851442

First published 2006

Printed in the United Kingdom at the University Press, Cambridge

A catalogue record for this publication is available from the British Library

ISBN-13 978-0-521-85144-2 hardback
ISBN-10 0-521-85144-0 hardback

Contents

Figures

Tables

Preface

In response to the sizeable proportion of national income devoted to the health care sector, policy makers in most high-income countries have become increasingly concerned with improving the efficiency of the health care sector. Meanwhile, econometricians, statisticians and management scientists have been developing increasingly sophisticated tools that seek to measure organisational efficiency. The question therefore arises: do these techniques offer policy makers useful tools with which to assess and regulate health care performance?

In collaboration with colleagues at the Centre for Health Economics and elsewhere, we have been involved in many studies seeking to address that question, and this book summarises our experience to date. As the reader will see, our findings are equivocal. We find much of value in the techniques of efficiency analysis, not least their rigour and the insights they give into complex data sets. These virtues deserve to be acknowledged. However, we also identify some important intellectual weaknesses and practical difficulties associated with implementing the techniques in health care, and we view with concern the claims made for them by some of their more ardent advocates.

This book therefore seeks to offer a balanced critique of the current state of the art of efficiency analysis as applied to health care. The intention is to offer analysts and policy makers a coherent view of the strengths and limitations of the techniques, both from a technical and a policy perspective. We assume the reader is comfortable with rudimentary mathematical exposition, but otherwise assume no familiarity with the analytic material. The breadth of the intended readership has nevertheless presented us with some challenges in choosing the level of technical detail to include in the exposition, and the chapters emphasise the technical and policy issues to different extents.

Chapters 1 and 2 offer a general introduction to the context and principles underlying the development of efficiency analysis, and should be accessible to all our intended readership. The core of the technical exposition is contained in chapters 3 and 4 (stochastic frontier analysis (SFA)) and chapters 5 and 6 (data envelopment analysis (DEA)). They are intended to stand on their own if the reader is interested in only one of the analytic approaches.

Chapter 7 offers a less technical comparison of the two techniques, and chapter 8, an assessment of their major weaknesses from a policy perspective. In the light of some of the concerns we raise, we present some tentative proposals for complementary analytic approaches in chapter 9. Finally, chapter 10 summarises what we feel is the current 'state of the art', emphasising our concern that – notwithstanding the need for good quantitative evidence – effective regulation of health care will always require a balanced range of analytic approaches.

Acknowledgements

Much of the work undertaken by the authors for this book has been as part of collaborative efforts with other researchers. We should like to acknowledge, in particular, Katharina Hauck, Steve Martin and Nigel Rice for their contributions to joint work in chapter 9.

Our research as members of the Health Policy team in the Centre for Health Economics has greatly benefited from the involvement and support of many CHE colleagues and of the wider research community at the University of York. Aspects of the work have been presented at numerous workshops and international conferences and we thank participants for discussions which helped improve our presentational clarity. In particular, members of the York Seminars in Health Econometrics have always provided extremely valuable comments. The material also benefited from comments received at a teaching workshop held at the University of York.

We are grateful to Gillian Robinson for her extraordinary efforts in formatting, correcting and compiling the manuscript and getting it into its present form. Thanks are also due to Chris Harrison and Lynn Dunlop at Cambridge University Press for their help with all aspects of bringing this book to fruition.

The authors acknowledge funding from the English Department of Health Policy Research Programme and the Economic and Social Research Council (Grant R000271253). Any errors in the text are solely our responsibility.

Abbreviations

A&E	Accident and Emergency
AE	allocative efficiency
B&C	Battese and Coelli model
BCC	Banker, Charnes and Cooper model
COLS	corrected ordinary least squares
CRS	constant returns to scale
DEA	data envelopment analysis
DMU	decision-making unit
DRG	diagnosis-related group
EE	economic efficiency
EQ5D	EuroQol five-dimensional health survey instrument
FE	fixed-effects
GDP	gross domestic product
GLS	generalised least squares
HRG	healthcare resource group
ITU	intensive care unit
MFF	market forces factor
ML	multilevel
MLE	maximum likelihood estimation
MVML	multivariate multilevel
NHS	National Health Service
NIRS	non-increasing returns to scale
OECD	Organisation for Economic Co-operation and Development
OFWAT	Office of Water Services
OLS	ordinary least squares
P&L	Pitt and Lee RE model
RE	random-effects
S&S	Schmidt and Sickles FE model
SE	scale efficiency
SF	stochastic frontier
SF36	Short Form 36 health survey instrument

SFA	stochastic frontier analysis
SUR	seemingly unrelated regression
T&O	Trauma and Orthopaedics
TE	technical efficiency
TFP	total factor productivity
UK	United Kingdom
VRS	variable returns to scale
WHO	World Health Organization

1 | Efficiency in health care

1.1 Introduction

T H E pursuit of efficiency has become a central objective of policy makers within most health systems. The reasons are manifest. In developed countries, expenditure on health care amounts to a sizeable proportion of gross domestic product. Policy makers need to be assured that such expenditure is in line with citizens' preferences, particularly when many sources of finance, such as tax revenues, are under acute pressure. On the supply side, health technologies are changing rapidly, and the pressures to introduce new technologies are often irresistible, even when there is uncertainty about cost-effectiveness. On the demand side, aging populations pose challenges for the design of health systems, and expectations are becoming ever more challenging. Finally, the revolution in information systems has made it feasible to measure aspects of system behaviour – most notably clinical activity – that until recently defied meaningful quantification.

The international concern was crystallised in the *World Health Report 2000* produced by the World Health Organization, which was devoted to the determinants and measurement of health system efficiency (World Health Organization 2000). The report stimulated a wide-ranging international debate, and a great deal of controversy (Williams 2001; Anand *et al.* 2002). However, its enduring legacy may be that it has helped policy makers to focus on the objectives of their health systems, on how achievement might be measured, and on whether resources are being deployed efficiently. A subsequent international conference organised by the Organization for Economic Co-operation and Development has confirmed the universal policy concern with performance measurement issues in health care (Smith 2002).

The analysis and measurement of efficiency is a complex undertaking, especially when there exist conceptual challenges, multiple objectives and great scope for measurement error. To address this complexity there has developed a flourishing research discipline of organisational efficiency analysis. Following pioneering studies by Farrell (1957), statisticians, econometricians and management scientists have developed tools to a high level of analytic sophistication that seek to measure the productive efficiency of organisations and systems. This book examines some of the most important techniques currently available to measure the efficiency of systems and organisations. It seeks to offer a critical assessment of the strengths and limitations of such tools applied to health and health care.

Throughout much of the book we take the view that health care objectives are known and agreed, and much of the discussion also assumes that the relative value placed on each objective is known. In practice, objectives and priorities are highly contested, and often not stated explicitly. A central purpose of this book is to examine how efficiency might be measured in the knowledge of objectives, but we also discuss the implications for efficiency analysis of failing to address priority setting explicitly.

Notwithstanding the apparent simplicity of the concept, there is a great deal of confusion in both popular and professional discussion about what is meant by efficiency in health care. In this opening chapter we first discuss the reasons for wishing to measure efficiency, and then define the concepts of organisational efficiency deployed in this book. Subsequently, we give a short summary of experience to date in measuring efficiency in the health sector. The chapter ends with an outline of the remainder of the book.

1.2 The demand for efficiency analysis in health care

The international explosion of interest in measuring the inputs, activities and outcomes of health systems can be attributed to heightened concerns with the costs of health care, increased demands for public accountability and improved capabilities for measuring performance (Smith 2002). Broadly speaking, the policy maker's notion of efficiency can be thought of as the extent to which objectives are achieved in relation to the resources consumed. There might also be some consideration of external circumstances that affect the ability of the system to achieve its objectives. This beguilingly simple notion of efficiency is analogous to the economist's concept of cost-effectiveness, or the accountant's concept of value for money. The potential customers for measures of efficiency include governments, regulators, health care purchasers, health care providers and the general public.

Governments clearly have an interest in assessing the efficiency of their health institutions. In all developed countries, public finance of one sort or another is the single most important source of health system funding, so national and local governments have a natural requirement to ensure that finance is deployed effectively. It is therefore not surprising to find that methodologies that offer insights into efficiency have attracted the interest of policy makers. Moreover, in most industrialised countries, a large element of the health care sector is provided by non-market organisations. Given the complexity of the functions undertaken by such institutions, and in the absence of the usual market signals, there is a clear need for instruments that offer insights into performance. The search for such technologies has been intensified by the almost universal concern with escalating health care costs and increased public pressure to ensure that expenditure on health systems is used effectively.

Given the absence of a competitive market in health care, all health systems require a regulator of some sort. A regulator is most obviously required when a significant proportion of health care is provided by the for-profit sector. However, the regulatory function might be incorporated implicitly into government surveillance of the health system if public provision predominates. As well as having an obvious role in promoting public safety, effective regulation requires the development of measures of comparative performance in order to set a level playing field for providers, a task to which efficiency models are in principle well-suited. Such interest is of course not limited to the health sector. For example, the UK water industry regulator (OFWAT) makes extensive use of efficiency analysis in determining its regulatory regime for water companies (Office of Water Services 1999).

Health care purchasers have a serious information difficulty when negotiating contracts with providers. In the absence of any meaningful market, they often find it difficult to judge whether providers are offering good value for money. Even in a competitive environment, it may be difficult for purchasers to discriminate between competing providers. Efficiency analysis can therefore help purchasers to understand better the performance of their local providers relative to best practice, and introduces an element of 'yardstick competition' into the purchasing function (Schleifer 1985). Likewise, even in non-competitive health care systems, providers have a natural interest in seeking out best practice and identifying scope for improvement.

Finally, there are increasing demands for offering the general public reliable information about the performance of its national and local health systems, and of individual providers (Atkinson 2005). Whilst the evidence hitherto suggests that it is difficult to stimulate public interest in this domain – and we are not aware of any major initiatives involving efficiency analysis – there are strong accountability arguments for seeking to place high-quality information in the public domain in order to enhance debates about value for money.

1.3 Organisational efficiency

The focus of efficiency analysis is as an organisational locus of production, often referred to as a decision-making unit (DMU). In health care, examples of DMUs include entire health systems, purchasing organisations, hospitals, physician practices and individual physicians. The DMUs consume various costly inputs (labour, capital etc.) and produce valued outputs. Efficiency analysis is centrally concerned with measuring the competence with which inputs are converted into valued outputs. In general, it treats the organisation as a black box, and does not seek to explain *why* it exhibits a particular level of efficiency (Fried, Lovell and Schmidt 1993).

The terms 'productivity' and 'efficiency' are often used interchangeably, which is unfortunate since they are not precisely the same thing. Productivity is the ratio of some (or all) valued outputs that an organisation produces to some (or all) inputs used in the production process. Thus the concept of productivity may embrace but is not confined to the notion of efficiency that is the topic of this book.

A starting point for examining the basic notion of efficiency is shown in Figure 1.1, which illustrates the case of just one input and one output. The line OC indicates the simplest of all technologies: no fixed costs and constant returns to scale. A technically efficient organisation would then produce somewhere on this line, which can be thought of as the production possibility frontier. Any element of inefficiency would result in an observation lying strictly below the line OC. For an inefficient organisation located at P_0, the ratio $X_0 P_0 / X_0 P_0^*$ offers an indication of how far short of the production frontier it is falling, and therefore a measure of its efficiency level.

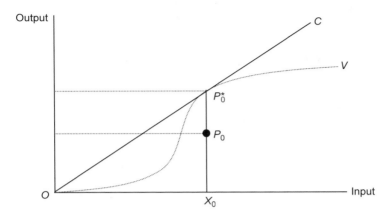

Figure 1.1. Efficiency measurement under constant returns to scale.

Many other technologies are possible. For example, the curve OV indicates a frontier with variable returns to scale. Up to the point P_0^*, the ratio of output to input decreases (increasing returns to scale), but thereafter it increases (decreasing returns to scale).

The notion of a production frontier can be extended to multiple outputs and a single input (say, costs). Figure 1.2 illustrates the case with two outputs. For the given technology, the isocost curve CC gives the feasible combination of outputs that can be secured for a given input. At a higher level of costs the isocost curve moves out to $C'C'$. These curves indicate the shape of the production possibility frontiers at given levels of input. An inefficient DMU lies inside this frontier. We define the marginal rate of transformation to be the sacrifice of output 2 required to produce a unit of output 1, indicated at any particular point on CC by the slope of the curve $-(P_2/P_1)$. It is usually assumed that – as in this figure – for a given level of input this becomes steeper as the volume of output 1 produced increases.

Likewise, in input space, we examine the case of two inputs and one output, as in Figure 1.3. The isoquant QQ indicates the feasible mix of inputs that can secure a given level of output, with inefficient DMUs lying beyond this curve.

Extending the analysis to the general case of multiple inputs and multiple outputs, we define the overall efficiency eff_0 of organisation 0 to be the ratio of a weighted sum of outputs to a weighted sum of inputs. Mathematically, if organisation 0 consumes a vector of

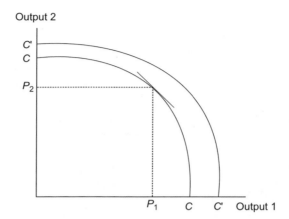

Figure 1.2. The case of two outputs.

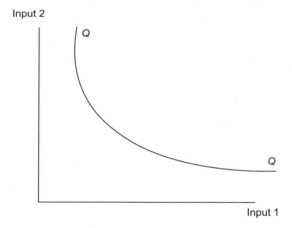

Figure 1.3. The case of two inputs.

M inputs $\mathbf{X}_0$ and produces a vector of S outputs $\mathbf{Y}_0$, its overall efficiency is measured by applying weight vectors $\mathbf{U}$ and $\mathbf{V}$ to yield:

$$eff_0 = \frac{\sum\limits_{s=1}^{S} U_s Y_{s0}}{\sum\limits_{m=1}^{M} V_m X_{m0}} \tag{1.1}$$

where:

> Y_{s0} is the amount of the sth output produced by organisation 0;
> U_s is the weight given to the sth output;
> X_{m0} is the amount of the mth input consumed by organisation 0;
> V_m is the weight given to the mth input.

The weights **U** and **V** indicate the relative importance of an additional unit of output or input. On the input side, the weights **V** might reflect the relative market prices of different inputs. It is often the case – with the notable exception of capital inputs – that these can be measured with some accuracy. Then, if the actual input costs incurred by organisation 0 are C_0, the ratio:

$$Ceff_0 = \frac{\sum_{m=1}^{M} V_m X_{m0}}{C_0} \tag{1.2}$$

indicates the extent to which the organisation is purchasing its chosen mix of inputs efficiently (that is, the extent to which it is purchasing its chosen inputs at lowest possible prices).

However, the organisation may not be using the correct mix of inputs. This can be illustrated using a simple two-input model. For some known production process, the isoquant QQ in Figure 1.4 shows the use of minimum inputs required to produce a unit of a single output. The points P_1 and P_2 lie on the isoquant and therefore – given the chosen mix of inputs – cannot produce more outputs.

When the unit costs of inputs are known, it is possible to examine the input price (or allocative) efficiency of the two units. Suppose the market prices are V_1^* and V_2^*. Then the cost-minimising point on the isoquant occurs where the slope is $-V_1^*/V_2^*$ (shown by the straight line BB). In Figure 1.4 this is the point P_1, which is input-price efficient. However, the point P_2 is not efficient with respect to prices, as a reduction in costs of $P_2 P_2^*$ is possible. The price efficiency of P_2 is therefore given by the ratio OP_2^*/OP_2.

Analogous arguments can be deployed to examine the allocative efficiency of organisations in output space. Figure 1.5 illustrates the case where a single input is used to produce two outputs. If the relative values U_1 and U_2 of the outputs are known, and the production possibilities are given by the curve CC, then organisation P_1 is producing

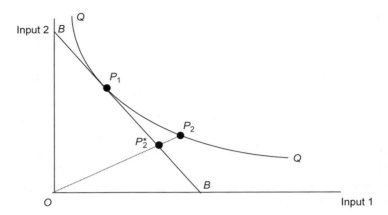

Figure 1.4. Allocative efficiency with two inputs.

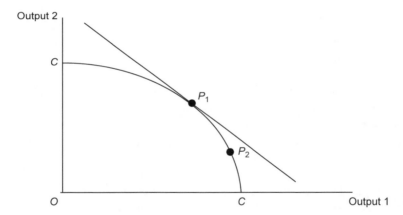

Figure 1.5. Allocative efficiency with two outputs.

at its allocatively efficient point while organisation P_2 exhibits some allocative inefficiency.

Although organisations may exhibit allocative inefficiency in purchasing the wrong mix of inputs or producing the wrong mix of outputs, we have so far explored only those organisations that lie on the frontier of technical production possibilities. However, it is likely that, particularly in a non-market environment, many organisations are not operating on the frontier. That is, they also exhibit an element

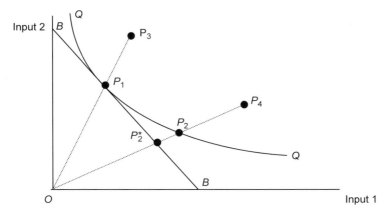

Figure 1.6. Technical and allocative inefficiency.

of technical inefficiency (also referred to as managerial inefficiency or X-inefficiency).

This is illustrated in Figure 1.6 by the points P_3 and P_4. Organisation P_3 purchases the correct mix of inputs, but lies inside the isoquant QQ. It therefore exhibits a degree of technical inefficiency, as indicated by the ratio OP_1/OP_3. Organisation P_4 both purchases an incorrect mix of inputs and lies inside the isoquant QQ. Its technical inefficiency is indicated by the ratio OP_2/OP_4. Thus its overall level of inefficiency OP_2^*/OP_4 can be thought of as the product of two components: technical inefficiency OP_2/OP_4 and allocative inefficiency OP_2^*/OP_2.

We have so far assumed constant returns to scale. That is, the production process is such that the optimal mix of inputs and outputs is independent of the scale of operation. In practice there exist important economies and diseconomies of scale in most production processes, so an important influence on *eff*$_0$ (from equation 1.1) may be the chosen scale of operation. This is illustrated in Figure 1.7 for the case of one input and one output. The production frontier is illustrated by the curve OV, which suggests regions of increasing and decreasing returns to scale. The optimal scale of production is at the point P^* where the ratio of output to input is maximised. Although lying on the frontier, the points P_1 and P_2 secure lower ratios because they are operating below and above (respectively) the scale-efficient point of production. They therefore exhibit levels of scale inefficiency given by:

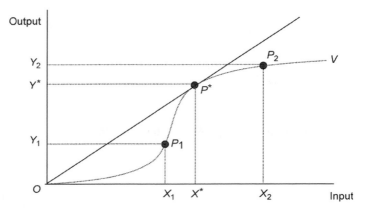

Figure 1.7. Economies of scale.

$$Seff_1 = \frac{OY_1/OX_1}{OY^*/OX^*} \text{ and } Seff_2 = \frac{OY_2/OX_2}{OY^*/OX^*} \tag{1.3}$$

1.4 Analytic efficiency measurement techniques

The fundamental building block of the economic analysis of organisational efficiency is the *cost function* (or its counterpart, the *production
function*). For the purposes of this exposition, we focus on the cost
function. This is probably more germane to the health care setting we
seek to analyse, in which it is usual to find multiple outputs quantified
on different measurement scales. The cost function simplifies the input
side of the production process by deploying a single measure of the
inputs used, rather than a vector. It indicates the minimum cost that an
organisation can incur in seeking to produce a set of valued outputs.
Using the notation introduced above, a cost function can be written in
general terms as $C_0^* = f(Y_0)$. Analogously, the production function
models the maximum (single) output an organisation could secure,
given its mix of inputs.

The cost function combines all inputs into a single metric (costs),
and does not model the mix of inputs employed, or their prices. In
practice, the costs incurred by an organisation might be higher than
those implied by the cost function for three reasons. First, it may
purchase inputs at higher than market prices (cost inefficiency). Second, given prevailing prices, it may employ an inefficient mix of inputs

(allocative inefficiency). And third, it may not secure the maximum output attainable given its inputs (technical inefficiency). However, if no measures of physical inputs are available, and only aggregate measures of costs are available, it is impossible to distinguish among these causes of deviation from the cost function. Therefore, notwithstanding its practical usefulness, a cost function offers little help with detailed understanding of the input side of efficiency.

Inefficiency can be defined as the extent to which an organisation's costs exceed those predicted by the cost function (or the extent to which its output falls short of that predicted by the production function). Inefficiency is inherently unobservable. This means that estimates of efficiency have to be derived indirectly after taking account of observable phenomena. This, very broadly, involves the following process:

1. Observable phenomena, such as outputs and inputs (costs), are measured.
2. Some form of relationship between these phenomena is specified. If a parametric method is used and differences in cost are the focus of the exercise, a cost function is estimated. If a non-parametric method is used, an efficiency frontier is derived.
3. Efficient behaviour is then predicted on the basis of the definition of technical efficiency.
4. The difference between each DMU's observed data and the optimum achievable as predicted by the cost function or frontier is then calculated.
5. The difference (or some portion of it) is defined as inefficiency.

A number of analytic techniques have been developed to estimate the form of cost and production frontiers and the associated inefficiency of individual organisations (Coelli, Rao and Battese 1998). These are covered in the subsequent chapters of this book, and can be divided into two broad categories: parametric methods, which use econometric techniques to estimate the parameters of a specific functional form of cost or production function, and non-parametric methods, which place no conditions on the functional form, and use observed data to infer the shape of the frontier.

The pre-eminent form of parametric method now in use is stochastic frontier analysis (SFA). This is similar to conventional regression analysis, but decomposes the unexplained error in the estimated function

into two components: inefficiency (which, in the case of a cost function, will always be positive), and the more conventional two-sided
random error. Cost functions are used extensively in parametric analysis of efficiency because the alternative strategy – estimating models
with both multiple inputs and multiple outputs – is methodologically
challenging, and demanding in terms of data requirements. In contrast,
univariate cost functions (and production functions) can be readily
estimated using standard econometric methods, or straightforward
variants. Parametric methods are introduced in chapter 3.

Most non-parametric methods take the form of data envelopment analysis (DEA) and its many variants. These were stimulated by
the pioneering work of Farrell (1957), later generalised by Charnes,
Cooper and Rhodes (1978). DEA uses linear programming methods
to infer a piecewise linear production possibility frontier, in effect
seeking out those efficient observations that dominate (or 'envelop')
the others. In contrast to parametric methods, DEA can handle multiple inputs and outputs without difficulty. DEA is introduced in
chapter 5.

The distinctive focus of modern efficiency analysis is to seek – in
addition to estimating the frontier – to provide an estimate of how far
each observation falls short of the estimated frontier. This emphasis
on the residual for each observation marks an unusual departure from
conventional statistical and econometric analyses, which are in the
main preoccupied with estimated coefficients (that is, relationships
displayed by the population of observations as a whole) rather than
individual observations. This novel focus gives rise to important
methodological complications, to which we return in chapter 8.

1.5 Experience with efficiency analysis in health care

All of the efficiency measurement tools we use in this book reflect the
efficiency framework sketched above. The differences between the
techniques arise from various assumptions about what lies within
the control of the organisations under scrutiny, and the constraints
imposed by data availability. The central technical requirements of
efficiency analysis are that there exist an adequate number of comparable units of observation, and that the salient dimensions of performance (inputs, outputs and environmental circumstances) are
satisfactorily measured.

Given these requirements, health care offers, in many respects, good opportunities for analysis. Entities such as insurers, purchasers, hospitals, clinics, diagnostic laboratories and general practices are present in large numbers in most health systems, and increasingly comprehensive performance data are available. Therefore – from a technical perspective – the feasibility of developing a wide range of efficiency models is beyond question. Furthermore, governments, regulators, purchasers and the public are asking searching questions about the performance of health care entities. Therefore, both the supply of and demand for efficiency analysis is increasing. However, compared with many other sectors of the economy, such as banks or schools, the development of efficiency measures in health and health care also poses enormous challenges, brought about by the complexity of the production process, the multiplicity of outputs produced, the strong influence of the organisational environment on performance, and the frequent absence of relevant or reliable data.

Hollingsworth describes progress reported in the public literature up to 2002 (Hollingsworth 2003). He examines published studies of cost and production functions in health and health care where examination of efficiency variation is a central concern, and identifies 189 relevant studies. About 50 per cent are in the hospital sector, reflecting its central policy importance and the ready availability of data. There are also significant numbers of studies of physicians, pharmacies, primary care organisations, nursing homes and purchasers. The great majority of studies have used DEA and its variants, probably reflecting its ease of use and flexibility. The use of SFA has become more widespread recently, but it is more demanding in terms of modelling and interpretive skills.

Early studies were content with merely estimating cost or production functions and inferring the distribution of efficiency variations from a cross-sectional sample. Recently, more creative uses of efficiency analysis have been reported, addressing issues such as productivity changes over time, and the effect of ownership and other institutional arrangements on efficiency.

1.6 This book

The purpose of this book is to describe economic and econometric approaches to modelling efficiency in the health sector, and to assess the usefulness of analytic techniques for policy purposes. The text draws on the authors' experience with case studies from the UK, and work for organisations such as the World Health Organization and the OECD. The intention is to cover the material for an informed but not necessarily specialist reader.

Chapter 2 covers principles of modelling, the purpose being to provide a framework to aid understanding of the production process employed by health care organisations. This entails consideration of the outputs from, and inputs to, the production process. Outputs can be defined as actions that seek to promote health system outcomes. Traditionally health outcomes are thought of in terms of increases in the length and quality of life. However, consideration must be given to non-health outcomes of health systems, such as their 'responsiveness', a term that embraces concepts such as autonomy, privacy, prompt attention, dignity and choice.

The input side is in some respects more straightforward. Although some studies require detailed examination of physical inputs, it is often enough to seek out costs as a proxy for inputs. Yet even here difficulties arise. The complexity of health care often necessitates detailed accounting rules to assign costs to particular activities or functions. Furthermore, one of the fundamental difficulties encountered in most efficiency analyses in the health sector is the need to adjust for uncontrollable external influences on performance. Such 'risk adjustment' is often essential, but methodologically extremely challenging.

Chapter 3 comprises a detailed treatment of stochastic frontier analysis of cross-sectional data. The chapter describes the key technical choices that have to be made when developing a stochastic frontier model. A case study from the English hospital sector is described. Chapter 4 describes how the stochastic frontier approach has been extended to exploit panels of data, where each organisation is observed more than once. Panel data give rise to exciting new possibilities in the examination of efficiency, but also introduce methodological challenges. Various stochastic frontier models have been developed for analysing panel data, and these are described and applied to a case study.

Chapters 5 and 6 consider data envelopment analysis (DEA), which applies non-parametric methods to efficiency analysis. Chapter 5 describes and illustrates the technique for cross-sectional data. Chapter 6 considers DEA when panel data are available. Chapter 7 concludes the expository material with a comparison of SFA and DEA.

Despite considerable recent advances in these analytical techniques, there remain a number of unresolved methodological challenges for efficiency analysis. These are discussed in chapter 8. Chapter 9 examines the potential for using other approaches to measuring organisational performance in a health setting, including the use of seemingly unrelated regression to analyse multiple objectives, and multilevel modelling techniques to exploit the hierarchical structure of many health care data. Chapter 10 concludes with some of the key challenges and messages for researchers, policy makers and regulators.

2 | *The components of an efficiency model*

2.1 Introduction

T HERE are numerous conceptual and practical issues to be clarified when seeking to undertake an empirical analysis of efficiency in health care. In this chapter we shall set aside philosophical issues concerning what is meant by 'efficiency', and conform to the concept discussed in chapter 1. That is, an organisation's efficiency is considered to be the ratio of the value of outputs it produces to the value of inputs it consumes. Figure 2.1 summarises the principles underlying this viewpoint. The organisation consumes a series of M physical resources, referred to as inputs, and valued in total as X by society. Some transformation process takes place, the details of which do not immediately concern us. This leads to the production of S outputs, which society values in aggregate as Y. Our summary measure of 'efficiency' is the ratio of Y to X – what might be more accurately referred to as cost-effectiveness.

Models of health care efficiency almost always entail consideration of multiple outputs. Central to the calculation of Y is therefore the relative weight U_s attached to each output s. These weights reflect the relative importance attached to an additional unit of production of each output, and allow us to calculate for organisation 0 the valuation of outputs $Y = \sum_{s=1}^{S} U_s Y_{s0}$ as discussed in chapter 1. In the same way, when there are multiple inputs, the relative weight V_m attached to input m allows us to calculate the valuation of inputs $X = \sum_{m=1}^{M} V_m X_{m0}$. If we have secure information on the magnitudes of U and V we can readily compute the efficiency as the ratio Y/X. In particular, in competitive markets, both U and V might be readily observed as prices. In such circumstances there may be no need to use the analytic techniques described in this book. Instead, comparative efficiency can be readily computed using the exogenously observed weights. However, in the health domain it is rarely the case that such

Figure 2.1. The naïve model of organisational performance.

prices are observed, particularly on the output side. It is in such circumstances that the analytic techniques can be deployed in order to furnish evidence on the weights U and V.

Although the framework is beguilingly simple, numerous complex issues are raised when seeking to use it to develop operational models of organisational efficiency in health care. The complexity involved in developing an operational framework reflects the complexity of the production process. The production of the majority of health care outputs rarely conforms to a production-line type technology, where a set of clearly identifiable inputs are used to produce a standard type of output. Rather than a production line, most health care is tailor-made to the specific needs of the individual recipient (Harris 1977). This means that the production process is much less clearly defined and there is the potential for considerable heterogeneity in what outputs are produced and how this is done. Contributions to the care process are often made by multiple agents or organisations, a 'package' of care may be delivered over multiple time periods and in different settings, and the responsibilities for delivery may vary from place to place and over time.

The purpose of this chapter is therefore to discuss the conceptual and practical issues that must be resolved in seeking to develop a satisfactory empirical model of efficiency in the health care sector. We address these model-building principles by considering five issues:

- What is the appropriate unit of analysis?
- What are the outputs of health care?
- What value should be attached to these outputs?
- What inputs are used in the production of these outputs and how should these be valued?
- What environmental constraints are faced?

We then discuss practical facets of undertaking efficiency analysis, which is often constrained by the scope and nature of data availability.

2.2 Unit of analysis

It is important that the boundaries of any efficiency analysis should be clearly defined. A fundamental question to ask is: what is the unit of organisation in which we are interested? Any efficiency analysis should have a clear idea of the entity it is examining, but should also recognise that its achievements are likely to be influenced by the actions of other organisations or by factors beyond its immediate control. This is especially likely when multiple agencies or organisations are involved in joint production. Three criteria should guide the choice of units.

1. The unit of analysis should capture the entire production process of interest. This may entail defining artificial units of analysis if there is variation among organisations in how the production process is organised.

2. They should be 'decision-making units' (DMUs). In a strict sense this requires that their function is to convert inputs into outputs, and that the DMUs have discretion about the technological process by which this conversion takes place. But a weaker definition of DMUs requires only that they play an organising function, establishing the rules and conditions to which producers have to adhere. This definition would allow government bodies to be considered as DMUs.

3. The units comprising the analytical sample should be comparable, particularly in the sense that they are seeking to produce the same set of outputs.

Making these criteria operational is not always straightforward, and the first and second, in particular, may conflict. This conflict is most likely where the production process is characterised by varying degrees of vertical integration. The pioneering work by Coase and Williamson identified the desire to minimise transaction costs as a factor in determining what range of the production process might be under the control of a single organisation (Coase 1937; Williamson 1973). Under some circumstances, organisations might 'vertically integrate' and assume control of the entire process. Under others, organisations may prefer to 'buy in' inputs from organisations further down the production process or 'sell on' to those further up the chain. If, as Coase and Williamson argue, transaction costs explain the desirability of vertical integration, this should be recognised in efficiency analysis.

Ensuring that the analytical DMU fully encompasses jointness in production is particularly important in contexts where there is variation in how the relative contributions to joint production are defined. This variation may be a major driver of the relative efficiency of DMUs. For example, suppose we are interested in analysing the efficiency of care delivered to patients who suffer head injury. The division of care between the trauma and orthopaedics (T&O) department and the intensive care unit (ITU) may differ substantially between one place and the next, with some T&O departments having invested more in step-down high-dependency beds in order to relieve pressure on the ITU. If the unit of analysis is confined to the T&O department and the contribution of the ITU is ignored, those T&O departments that have made greater investments in high-dependency beds will appear relatively inefficient, despite the joint production process actually being more effective.

This raises the question of where the boundaries of the production process should be drawn. At one extreme, the decision-making unit could be thought of as the entire health system, defined by the World Health Organization as 'all the activities whose primary purpose is to promote, restore or maintain health' (World Health Organization 2000). This is perhaps the loosest definition of a DMU that it is possible to adopt, but is one that was employed by the WHO in its analysis of the relative performance of national health systems.

Yet while in principle it may often be desirable to adopt such a 'whole-system' approach, in practice it is usually infeasible and often unhelpful because of the difficulties of defining the system, identifying its primary decision-makers and specifying its inputs. It is therefore usual to circumscribe the analysis to more clearly defined organisations within the health system.

At the opposite extreme to a whole-system approach, interest may be on the actions of individuals or groups of individuals working together within larger organisations. For example, we might be interested in the efficiency of individual general practitioners, or of the general practice of which they are a part, or of trauma and orthopaedics specialities in hospitals. For several reasons, taking the individual or team as the unit of analysis has much to recommend it in comparison with larger organisational aggregations:

- their activities and outputs are likely to be of a more limited range, so comparability among units is more easily secured;
- dedicated inputs should be identifiable more accurately;
- the likelihood of assigning personal responsibility for performance is higher, leading to greater promise that the analysis will secure favourable change in behaviour.

But there are drawbacks to the analysis of individuals or teams within organisations or even of organisations in isolation from the other organisations with which they interact. Many outputs are produced by different teams working together. For example, staff from a variety of hospital specialities contribute to providing care to each patient admitted to hospital. Or the functioning of mental health hospitals might be inherently linked to the actions of local social care agencies. In such circumstances assessing the relative contribution of each team or organisation is not straightforward.

Again, teams within organisations usually draw on joint resources. For instance, some staff may work in more than one team, such as when a urologist works partly in general surgery. It may be difficult to determine accurately what proportion of this shared input is associated with each team.

Thus, larger aggregations of individuals or teams may be appropriate for analytical purposes when outputs are the result of joint production decisions, even if this means that the analytical DMU does not correspond precisely to a single organisational entity.

The final crucial criterion to guide the choice of analytical unit is that the units being compared are seeking to deliver the same set of health care outputs. As will be seen through the course of the book, strict comparability is difficult to achieve: almost every organisation can claim unique features that mark it as different. Yet if all such claims were accepted, there would be no legitimate basis for comparing organisations at all. So evaluating the reasonableness of claims of 'non-comparability', and taking them properly into account, are among the most challenging political and technical tasks associated with efficiency measurement.

2.3 What are outputs in health care?

In competitive industries the physical output of the organisation is usually a traded product. Of course, even in a reasonably homogeneous market, such products (say, a refrigerator) can vary enormously on various dimensions of 'quality', such as reliability, looks and temperature range. The quality of the product is intrinsic to its social value, but that value can be readily inferred by observing the price people are prepared to pay. Usually, therefore, there is no need explicitly to consider the ultimate 'outcome' of the product, in terms of the value it bestows on the consumer.

In many parts of the economy, however, not only do prices not exist, but outputs are difficult to define. In particular this is true for many of the goods and services to which government spending is devoted (Atkinson 2005). Defining the outputs of the health care sector is particularly challenging. 'Health' is a complex concept for which there has been no readily available valuation, and there is no market for health in the conventional sense. In the context of efficiency analysis, two fundamental issues need to be considered. How should the outputs of the health care sector be defined? And what value should be attached to these outputs?

Defining outputs of the health sector is problematic because health care is rarely demanded for its own sake. Rather, demand derives from the belief that health care will make a positive contribution to health status. This suggests that health care outputs should properly be defined in terms of the health outcomes produced. However, rarely do organisations collect routine information about what health outcomes they produce. More commonly the analyst is forced to rely on comparing health care organisations in terms of the quantity and type of activities they undertake. The remainder of this section considers the issues and relative merits of using health outcomes and health care activities as ways of measuring what health care organisations produce.

2.3.1 Health outcomes

The output of health care can be considered in two broad categories:

- the additional health conferred on the patient; and
- broader patient satisfaction over and above that related to the health effect.

The 'outcomes' of health care can then be considered to be the quality-adjusted physical outputs.

The case in favour of defining output in terms of health outcomes is manifest. For most patients and carers, health gain is the central indicator of the success of an intervention. A focus on outcomes directs attention towards the patient (rather than the services provided by the organisation). Moreover, some widely accepted measures of health outcome (such as gains in quality-adjusted life years) are independent of the technologies used to deliver care, obviating the need for detailed scrutiny of the physical actions of the organisations.

In principle the measure of health outcome should indicate the 'value-added' to health as a result of contact with the health system. Such measures of added value are routinely deployed in other sectors, such as school education. A central measure of school performance is the contribution made to improving the educational attainment of pupils. One measure of educational attainment is the exam grades obtained. But exam grades are partly a function of the efforts of the school and partly a reflection of the inherent ability of the pupil, and there are great variations in the abilities of pupils taught by different schools. Schools therefore cannot be compared solely on the basis of crude exam results: a school that attracts pupils of high ability will report better exam grades than one that caters for pupils of lesser ability, even though both schools work equally hard and are equally well organised. To make an appropriate comparison, the ability of pupils must be separated from the school effect. This can be done by measuring pupil ability at entry to each school, and then comparing subsequent exam grades in relation to this baseline, yielding a measure of educational 'value-added' (Goldstein and Spiegelhalter 1996).

While the concept of value-added is relatively straightforward in the education sector, the construct has proved more challenging to make operational in the health sector, because of the much greater heterogeneity of service users and the intrinsic measurement difficulties. The fundamental difficulty is that it is rarely possible to observe a baseline, or counterfactual – the health status that would have been secured in the absence of an intervention. Although health status measurement is becoming increasingly routine in many health care settings, it tends merely to involve comparisons of health states before and after the intervention. Yet the with/without and before/after measures of the added value of treatment are unlikely to be equivalent. Most importantly for our purposes, reliance on before/after measures will tend to undervalue the contribution of organisations that focus primarily on interventions designed to slow deterioration in health status rather than on those designed to make people better.

To see why, consider two alternative baselines against which to compare post-intervention health status:

- The health status that the patient would have experienced had there been no intervention. Let h_j^0 be the health status if the individual had not been treated. Then the outcome is measured as $\Delta h_j'' = h_{jt} - h_j^0$.
- Pre-treatment health status. Let h_{jt-1} be the pre-treatment and h_{jt} the post-treatment health status so that the measured outcome is $\Delta h_j' = h_{jt} - h_{jt-1}$.

The choice of baseline will yield different estimates of the health effect of interventions.

To illustrate this, consider two interventions, a and b, with the same cost, suitable respectively for two individuals, A and B, who suffer different conditions but who, prior to the intervention, have similarly poor health status, $h_{jt-1} = 0.5$, where $j = a,b$.

For individual A, intervention a yields no change in health status at time t relative to $t-1$, hence $\Delta h_a' = 0$, as shown in Figure 2.2. For individual B, intervention b delivers an improvement in health status such that $h_{bt} = 0.7$, hence $\Delta h_b' = 0.2$. On this basis an organisation that treats proportionately more patients of type B will appear more efficient – producing more health outcome – than one that treats more of type A.

The true effect of the intervention is the change in health status with and without the intervention. This is not measured by the change in health status before and after treatment unless the individual's health without treatment would not have deteriorated (or improved). Suppose that the natural, untreated, course of disease for the conditions of individuals A and B differs. Untreated, the health status of individual B would not change from one period to the next, with $h_b^0 = 0.5$ shown by the horizontal dashed line in Figure 2.3. The net treatment effect, therefore, amounts to $\Delta h_b'' = 0.2$.

Individual A, in contrast, suffers a debilitating disease, likely to result in a major deterioration in health status by time t, equivalent to $h_a^0 = 0.2$ if untreated. The role of the intervention in this case is not to improve health status, but to stabilise the condition. If the value of interventions is assessed on the basis of this net treatment effect,

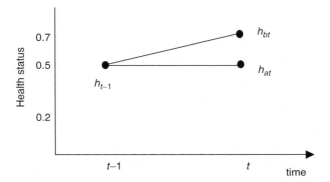

Figure 2.2. Change in health status: before and after intervention.

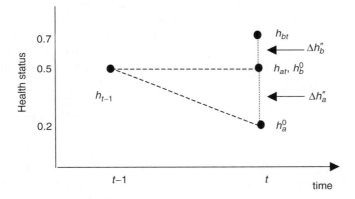

Figure 2.3. Change in health status: with and without intervention.

intervention a would be more highly valued with $\Delta h_a'' = 0.3$. Accordingly, organisations that treat more type A patients would appear more efficient.

The tension between before/after and with/without measurement is, to a great extent, unresolvable because without-treatment health profiles are rarely observable. The only practical option, then, is to rely on before/after measurement, but to recognise that this has the potential to introduce bias into the comparative analysis and, accordingly, to make a cautious interpretation of the results.

A number of well-established measurement instruments have been developed which could be used to collect before/after measures of treatment effects, such as the EQ5D and SF36 (EuroQol Group 1990; Ware and Sherbourne 1992). Although there remain many unresolved issues surrounding the precise specification and analysis of such instruments, their use should be considered whenever there are likely to be material differences in the clinical quality of different organisations. Moreover, where organisations treat a heterogeneous mix of patients, the use of a generic measure of health gain represents one way of adjusting for any differences in case mix between organisations.

Quite apart from health gain, patients in developed countries are becoming increasingly vocal in demanding that health care should be responsive to concerns over and above the health outcomes resulting from treatments. This concern with the 'patient experience' covers issues as diverse as promptness, autonomy, empowerment, privacy and choice, and should also be incorporated into any efficiency analysis, particularly when there are large variations in the responsiveness of organisations, such as in hospital waiting times in many publicly funded health systems.

However, it is unusual for efficiency studies to incorporate such information (Pedraja-Chaparro, Salinas-Jiménez and Smith 1999). An important exception was the World Health Organization's examination of the efficiency of national health systems (World Health Organization 2000). In the *World Health Report 2000*, the WHO developed the concept of the 'responsiveness' of the health system. This seeks to reflect the extent to which the health system succeeds in being user-oriented. However, although the *World Health Report 2000* contained a useful discussion of the concept of responsiveness, the WHO contribution was undermined by the weak measurement methods used. More recent work with the World Health Survey is seeking to address the issue of responsiveness more satisfactorily (Üstün *et al.* 2003).

Notwithstanding the complexity of the concept of responsiveness, many survey instruments are now being deployed routinely to measure the patient experience. These are often extensive in scope, and therefore difficult to incorporate directly into an operational efficiency analysis. However, they contain a great deal of information that could be used, providing that the mass of data contained in the surveys can be condensed satisfactorily to a small number of summary measures of responsiveness (Coulter and Magee 2003).

2.3.2 Health care activities

Although efficiency analysis should be based on the outcomes of care discussed above, analysts are often constrained in practice to examining efficiency on the basis of measures of activities, for example in the form of patients treated, operations undertaken or outpatients seen. Such measures are manifestly inadequate, as they fail to capture variations in the effectiveness (or quality) of the health care delivered. Yet, despite the growing move towards measuring the outcomes of care, there is often no alternative to using such crude measures of activity as proxies for health care outcomes. For example, some health outcomes may take years to be realised, and it is clearly impractical to wait for them to emerge before attempting to assess performance. Furthermore, collection of outcome data may impose impractically high costs on the health system. In such circumstances, it becomes necessary to rely on measures of the activities of care as proxies for outcome.

Measuring activities can also address a fundamental difficulty of outcome measurement – identifying how much of the variation in outcomes is directly attributable to the actions of the health care organisation. For example, mortality after a surgical procedure is likely to be influenced by numerous factors beyond the control of health care. In some circumstances such considerations can be accommodated by careful use of risk adjustment methods (see section 2.6). However, there is sometimes no analytically satisfactory way of adjusting for environmental influences on outcomes, in which case analysing instead the activities of care may offer a more meaningful insight into organisational performance.

Reliance on counts of activities may be unproblematic when there is good research evidence that the activities (such as an inpatient procedure) lead, on average, to health improvement. Measuring such activities will give a strong indication of expected health outcomes. However, it is important to note that, when using such measures as the basis for efficiency measurement, one is implicitly assuming that there is no difference between organisations in the effectiveness with which they implement the procedure. Where such differences are suspected, it becomes imperative to augment activity counts with measures of the quality of outcome. Ideally these would indicate health gain, but more readily measured proxies, such as mortality rates or readmission rates, are often used instead for such purposes.

Thus, although the use of measures of activity is often the only practical option available to the analyst, it is important to keep in mind the limitations it imposes. In particular, one should beware of two classes of misinterpretation that commonly result from the efficiency analysis because of lost outcome information. First, all else being equal, organisations that undertake more activities will be rated as more efficient. But some organisations may have developed care pathways and protocols that minimise the number of activities required to deliver care to a patient. This may eliminate unnecessary diagnostic tests, for example, and may be an efficient way of organising care. However, an activity-based efficiency analysis will penalise such organisations. Second, the effectiveness (or quality) of the health care delivered is not captured by a count of activities. For instance, an activity-based analysis will consider operating theatres that undertake the same number of operations to be equivalent, even if patients are more likely to suffer complications or die if treated in one theatre rather than the other.

The efficiency literature examined in this book makes little distinction between activities, outputs and outcomes, referring loosely to all as 'outputs'. In the context of health care this is unfortunate, as it suggests a lack of interest in seeking to move towards a concept of efficiency based on outcomes. However, in the interests of conciseness, and consistency with the literature, we shall refer throughout much of the book to activities, outputs and outcomes as 'outputs'.

2.4 Valuing health care outputs

Measuring the outputs produced by health care organisations would be difficult enough if those organisations were seeking to provide a single and relatively homogeneous product (such as a hip replacement operation). But health care organisations are immensely complex entities, undertaking numerous activities and therefore producing multiple outputs. A further difficulty therefore emerges: how are we to assess the relative value of different types of output (comparing, for example, hip replacements with pacemaker insertions)? The use of generic measures of health gain is one approach to addressing this problem, but as discussed above this is often infeasible.

What health care outputs are valued – and how much they are valued – are in the first instance personal judgements, and there is evidence to suggest that there is great variation among individual citizens as to what is valued in health care. Some focus principally on health gain, while others place great weight on aspects of responsiveness, such as being treated with dignity and respect, and being able to make informed choices. For the purposes of meaningful comparison, in the absence of market valuations (such as prices), someone on behalf of society has to decide what is valued. That is rarely a role for analysts or researchers – rather, it is the legitimate role of politicians. In developing an efficiency model, an important requirement is to seek out a clear political statement on what is valued from legitimate stakeholders. This will usually take the form of some statement of the objectives of the health system or its constituent organisations. We shall discuss the issue of valuation at greater length in chapter 8.

2.5 Specifying inputs

The input side of efficiency analysis is usually considered less problematic than the output side. Physical inputs can often be measured more accurately than outputs, or can be summarised in the form of a measure of costs. However, even the specification of inputs can give rise to serious conceptual and practical difficulties in efficiency analysis. This section briefly summarises some of the major issues.

A fundamental decision that must be taken is the level of disaggregation of inputs to be specified. At one extreme, a single measure of aggregate inputs (in the form of total costs) might be used. The efficiency model then effectively becomes a cost function. This approach assumes that the organisations under scrutiny are free to deploy inputs efficiently, taking account of relative prices. Any failure to do so (price inefficiency) will be reflected in a lower estimate of measured efficiency. Use of a single measure of costs therefore takes a long-term perspective as it assumes, for example, that organisations can freely adopt an optimal mix of capital and labour.

It may also be important to consider a short-term perspective, in which certain aspects of the input mix are considered beyond the control of the organisation. In these circumstances, it becomes necessary to disaggregate the inputs to some extent in order to capture the different input mixes that organisations have inherited. In particular, disaggregation of labour and capital may be required. We consider these two classes of input in turn.

2.5.1 Labour inputs

Labour inputs can usually be measured with some degree of accuracy, often disaggregated by skill level. An important issue is then how much aggregation of labour inputs to use before pursuing an efficiency analysis. Unless there is a specific interest in the deployment of different labour types, it may be appropriate to aggregate into a single measure of labour input, weighting the various labour inputs by their relative wages. A central contribution of the techniques discussed in this book is to offer evidence on efficiency when there is no direct information on the relative value placed on inputs or outputs. Where such evidence does exist, as for example on the market price of inputs, there may be little merit in disaggregation unless there is a specific interest in input allocative efficiency. Aggregation leads to a more parsimonious model, thereby allowing the analyst to focus attention on aspects of the production process where there is less secure evidence on weightings.

However, there may be an interest in the relationship between efficiency and the mix of labour inputs employed. Under such circumstances, a short-run model using measures of labour input disaggregated by skill type may be valuable. Such modelling assumes that organisations are constrained in their ability to alter skill mix, and can yield useful policy recommendations about (say) substituting one type of labour for another.

It may be that labour inputs are measured in either physical units (hours of labour) or costs of labour. Which should be used in an efficiency analysis depends on the context. The use of physical inputs will fail to capture any variations in organisations' wage rates. This may be desirable (for example, if there are variations in pay levels beyond the control of organisations) or undesirable (if there is believed to be input price inefficiency, in the form of different pay levels for identical workers).

Although labour inputs can be measured readily at an organisational level, problems may arise if the purpose of the study is to examine the efficiency of sub-units within organisations, such as operating theatres within hospitals. It becomes increasingly difficult to attribute labour inputs, when the unit of observation within the hospital becomes smaller (department, team, surgeon and patient). Staff often work across sub-units, but information or financial systems cannot track their input across these units with any accuracy. In particular, hospital specialists often work across specialities. For instance, a general surgeon may have an interest in urology; or a plastic surgeon may spend some time working in dermatology. Their measured contribution to each speciality then relies on arbitrary accounting choices that may vary considerably between units being compared. Particular care should be exercised when developing organisational efficiency models relying heavily for input measures on self-reported allocations of professional time.

One final consideration on labour inputs is that organisations may vary in the extent to which they 'buy in' certain services, rather than directly employ labour. For example, some hospitals may purchase cleaning services from independent contractors and have little idea of the associated labour inputs. Cleaning services might therefore appear as a 'goods and services purchased' input rather than labour and capital inputs. If other hospitals directly employ cleaning personnel, it may be the case that such inputs are not being treated on a strictly comparable basis. In such circumstances, the analyst may need to resort to a single measure of inputs, in the form of total costs.

2.5.2 *Capital inputs*

Incorporating measures of capital into the efficiency analysis is more challenging. This is partly because of the difficulty of measuring capital stock and partly due to problems in attributing its use to any particular period.

Measures of capital are often very rudimentary, and even misleading. For example, accounting measures of the depreciation of physical stock usually offer little meaningful indication of capital consumed. Indeed, in practice, analysts may have to resort to very crude measures; for example, the number of hospital beds or floorspace as a proxy for physical capital. Furthermore, health care often invests in important non-physical capital inputs, such as health promotion efforts.

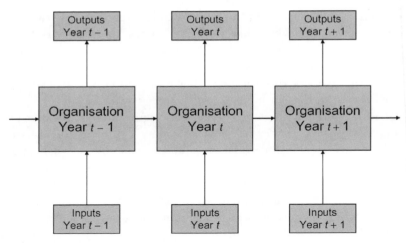

Figure 2.4. The dynamic nature of organisational performance.

In principle, an efficiency model should use the capital consumed in the current period as an input to the production process. But capital is by its nature deployed across time. On the one hand, contemporary output may rely on capital investment that took place in previous periods, while on the other, some current activities are investments that are intended to contribute to future rather than contemporary outputs.

The accounting difficulties capital inputs give rise to can be summarised in the form of a diagram, as shown in Figure 2.4. In each period, inputs are consumed and direct outputs emerge from the organisation. A rudimentary efficiency analysis will examine the ratio of outputs to inputs for only a single time period t. Yet crucially the organisation in year t has enjoyed the benefits of past investments. And it also leaves an 'endowment' for future periods in the form of investments undertaken in this and preceding periods. The endowment might be in the form of real capital (buildings or personnel) or investment in health 'capital' through (say) preventive medicine. In principle, the endowment may be an important aspect of both the inputs to and outputs of the health system. In practice it can be very difficult to measure.

A central issue in the treatment of capital is the extent to which short-run or long-run efficiency is under scrutiny. In the short run, it

makes sense for organisations to take advantage of whatever investment infrastructure they have available, and to optimise subject to
any constraints imposed by that infrastructure. So, for example, short-
run efficiency should be judged in the light of the capital configuration
that a hospital has available. Yet in the longer run one might expect
the hospital to reconfigure its capital resources when this can bring
about efficiency improvements.

2.5.3 Summary

As with all modelling, efficiency models should be developed according to the intentions of the analysis. If the interest is in narrow short-
run use of existing resources, then it may be relevant to disaggregate
inputs in order to reflect the resources currently at the disposal of
management. If a longer-term, less constrained analysis is required,
then a single measure of 'total costs' may be a perfectly adequate
indicator of physical organisational inputs.

2.6 Environmental constraints

In many contexts, a separate class of factor affects organisational
capacity, which we classify as the 'environmental' determinants of
performance. These are exogenous influences on the organisation's
production function, beyond its control, that reflect the external environment within which it must operate. In particular, many of the
outcomes secured by health care organisations are highly dependent
on the characteristics of the population group they serve. For example:

- population mortality rates are heavily dependent on the demographic structure of the population under consideration;
- surgical outcomes are often highly contingent on the severity of
  disease of patients;
- hospital performance may be related to how care is organised in
  the local community;
- the performance of emergency ambulance services may depend on
  local geography and settlement patterns.

There is often considerable debate as to which environmental factors can be considered 'controllable'. For example, responses to the
World Health Report 2000 argued that the HIV/AIDS epidemic was

important in the poor measured performance of many low-income health systems, but had not been taken into account (World Health Organization 2001). Conversely, the World Health Organization argued that control of the epidemic had been amenable to intervention, and so efficiency should be judged without adjustment. In the same vein, hospital outcomes may be strongly related to infection rates, and there may be debate on the extent to which these are within the hospital's control. The analyst's choice is likely to be heavily dependent on whether the purpose of the analysis is short-run and tactical, or longer-run and strategic. In many circumstances it will be appropriate to undertake both short-run and long-run analysis.

The performance of many health care organisations is in part dependent on inputs from outside agencies, such as social care, housing organisations or private families. In principle we should recognise this in modelling efficiency. For example, many patient outcomes rely on the co-ordinated contributions of a number of organisations, in the form of integrated care. If the performance of only one of these organisations is under scrutiny, there may be a difficulty in identifying the element of patient outcome that is attributable specifically to its endeavours. The danger is either (i) its contribution towards integrated care is ignored in the analysis (under-attribution) or (ii) the contribution of other external agencies towards outcome is ignored (over-attribution). Again, whether these external efforts should be treated as exogenous depends on the extent to which the behaviour of external agencies is amenable to influence by the organisation under scrutiny.

Broadly speaking, there are three ways in which environmental factors can be taken into account in efficiency analyses:

- restrict comparison only to organisations within a similarly constrained environment;
- model the constraints explicitly, as being analogous to 'factors' in the production process;
- undertake risk adjustment.

The first approach to accommodating environmental influences is to cluster organisations into similar 'families', using techniques such as cluster analysis (Everitt, Landau and Leese 2001). The intention is then to compare only like with like. Of course, this begs the question as to what criteria are to be used to create the families. Statistical examination of the link between putative exogenous influences and performance is often ruled out because efficiency too is correlated with performance. Unless exogenous influences are known to be entirely independent of efficiency levels, it becomes impossible to determine whether a correlation with performance is reflecting exogenous influences or efficiency variations. The analyst will therefore often have to resort to informed judgement in choosing the basis for creating families.

A further problem with the use of families is that it will reduce sample size, as it rules out extrapolation of performance of one type of organisation as a basis for comparison with another type. This may be appropriate to ensure robust comparisons, but with parametric methods can seriously affect the confidence with which efficiency judgements can be made, for example by leading to smaller samples and larger standard errors. Furthermore, of course, useful lessons that organisations might learn from being compared to a more heterogeneous sample will be lost.

The second approach is to incorporate environmental factors directly into the production model, often treating them as an exogenous 'input' analogous to labour or capital. This approach effectively generalises the clustering approach by allowing extrapolation from one class of organisation to another. For example, an environmental factor might be included as an explanatory variable in the parametric modelling approach (chapter 3) or as an input or output in the non-parametric approach (chapter 5). Whilst leading to a more general specification of the efficiency model than the clustering approach, the direct incorporation of environmental factors into the efficiency model leads to new modelling challenges that are discussed in detail in the chapters that follow.

The final method to control for variation in environmental circumstances is the family of techniques known as 'risk adjustment'. These methods adjust organisational outputs for differences in circumstances before they are deployed in an efficiency model, and are – where feasible – often the most sensible approach to treating environmental factors. In particular, they permit the analyst to adjust each output for only those factors that apply specifically to that output, rather than to use environmental factors as a general adjustment for all outputs.

Well-understood forms of risk adjustment include the various types of standardised mortality rates routinely deployed in studies of population outcomes. These adjust observed mortality rates for the demographic structure of the population, thereby seeking to account for the higher risk of mortality among older people. Likewise, surgical outcomes might be adjusted for the severity of risk factors, such as age, co-morbidities and smoking status of the patients treated.

The methods of risk adjustment are often a highly efficient means of controlling an output measure for a multiplicity of environmental factors. The risk-adjusted output can then be entered into the efficiency model without any further need to enter environmental factors. The methods of risk adjustment have been developed to a high level of refinement (Iezzoni 2003). However, it must be noted that risk adjustment usually has demanding data requirements, in the form of information on the circumstances of individual patients. And even when adequate data do exist it is often difficult to secure scientific consensus on the most appropriate way of undertaking the risk adjustment.

Including a factor in a risk-adjusted output measure should preclude the need to consider the factor further in any efficiency analysis. It therefore considerably simplifies the efficiency modelling process. Yet it is important to bear in mind that conventional risk adjustment usually requires the assumption that the sample average outcome for a particular population group (say, population aged 65–74, non-smoking) is a suitable benchmark against which individual or organisational performance can be measured. If for some reason certain population groups receive systematically poor care, it may be inappropriate to include such groups in the risk adjustment process, particularly if the intention is to highlight such underperformance and promote better performance among practitioners caring for such groups.

For example, in Australia, aboriginal population groups suffer substantially poorer life expectancy than most other ethnic groups (Zhao *et al.* 2004). Therefore, if standardised mortality rates are to be used as an indicator of public health authorities' performance, a critical policy decision is whether or not to include aboriginal ethnic origin in the risk adjustment process. If it is included, the effect of ethnicity on health authority performance will not be identified explicitly. If it is not included, health authorities with large aboriginal populations will exhibit poor outcomes, stimulating a debate as to whether this is beyond health authority control. The technical choice of risk adjustment methodology should therefore be driven by the policy intentions underlying the analysis.

One particularly important situation arises when organisations have been allocated funds to deliver some standard level of care, for example using risk-adjusted capitation formulae. The purpose of such formulae is to adjust for legitimate environmental circumstances, so that in principle all organisations are operating on a 'level playing-field' (Smith 2003). In these special circumstances there may be no need explicitly to consider any exogenous variables at all on the input side. Efficiency analysis should focus solely on variations in organisational outputs, as all inputs have been equalised. This argument, of course, presumes that the funding formulae have been correctly designed.

In chapter 8, we shall return to the issue of environmental constraints, with a discussion of the inferential implications arising from how most SFA and DEA models deal with the issue.

2.7 Practical challenges

Notwithstanding the important model-building considerations discussed in this chapter, it is often the case that the most serious difficulties for the analyst arise from the scope and nature of the available data sources. Numerous difficulties can arise:

- In health care, there is often a serious lack of information on some important dimensions of performance, most notably the quality of care. This is especially problematic in efficiency analysis, when the ambition is to present a rounded view of performance.
- Where measurement instruments are available, they may be incomplete or highly imperfect metrics with large random elements.
- Time series are often short, or interrupted by structural changes, such as hospital mergers.
- As always, there may be missing data for some observations, leading to difficult technical choices as to whether to broaden the scope of the model (and so effectively reduce sample size) or to use a more circumscribed model with a larger sample.
- More generally, given the complexity of the production process in much of health care, sample sizes may often be too small to draw secure inferences on the nature of the preferred model.

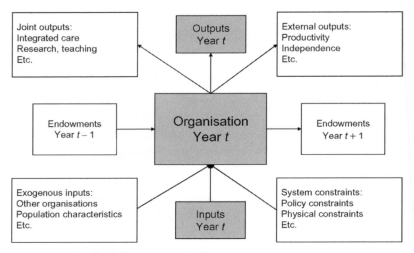

Figure 2.5. The broader context of efficiency analysis.

Such difficulties will be familiar to those working in most domains of quantitative analysis. However, they can become particularly problematic in efficiency analysis because of the great attention placed on unexplained variations from the estimated frontier.

These issues are discussed in more detail in chapter 8. Here we merely emphasise the potentially high sensitivity of results to model specification and data errors. This suggests a need for great attention to sensitivity analysis, experimentation with different model specifications, and caution about drawing definitive judgements on the efficiency of individual organisations. It is important to bear in mind that a great deal of conventional uncertainty analysis merely models uncertainty in the data, and not the implications of wrongly specifying the underlying model (Smith 1997). Conventional measures of uncertainty may therefore seriously overestimate the degree of confidence in efficiency scores, and should be viewed with caution.

In short, data constraints will often circumscribe the ability to answer the questions of health care regulators in their entirety. Instead, the analyst must adopt pragmatic solutions to otherwise infeasible modelling demands. Under these circumstances, it is imperative to state what technical assumptions have been made, and to communicate clearly the limitations of the analysis.

2.8 Conclusions

The beguilingly simple notion of efficiency disguises a series of thorny conceptual and methodological problems. Setting aside the obvious measurement difficulties, the structural problem can be illustrated as in Figure 2.5. Naïve efficiency analysis involves examining the ratio of health system outputs to health system inputs (the shaded boxes). Yet system inputs should also incorporate previous investments (endowments) and exogenous inputs (such as other organisations and patient characteristics). And system outputs should also include endowments for the future, joint outputs and outputs not directly related to health, such as enhanced productivity.

It will never be feasible to accommodate all the issues summarised in Figure 2.5 into an efficiency analysis. Rather, the analyst should be aware of which factors are likely to be material for the application under consideration, and seek to offer guidance on the implications of serious omissions from the efficiency model.

3 | Stochastic frontier analysis of cross-sectional data

3.1 Introduction

THIS chapter is concerned with the econometric approach to efficiency measurement when the analyst has only a single observation for each organisation – in other words, a cross-sectional data set. The subsequent chapter discusses the panel data techniques that can be used to exploit the additional information that is available when organisations are observed at more than a single point in time. When only cross-sectional data are available there are two classes of econometric technique available for efficiency analysis: corrected ordinary least squares (COLS) and stochastic frontier analysis (SFA). Both follow the conventional statistical process of specifying an econometric model of the general form:

$$y_i = \alpha + \beta x_i + \varepsilon_i \tag{3.1}$$

where y indicates either output (Y) or cost (C); i indicates the number of observations, $i = 1, \ldots, I$; α is a constant; x is a vector of explanatory variables; and β captures the relationship between the dependent and explanatory variables. The residual ε represents the deviation between the observed data and the relationship predicted by the explanatory variables in the model. In most statistical or econometric models of this form, the relationships between y and x are the primary focus. Generally, the residual is not afforded attention in its own right, with researchers interested only that it satisfies classical assumptions of having zero mean and constant variance (Cook and Weisberg 1982). In efficiency analyses, by contrast, the residual is often the only 'parameter' of interest – it is from the residual that estimates of efficiency are derived. The difference between COLS and SFA rests upon the interpretation accorded to the residual. In COLS, the entire residual is interpreted as arising from inefficiency. In SFA, the residual comprises a mixture of inefficiency and measurement error.

3.2 Considerations in stochastic frontier analysis

There are a number of considerations when estimating an efficiency model of the above form:

- whether to estimate a production or a cost function;
- whether to transform variables;
- whether to estimate a total or an average function;
- which explanatory variables to include;
- how to model the residual;
- how to extract the efficiency estimates.

These issues are discussed in the first half of the chapter before being illustrated using case study material.

3.2.1 Whether to estimate a production or a cost function

The first decision facing the analyst is whether to estimate a production or a cost function. If the purpose of the analysis is to explore differences in output, Y, the econometric model of (3.1) takes the revised form:

$$Y_i = \alpha + \beta x_i + \varepsilon_i \qquad (3.2)$$

In many industries, estimation of a production function poses serious practical difficulties (Intriligator 1978). In particular, where organisations produce multiple outputs, it is a challenge to derive a composite measure of output without loss of information. Most econometric attempts to deal with this problem reduce to estimation of a single output, conditioned in some way on the other outputs. This is not particularly satisfactory because the estimates of efficiency tend to be sensitive to which output is chosen to represent Y (Fernández, Koop and Steel 2000). A different approach is described by these authors in which Bayesian methods are implemented using a Markov chain Monte Carlo algorithm to transform multiple outputs into an equivalent univariate production function (Fernández, Koop and Steel 2000). As will be shown in chapter 5, data envelopment analysis has a clear advantage over econometric methods in its ability to handle multiple outputs. In chapter 9, we describe the use of multivariate models to analyse multiple objectives using econometric methods.

Faced with multiple outputs, most researchers find it more convenient to work with a cost function because it allows a single dependent variable, cost (C), to be estimated. Information about different outputs can be included as a vector of explanatory variables $Y = Y(Y_1, Y_2, \ldots, Y_S)$, hence:

$$C_i = \alpha + \beta_1 Y_i + \beta_2 x_i + \varepsilon_i \tag{3.3}$$

If cost-minimising behaviour can be assumed, the cost function is usually the dual of the production function, making the two approaches equivalent. However, duality does not hold for all functional forms, particularly if higher-order powers are included (Burgess 1975; Christensen and Greene 1976). Moreover, cost-minimising behaviour may be a strong assumption in some sectors of the economy, such as the health sector (Varian 1978).

3.2.2 Whether to transform variables

The second question concerns the form of the functional relationship between the dependent and explanatory variables. This functional form can be specified in a variety of ways, some of which are considered later. For the moment, we focus on the implications of using variables in their natural units or of transforming them into logarithmic form.

Using variables in their natural units assumes that the explanatory variables are related linearly to the dependent variable. Suppose that the main determinant of total hospital cost is the scale of activity, measured by the number of inpatients treated. The model would yield estimates of the relationship between cost and activity suggesting that, whatever the scale of operation, an additional patient treated would make the same contribution to total cost. This is illustrated as line A in Figure 3.1.

The assumption of a constant rate of change in costs as the scale of activity changes may not hold in practice. Marginal costs will be higher than average costs in the presence of diminishing factor productivity or decreasing returns to scale. In such circumstances, the overall cost impact of, for instance, treating an additional patient, would be lower in organisations with a small level of activity than in those treating greater numbers. One way to model this relationship is by taking logarithms of the variables. This may produce a function similar to curve B in Figure 3.1. The interpretation of the coefficients under a logarithmic form also change from natural units to elasticities or percentage changes.

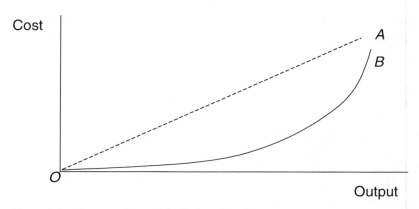

Figure 3.1. Linear and logarithmic functional forms.

The Davidson–MacKinnon P_E-test can be used to test for non-linear functional forms (Davidson and MacKinnon 1985). Obviously, other functional forms can be specified, for instance by including higher-order powers of explanatory variables. The appropriateness of their inclusion can be ascertained simply by application of a t-test.

3.2.3 Whether to estimate a total or an average function

The choice between working with total or average output/cost depends on the assumptions made about the relationship between the dependent and explanatory variables. Organisations can change their output or cost levels in two ways: by changing the *scale* of production, making proportionate changes in the quantities of inputs employed; or by altering the *mix* of inputs used.

The impact of altering input quantities depends on the scale properties – or degree of homogeneity – of the function. The production function is homogeneous of degree h if

$$\kappa^h Y = f(\kappa x_1, \kappa x_2) = \kappa^h f(x_1, x_2), \quad \text{for all } \kappa > 0, \\ \text{for all } \mathbf{x} \tag{3.4}$$

where κ is any scalar and x_1 and x_2 are different inputs. A special case is where $h = 1$, where the function is homogeneous of degree 1, or linearly homogeneous. In this situation, the production function displays constant returns to scale, whereby a proportionate change in the use of inputs leads to a change in output by the same proportion. For instance, for an organisation operating under constant returns to scale, doubling the use of inputs would lead to twice as much output. Where $h > 1$, the function displays increasing returns to scale and where $h < 1$, it displays decreasing returns to scale. Only in the presence of constant returns to scale will the estimation of total and average functions yield equivalent results.

Scale properties aside, estimation of an average function may be preferable if the data being analysed are subject to heteroscedasticity. Heteroscedasticity arises if the variance of the residual ε_i is not constant. The error term ε_i is based on an underlying probability distribution, assumed to have zero mean and constant variance. Heteroscedasticity may occur where, for instance, the variance of the residuals varies systematically with one of the explanatory variables, such as size (Pindyck and Rubinfeld 1991). Observed data for (say) larger organisations thus lie further from the regression line than they do for small organisations, as illustrated in Figure 3.2. One reason why this may occur is that the contribution made by labour to output may be a function of skill e: $Y = eL$. Staff are likely to have different levels of skill, even if they are paid similarly, but this is unlikely to be observable to the researcher. Smaller organisations will experience less variation in e for the simple reason that they employ fewer people, so their observed data will lie closer to the regression line, with observations fanning out from the regression line as the size of the workforce and, hence, output increases.

Heteroscedasticity has two implications. First, ordinary least squares (OLS) regression estimates will no longer provide minimum variance (they will be inefficient) and so they will not provide 'best' estimates of the hypothesised relationship. Second, the estimated variances of the OLS estimators will be biased, invalidating tests of statistical significance.

If present, heteroscedasticity can be reduced by working with average rather than total functions because, by estimating the ratio of output or cost to a deflating variable, the residual is more likely to display homoscedasticity (Intriligator 1978). But in specifying an average cost function a deflating variable has to be selected. One option is to use a measure of organisational size, thereby making the dependent variable an average cost per unit of size. Deflating by size would be appropriate only in the presence of constant returns to scale.

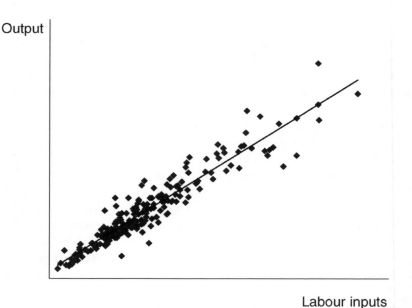

Figure 3.2. Illustration of heteroscedastic data.

Alternatively, output might be used for deflating purposes, to make the dependent variable cost per unit of output, say. This is problematic in the context of multiple outputs because efficiency estimates will be sensitive to which output is chosen for deflation. The total cost function has the advantage of incorporating the various types of output as separate explanatory variables.

It is important to test for heteroscedasticity of the total function before proceeding with deflation – if the undeflated series was homoscedastic, deflation would introduce heteroscedasticity because the error term is transformed by deflation (Kuh and Meyer 1955). Moreover, the average function may not resolve the problem of biased estimation (Hough 1985). Indeed, a new source of bias may arise if the variable used for deflation on the left-hand side of the equation as the denominator (say number of cases) is multicollinear with one of the explanatory variables on the right-hand side of the equation (Kuh and Meyer 1955).

There are other ways to deal with heteroscedasticity other than by estimating an average function. Logarithmic functions are likely to be less susceptible to heteroscedasticity because by transforming variables into their logarithmic form their distribution is likely to approach normalisation (Maddala 1988). Another approach is to correct for heteroscedasticity using a robust estimator (White 1980).

3.2.4 Which explanatory variables to include

Explanatory variables, **x**, are used to explain differences among organisations in their observed levels of output or cost. The choice about what constitute appropriate explanatory variables depends on the purpose or perspective of the analysis. Broadly, the literature can be divided into two camps: technological functions derived from the theory of the firm; and behavioural functions that can be (loosely) categorised as stemming from theories of regulation.

If the research interest is in analysing production from the perspective of the organisations under consideration, the neo-classical theory of the firm is an appropriate framework. This type of specification facilitates investigation of questions such as how output might vary following changes in the level or mix of inputs. Candidate explanatory variables will measure the input choices made by – or endogenous to – the organisations themselves. These variables might be supplemented by others measuring unavoidable organisational constraints that, in the short term at least, are exogenous to managerial control.

In contrast, many efficiency studies are conducted from the perspective of a regulator. The regulator might be interested in assessing organisational effort and efficiency, recognising that organisations face different and, sometimes, unavoidable operational or environmental constraints. The regulatory objective will be to control for these exogenous constraints before making judgements about the level of effort expended. Endogenous factors that influence production or costs, such as the choice about what technical production process to employ, would be excluded from the model on the grounds that these are decided by the organisation. The analytical task is to construct a behavioural function that reflects feasible production possibilities within a constrained environment (Smith 1981).

Many studies of health care organisations adopt a neo-classical approach (Schmidt and Lovell 1980; Vitaliano 1987; Zuckerman, Hadley and Lezzoni 1994; Linna 1998; Folland and Hofler 2001; Rosko 2001). Here, the production function summarises a technical relationship among the maximum outputs attainable for different combinations of all possible factors of production. For example, suppose hospital output is measured as the total number of patients treated (Y) and that there are two factors of production, labour (L) and capital (K). Then the production function would be written as:

$$Y = f(L, K) \tag{3.5}$$

where $f(.)$ describes the functional relationship between output and different mixes of labour and capital.

One of the most widely used production functions is the Cobb–Douglas, which takes a logarithmic form and can be written as:

$$Y = \alpha L^{\beta_1} K^{\beta_2} \tag{3.6}$$

and estimated as:

$$\ln Y_i = \alpha + \beta_1 \ln L_i + \beta_2 \ln K_i + \varepsilon_i \tag{3.7}$$

where β_1 and β_2 are parameters describing the contributions to output made by labour and capital respectively. The logarithmic form allows these parameters to be interpreted as elasticities: a 1 per cent increase in the amount of labour employed is predicted to lead to a percentage increase in output to the value of β_1.

Another commonly estimated production function is the transcendental logarithmic function – the translog (Christensen, Jorgenson and Lau 1973). The attraction of the translog is its flexibility – it can approximate virtually any functional form (Intriligator 1978). The translog is estimated by including squares and cross-products of the explanatory variables. Thus the production function of (3.5) would be estimated as:

$$\ln Y_i = \alpha + \beta_1 \ln L_i + \beta_2 \ln K_i$$
$$+ \frac{1}{2}\beta_3 (\ln L_i)^2 + \frac{1}{2}\beta_4 (\ln K_i)^2 + \beta_5 \ln L_i \ln K_i + \varepsilon_i \tag{3.8}$$

If the parameters β_3, β_4 and β_5 are not significantly different from zero, the function reduces to a Cobb–Douglas.

One of the drawbacks of the translog is that there are likely to be a large number of parameters to be estimated: for every additional variable added to the model, it is necessary to include a squared term and cross-products with the existing variables. If π represents the sum of variables, the number of parameters amounts to approximately

$\pi(\pi + 1)/2$, with a consequent reduction in the degrees of freedom available (Newhouse 1994). A compromise might be to include only broad descriptions of the factors of production. For instance, estimation may be based on total number of staff, rather than specific details about medical or nursing staff complements, although this would imply a loss of information relating to skill mix.

The cost function equivalent to the production function of (3.5) can be written as:

$$C = f(Y, w, r) \tag{3.9}$$

where w and r represent input prices for labour (wages) and capital (rent) respectively. The cost function equivalent to the Cobb–Douglas production function is:

$$C(Y, w, r) = \alpha'(Yw^{\beta_1}r^{\beta_2})^{1/(\beta_1 + \beta_2)} \tag{3.10}$$

The elasticities β_1 and β_2 can be estimated from a linear model of the following form:

$$\ln C_i = \alpha + \frac{1}{\beta_1 + \beta_2}\ln Y_i + \frac{\beta_1}{\beta_1 + \beta_2}\ln w_i + \frac{\beta_2}{\beta_1 + \beta_2}\ln r_i + \varepsilon_i \tag{3.11}$$

where w and r are the unit prices of each factor of production. The translog cost function can be expressed in the following manner (Greene 2000):

$$\begin{aligned}\ln C_i = {} & \alpha + \beta_0\ln Y_i + \beta_1\ln w_i + \beta_2\ln r_i \\ & + \frac{1}{2}\beta_3(\ln Y_i)^2 + \frac{1}{2}\beta_4(\ln w_i)^2 + \frac{1}{2}\beta_5(\ln r_i)^2 \\ & + \beta_6\ln Y_i\ln w_i + \beta_7\ln Y_i\ln r_i + \beta_8\ln w_i\ln r_i + \varepsilon_i \end{aligned} \tag{3.12}$$

This will correspond to the translog production function (3.8) only if factor markets are competitive and the cost function displays constant returns to scale, with total costs increasing proportionally when all prices increase proportionally, given the level of output (Christensen and Greene 1976). If these conditions do not hold, estimation will be sensitive to the choice of a translog production function or translog cost function (Burgess 1975).

Direct estimation of the production or cost function gives rise to two potential problems. First, L and K are unlikely to be independent of each other, leading to problems of multicollinearity. This makes it difficult to disentangle the separate contributions of each explanatory variable to the dependent variable (Maddala 1988). Second, the explanatory variables may be jointly determined (i.e. endogenous), implying a simultaneous (two-way) relationship between the dependent variable and the explanatory variables (Intriligator 1978). For instance, the decision to expand output may imply the greater use of inputs (cost) and the greater use of inputs (cost) may imply output expansion. In effect, the two sides of the equation are jointly determined. These problems are not encountered under the alternative approach to model specification, informed by the theory of regulation, to which we now turn.

Regulators of industries that face little competition often wish to exert downward pressure on costs by regulating prices or setting efficiency targets. The regulator may wish to examine output or costs in order to make inferences about the level of effort applied by the organisations being regulated. Below average costs may be observed in organisations that expend more effort in searching for and applying efficient modes of operation. However, observed costs may not be related to effort alone, particularly if firms face different operating environments or other influences on their costs that are not subject to managerial control. To be able to draw accurate inferences about the relationship between output or costs and effort, the regulator would want to include variables in the parametric model that control for these exogenous influences (Schleifer 1985). In fact, it has been argued that if the objective of the exercise is to make inferences about relative efficiency, a necessary condition is that *all* variables included as regressors are exogenous to managerial influence (Giuffrida, Gravelle and Sutton 2000). The task for the analyst, then, is to determine which are valid exogenous variables and over what time-frame the constraints are binding. Obviously, such constraints will be highly context-specific and, in all likelihood, an area of contention between the regulator and the regulated organisations.

3.2.5 How to model the residual

The specifications outlined thus far describe 'sample average' relationships between output or costs and a set of explanatory variables. The fundamental requirement for efficiency analysis is some indication of what constitutes 'best practice'. Farrell argues that it is possible to analyse technical efficiency by examining the residuals, ε_i, from regression equations (Farrell 1957). In standard econometric analysis, the residual would not be accorded special attention. Rather, it represents merely the deviation between the observed data and the relationship predicted by the model and can be interpreted as statistical error, caused by measurement inaccuracies or unobservable heterogeneity.

However, Farrell suggested a different interpretation: the residual can be used to describe the extent to which an organisation operates from best practice. The difference between observed costs (or output) and that predicted by a correctly specified model is due to inefficient behaviour. In the case of a cost function, an organisation with a residual of zero is interpreted as displaying average efficiency, while organisations with negative (positive) residuals are deemed to be of above (below) average efficiency. (If Y represents output, the interpretations are reversed).

This suggests that observations can be ranked according to their average efficiency, as in an early study of National Health Service (NHS) hospital costs (Feldstein 1967). The observation with a residual lying the greatest distance below the cost function is defined as being the most efficient in the sample. Given the relationship specified by the model, its costs are lower than that for any other observation in the sample. In this respect, the observation represents 'best practice' cost-minimising behaviour. Accordingly, the observation can be thought of as lying on the 'frontier' of the sample.

This implies that a cost (or production) *frontier* can be estimated. For a cost function, this is done by adding $\min(\varepsilon_i)$ to the intercept and subtracting it from the residuals, a procedure referred to as corrected ordinary least squares (COLS). The intention is to shift an OLS regression line that originally fell through the centre of a cloud of observed data so that it passes through the observation displaying minimum cost. The process is reversed for a production function.

A stylised example of this procedure is illustrated in Figure 3.3 for a single explanatory variable regressed on costs. The upper figure shows the fitted OLS function through the set of observations. Under the COLS approach, in the case of a cost function, the organisation with the lowest residual value is defined as being fully efficient – its costs are lower than those for any other observation, holding constant the variables in the model. This implies that the COLS efficiency

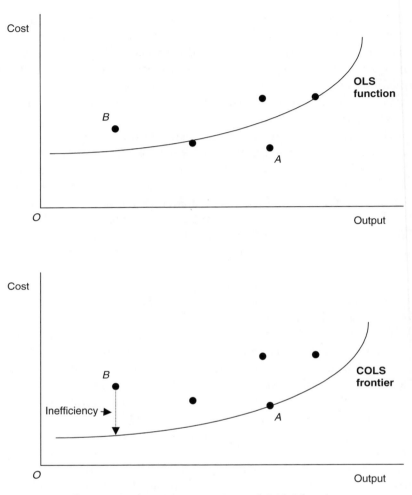

Figure 3.3. Illustration of an OLS regression and COLS frontier.

frontier is located by shifting the OLS regression line so that it passes through this fully efficient observation. This is illustrated in the lower half of the figure, where observation *A* is efficient. For an organisation lying above the COLS frontier, it is predicted that it would be able to reduce costs to the level predicted by the best-practice frontier without having to reduce output. The inefficiency of such an organisation can be measured as the vertical distance between its observed data and the frontier below, as shown for observation *B*.

The COLS approach implies that the residual is due solely to inefficiency. A contrasting viewpoint would be that the entire residual is due to random influences or measurement error. For instance, this interpretation would apply when analysing firms operating in a perfectly competitive environment, in which they are forced to operate at minimum cost levels.

Recognising that there are these two diametrically opposed interpretations of the residual it has been suggested that it might comprise both these components: inefficiency and random (stochastic) error. The econometric technique known as stochastic frontier analysis (SFA) has been developed to provide separate estimates of these two components.

The key assumption underlying SFA is that the inefficiency component and the random component of the residual will be distributed differently. In particular, the random component is assumed to be distributed normally, as is consistent with the classical OLS model. If ε_i is normally distributed, all residual variance is interpreted as arising from random noise and measurement error (Wagstaff 1989). If ε_i is skewed, this is taken as evidence that there is inefficiency in the sample (Schmidt and Lin 1984). Subject to ε_i being skewed, stochastic frontier analysis decomposes the error term into two parts with zero covariance:

$$\varepsilon_i = v_i + u_i, \quad \text{cov}(v_i, u_i) = 0 \tag{3.13}$$

The dual specification is defended on the grounds that each component represents an economically distinct disturbance (Aigner, Lovell and Schmidt 1977). v_i can be interpreted as stochastic (random) events not under the control of the organisation, such as climatic conditions (Aigner, Lovell and Schmidt 1977), random equipment failure (Greene 1993), errors in identifying or measuring explanatory variables (Timmer 1971) or just pure chance.

u is a non-negative term that captures the cost of inefficiency in production, with u_i defining how far the organisation operates above the cost frontier. Diagrammatically, this might result in a cost function similar to that depicted in Figure 3.4. The stochastic frontier has two notable features. First, it does not correspond to the 'line of best fit' through the observations that would be produced by a simple linear regression model. Second, the frontier does not (necessarily) pass through the observation that has lowest cost, conditional upon model

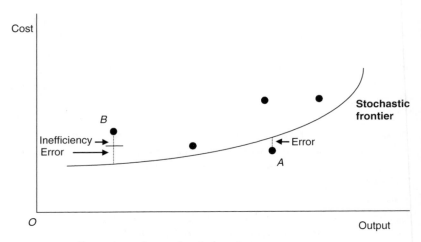

Figure 3.4. Illustration of a stochastic frontier.

specification (observation A). This is because the frontier is estimated after recognising that the difference between observed output and the level of output predicted by the explanatory variables is not due solely to inefficiency. Some of the difference may be due to measurement error and omitted variables. In Figure 3.4, observation A lies below the estimated frontier. The distance of this point from the stochastic cost frontier is attributable to random error, v_i. For observations lying above the frontier, the distance comprises both measurement error and inefficiency, as illustrated for observation B.

In estimating the stochastic frontier for cross-sectional data, it is necessary to specify the distributional characteristics of the two components of the residual. These distributions must be different in order to distinguish them econometrically. In common with classical assumptions it is usual to assume that v_i is normally distributed with zero mean and constant variance, hence $v_i \sim N(0, \sigma_i^2)$.

No economic criteria are available to guide the choice of distribution to apply to u_i (Schmidt and Sickles 1984). Standard computer software allows four options: a half-normal, truncated normal, exponential and gamma (Greene 2002). The half-normal is a special case of the truncated normal and in some data sets statistical criteria can be used to discriminate between these two options.

The u_i must be observed indirectly since direct estimates of only ε_i are available. The procedure for decomposing ε_i into its two components v_i and u_i relies on considering the expected value of u_i conditional upon $\varepsilon_i (= v_i + u_i)$. Jondrow *et al.* (1982) were the first to specify a half-normal distribution for the one-sided inefficiency component and to derive the conditional distribution $(u_i | v_i + u_i)$. Under this formulation of the half-normal distribution, the expected mean value of inefficiency, conditional upon the composite residual, is defined as:

$$E[u_i | \varepsilon_i] = \frac{\sigma \lambda}{(1 + \lambda^2)} \left[\frac{\phi(\varepsilon_i \lambda / \sigma)}{\Phi(-\varepsilon_i \lambda / \sigma)} - \frac{\varepsilon_i \lambda}{\sigma} \right] \tag{3.14}$$

where $\sigma^2 = \sigma_u^2 + \sigma_v^2$. $\lambda = \sigma_u / \sigma_v$ and captures inefficiency. Where $\lambda = 0$, every observation would lie on the frontier (Greene 1993). $\phi(.)$ and $\Phi(.)$ are, respectively, the probability density function and cumulative distribution function of the standard normal distribution.

The truncated normal model is a more general form of the half-normal, where u is distributed with a modal value of μ (Stevenson 1980). The explicit form for the conditional expectation is obtained by replacing the $\varepsilon_i \lambda / \sigma$ in the half-normal model with:

$$u_i^* = \frac{\varepsilon_i \lambda}{\sigma} + \frac{\mu}{\sigma \lambda} \tag{3.15}$$

If μ is not significantly different from zero, the model collapses to the half-normal.

If an exponential distribution is imposed, with a density function of the general form $f(u_i) = \theta exp^{-\theta u_i}$, the conditional expectation is expressed as (Greene 1995):

$$E[u_i | \varepsilon_i] = (\varepsilon_i - \theta \sigma_v^2) + \frac{\sigma_v \phi[(\varepsilon_i - \theta \sigma_v^2) / \sigma_v]}{\Phi[(\varepsilon_i - \theta \sigma_v^2) / \sigma_v]} \tag{3.16}$$

in which θ is the distribution parameter to be estimated.

The more general gamma distribution is formed by adding an additional parameter P to the exponential formulation, such that $f(u_i) = \frac{\theta^P}{\Gamma(P)} u^{P-1} exp^{-\theta u_i}$ with $u_i \sim G[\theta, P]$ (Greene 1990).

These formulations produce an unbiased but inconsistent estimator of u_i because, regardless of the sample size, the variance of the estimate remains non-zero (Greene 1993). The inconsistency of the estimator u_i is unfortunate in view of the fact that the purpose of the estimation is to approximate inefficiency. However, no improvements on this

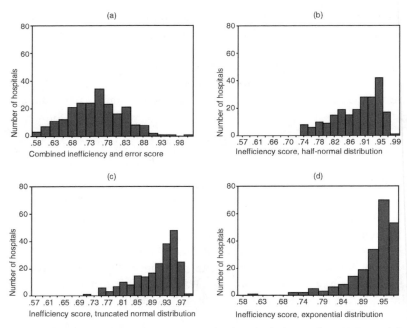

Figure 3.5. Histograms showing (a) the residual from the OLS model; (b) the inefficiency term from the half-normal model; (c) the inefficiency term from the truncated model; (d) the inefficiency term from the exponential model.

measure have yet been forthcoming in the literature for single-equation cross-sectional studies.

The choice of distribution will yield different estimates of inefficiency, both in the sample as a whole and for individual organisations. For example, the exponential distribution will impose a highly skewed relationship, and in many data sets this will imply that most observations are clustered close to the frontier with a long tail of observations further away.

Figure 3.5 provides a visual example of three distributions of u_i, together with the distribution from an OLS model, where v_i and u_i are combined. These histograms are taken from the case study used in the latter half of this chapter. The histograms are scaled such that estimated efficiency increases along the horizontal axis. The COLS histogram, in the top left-hand corner, suggests that few organisations are

Table 3.1. Calculating individual efficiency estimates for each organisation

Production or cost function?	Logged dependent variable?	Efficiency
Production	yes	$\exp(-u_i)$
Cost	yes	$\exp(u_i)$
Production	no	$(\beta x_i - u_i) / (\beta x_i)$
Cost	no	$(\beta x_i + u_i) / (\beta x_i)$

efficient, with inefficiency distributed not quite normally among the sample. The alternative specifications derived from the stochastic frontier models imply that most organisations are (or are close to being) relatively efficient as they are clustered to the right-hand side of the distribution. The exponential distribution, in the bottom right-hand corner, with its more pronounced negative skew, implies that inefficiency is less widespread than is assumed under the alternative specifications.

For most data sets, results will be more sensitive to the decision on whether to estimate a stochastic frontier instead of a COLS frontier and less sensitive to the choice of distribution of u_i within the stochastic frontier framework. Invariably COLS will yield lower levels of average efficiency because the entire residual is attributed to inefficiency (Schmidt 1985).

3.2.6 How to extract the efficiency estimates

The measure of efficiency for each organisation i, eff_i, depends on the type of function estimated. Details of how to calculate predictions for each organisation are given in Table 3.1 (Coelli 1996a). In the case of a production function, eff_i will lie between 0 and 1. For the cost function, values will fall between 1 and infinity, so when reporting results it is usual to invert the values such that $0 < \frac{1}{eff_i} < 1$. The efficiency estimates derived from a model with untransformed variables can be interpreted as absolute distances from the frontier. Estimates from a logarithmic model represent percentage distances from the frontier.

3.3 Application to acute hospitals in England

The considerations discussed above in estimating an efficiency model
are illustrated using a data set and model specification developed
by the Department of Health in England to analyse the efficiency of
acute hospitals (Audit Commission and Department of Health 1999).
Data for 226 hospitals were compiled for the year 1995/96 from a
variety of publicly available sources (Söderlund and van der Merwe
1999). As discussed in section 2.3.2 we ideally wish to measure outcomes of health care, but in the case of this data set we are constrained
to measuring health care activities. The variables in the data set are
described in more detail in the Appendix.

The dependent variable in the average cost function, AC, is a case
mix cost index, the ratio of actual costs to cost-weighted output. Output includes inpatient admissions (adjusted for case mix differences),
outpatient visits and A&E attendances. This case mix cost index
has been regressed against a set of variables x that seek to explain
variations in index scores, using a model of the form:

$$AC_i = \alpha + \beta_1 x_i + \varepsilon_i \qquad (3.17)$$

The results from this equation are compared to those where total
costs, C, enter as the dependent variable, with the various dimensions
of output (inpatient admissions, outpatient and A&E attendances)
included as an additional vector of explanatory variables, Y:

$$C_i = \alpha + \beta_1 x_i + \beta_2 Y_i + \varepsilon_i \qquad (3.18)$$

The variables included in the vector x conform to the regulatory rather
than the neo-classical framework discussed earlier. A neo-classical
formulation would require that the cost implications of choosing a
particular production process should be captured by the model parameters, not by the residual. The rationale for not including capital
and labour prices as explanatory variables is that the amount and mix
of inputs is determined by hospital managers, so any sub-optimality
arising from the employment of these resources should be considered
as indicative of inefficiency. In addition, within the NHS, factor prices
w and r are set through the central bargaining processes and, in
essence, display very little variation.

The 'behavioural' formulation adopted by the Department of
Health stems from a desire to isolate those cost-influencing factors

over which hospitals have no control so that their influence on costs can be eliminated when using the information to guide regulatory policy. Cost differences remaining over and above those 'explained' by the econometric model are deemed to reflect differences in organisational effort and the choice of what technical production process to employ.

The variables included in the model are listed in Table 3.2, together with descriptive statistics, for 226 hospitals. These data exclude outliers, identified by applying the DFFITS procedure to the total cost function, and setting a cut-off point of DFFITS $> 3(k/i)^{0.5}$ where k is the number of parameters estimated and i the number of observations (Söderlund and van der Merwe 1999).

Table 3.3 presents the regression results for the average cost function. The COLS model implies a mean level of 'inefficiency' of around 70 per cent, with the least efficient hospital estimated to be operating at 50 per cent efficiency. The majority of variables are significant influences on cost. For example, hospitals receiving more patients transferred from other hospitals (TRANS-IN) or treating more patients with multiple problems (EP_SPELL) tend to have higher average costs. Hospitals treating higher proportions of female (P-FEM), old (P-60), and young (P-15) patients are more likely to incur lower average costs, these seemingly counter-intuitive results probably arising from an overcompensation for these characteristics in the adjustment for case mix complexity.

The coefficient of skewness, $\sqrt{b_1}$, suggests that the residuals are significantly skewed. The COLS results are accompanied by the stochastic cost frontier regression estimations, corresponding to the half-normal, truncated normal and exponential error distributions. The distribution parameters of both the half-normal and exponential models (λ and θ respectively) are significant, suggesting that these models are an improvement on COLS estimation. In contrast, the truncated normal model yields a value for μ that is not significantly different from zero, making it equivalent to the half-normal model. The coefficients and the significance of the explanatory variables are broadly similar across all specifications. This is to be expected, since both the OLS estimates (which provide the starting values for the iterations) and the maximum likelihood estimates used in the stochastic frontier (SF) regressions are consistent estimators (Greene 1993).

Table 3.2. *Descriptive statistics*

Description		Mean	Std Dev.	Min.	Max.
Dependent variables					
C	Total cost (£m)	52.362	27.452	7.859	166.189
AC	Case mix cost index	1.000	0.187	0.531	2.166
Explanatory variables					
INPATIENTS	Number of inpatients, adjusted for case mix complexity using HRGs (000s)	42.478	24.041	3.928	136.041
OUTPATIENTS	Number of first outpatient attendances, weighted by speciality (000s)	46.330	27.342	0	148.817
A&E	Number of first accident and emergency attendances (000s)	45.894	29.341	0	157.042
EP_SPELL	Episodes per spell	1.068	0.118	0.785	1.661
TRANS-IN	Transfers in to hospital per spell	0.016	0.030	0.000	0.241
TRANS-OUT	Transfers out of hospital per spell	0.021	0.015	0.000	0.125
EMERGENCY	Emergency admissions per spell	0.346	0.087	0.020	0.549
FCE	Finished consultant episodes per spell	0.020	0.014	0.000	0.114
FU-OUTPTS	Follow-up outpatient attendances per inpatient spell	2.923	0.833	0.797	7.847
EMERINDX	Standardised index of unexpected emergency admissions/total emergency admissions	0.058	0.015	0.016	0.150
P-15	Proportion of patients under 15 years of age	0.094	0.101	0.000	0.838
P-60	Proportion of patients 60 years or older	0.340	0.083	0.000	0.590

Description		Mean	Std Dev.	Min.	Max.
P-FEM	Proportion of female patients	0.572	0.056	0.308	0.897
STUDENTS	Medical students per inpatient spell	0.001	0.001	0.000	0.012
RESEARCH	Percentage of total revenue spent on research	1.750	6.090	0.000	73.065
MFF	Market forces factor – weighted average of staff, land, buildings and London weighting factors	87.479	9.902	75.817	132.789

Table 3.3 indicates that the mean level of efficiency is similar across the SF error distributions, ranging from 85 to 90 per cent. This is considerably higher than was implied by the COLS model. This is expected because the COLS residual comprises both inefficiency and random error and, hence, yields lower estimates of efficiency (Schmidt 1985).

The correlations between the point estimates of efficiency and the relative rank of each hospital under each specification (with the exception of the truncated normal) are provided in Table 3.4. Two points are noteworthy. First, estimates are more sensitive to the choice between a COLS and SF specification than they are to the choice concerning the distribution of inefficiency within the SF framework. Second, differences are greatest when comparing COLS and SF results from an exponential distribution, as would be expected given the highly skewed distribution adopted by the latter specification.

Regression results pertaining to the total cost function are reported in Table 3.5, which includes measures of activity as additional explanatory variables. Treating an additional (case mix weighted) inpatient is estimated to increase total costs by upwards of £900, with an additional outpatient adding around £170 to total costs. Switching from an average to a total cost function has some influence on the significance of some of the explanatory variables but results are fairly stable.

The estimates of the mean level of efficiency in the sample are similar to those arising from estimating an average cost function. However, the distribution of efficiency is now wider, with the least efficient hospitals having lower point estimates than was apparent under the average cost function. Correlations of the efficiency estimates and ranks across the different specifications of the total cost function are provided in Table 3.6 and are similar to those under the average cost specifications.

Table 3.7 presents the correlation coefficients relating to a comparison of the efficiency estimates and ranks produced by the average and total cost functions. These coefficients, while still significant, are substantially lower than those reported in Tables 3.4 and 3.6. This suggests that results for these data are more sensitive to the choice between estimating a total or an average cost function than they are to choices about how inefficiency is distributed.

Table 3.3. Regression results for average cost function

Average cost	COLS			Half-normal			Truncated normal			Exponential		
	Coeff.	s.e.	t	Coeff.	s.e.	t	Coeff.	s.e.	t	Coeff.	s.e.	t
CONSTANT	0.738	0.254	4.595	0.766	0.239	3.201	0.516	0.262	1.968	0.624	0.230	2.708
EP_SPELL	0.202	0.093	2.172	0.119	0.087	1.375	0.089	0.094	0.938	0.085	0.080	1.058
TRANS-IN	0.776	0.434	1.788	0.731	0.385	1.899	0.873	0.309	2.821	1.283	0.272	4.707
TRANS-OUT	−2.648	0.790	−3.354	−2.469	0.683	−3.615	−2.340	0.621	−3.770	−2.404	0.548	−4.387
EMERGENCY	−0.234	0.146	−1.603	−0.029	0.126	−0.233	0.124	0.098	1.270	0.102	0.105	0.971
FCE	1.097	0.759	1.445	1.822	0.640	2.846	2.109	0.743	2.837	1.846	0.720	2.564
FU-OUTPTS	0.073	0.010	7.386	0.053	0.009	5.903	0.044	0.009	5.228	0.036	0.008	4.596
EMERINDX	0.423	0.745	0.568	0.210	0.496	0.423	0.304	0.489	0.623	−0.046	0.561	−0.081
P-15	−0.374	0.132	−2.843	−0.252	0.105	−2.406	−0.206	0.132	−1.560	−0.163	0.104	−1.560
P-60	−0.569	0.161	−3.539	−0.375	0.142	−2.636	−0.257	0.173	−1.484	−0.197	0.154	−1.280
P-FEM	−0.824	0.233	−3.535	−0.534	0.231	−2.318	−0.274	0.245	−1.120	−0.304	0.222	−1.365
STUDENTS	10.122	10.215	0.991	12.371	9.727	1.272	9.885	12.767	0.774	16.227	11.311	1.435
RESEARCH	−0.002	0.001	−1.810	−0.003	0.001	−3.385	−0.003	0.001	−3.422	−0.003	0.001	−3.687
MFF	0.002	0.001	1.485	0.003	0.001	2.410	0.004	0.001	2.797	0.003	0.001	2.678
λ				0.907	0.044	20.830	5.450	1.294	4.213			
μ/σ_u							−1.178	1.155	−1.020			
θ										8.573	0.864	9.918
σ_v^2							0.003			0.005		
σ_u^2							0.103			0.014		

Table 3.3. (continued)

Average cost	COLS Coeff.	s.e.	t	Half-normal Coeff.	s.e.	t	Truncated normal Coeff.	s.e.	t	Exponential Coeff.	s.e.	t
Log-likelihood					136.439			141.253			149.687	
Adj. R^2		0.408										
Efficiency												
mean		0.704			0.852			0.878			0.904	
s.d.		0.071			0.08			0.085			0.071	
min.–max.	0.504–1.000			0.514–0.980			0.493–0.981			0.527–0.983		

Table 3.4. Correlations across average cost specifications

Average cost	COLS	Half-normal	Exponential
Scores			
COLS	1.000		
Half-normal	0.855*	1.000	
Exponential	0.679*	0.934*	1.000
Ranks			
COLS	1.000		
Half-normal	0.916*	1.000	
Exponential	0.839*	0.973*	1.000

Note:
* Significant at 0.01 level.

Of even greater significance is the choice of whether to work in natural units or to use logarithmic transformations. Rather than specifying costs in original units, it is more conventional in productivity and cost analyses to adopt a logarithmic functional form, thereby relaxing the assumption that the rate of change in costs is constant over the entire range to be evaluated (Breyer 1987). But by transforming variables into logarithmic form, their distribution is likely to approach normalisation and, by implication, the residual is also likely to exhibit a less skewed distribution. Following logarithmic transformation of these data, OLS estimation yields a coefficient of skewness suggesting that the residual is normally distributed, thereby making it impossible to perform stochastic frontier analysis. In cases such as this, all residual variance should be interpreted as noise (Wagstaff 1989). This result suggests that the appearance of 'inefficiency' in a linear model might be banished following transformation.

3.4 Conclusions

This chapter has outlined the main issues involved in specifying an econometric model to assess efficiency using cross-sectional data. The analyst faces a number of decisions regarding the type of function to be estimated, the functional form of the model, the choice of explanatory variables and how to model inefficiency. It may be possible to apply statistical criteria to make some of these choices but for others

Table 3.5. *Regression results for total cost function*

Total cost	COLS			Half-normal			Truncated normal			Exponential		
	Coeff.	s.e.	t	Coeff.	s.e.	t	Coeff.	s.e.	t	Coeff.	s.e.	t
CONSTANT	16.115	11.240	3.194	32.283	12.051	2.679	30.268	13.110	2.309	35.477	11.368	3.121
INPATIENTS	0.970	0.041	23.896	0.927	0.038	24.153	0.938	0.040	23.375	0.910	0.039	23.245
OUTPATIENTS	0.157	0.031	5.019	0.176	0.033	5.348	0.171	0.035	4.893	0.182	0.031	5.904
A&E	0.036	0.019	1.900	0.029	0.023	1.252	0.033	0.023	1.440	0.024	0.021	1.143
EP_SPELL	−29.575	4.799	−6.163	−32.327	4.055	−7.971	−29.536	4.310	−6.853	−32.544	4.139	−7.862
TRANS-IN	64.394	19.341	3.329	56.625	17.848	3.173	64.387	16.664	3.864	53.178	16.613	3.201
TRANS-OUT	−147.887	35.079	−4.216	−143.533	33.332	−4.306	−147.881	33.062	−4.473	−129.893	30.479	−4.262
EMERGENCY	20.020	6.832	2.930	19.607	7.692	2.549	20.112	8.053	2.497	18.445	7.260	2.541
FCE	76.637	34.122	2.246	96.344	43.935	2.193	76.644	41.787	1.834	103.534	43.477	2.381
FU-OUTPTS	2.254	0.452	4.991	2.057	0.424	4.848	2.059	0.443	4.650	1.872	0.396	4.729
EMERINDX	−75.196	33.218	−2.264	−52.414	43.175	−1.214	−75.176	49.389	−1.522	−50.225	38.350	−1.310
P-15	−15.374	5.834	−2.635	−13.249	6.788	−1.952	−15.341	7.675	−1.999	−12.366	5.585	−2.214
P-60	−18.160	7.069	−2.569	−15.284	8.528	−1.792	−18.090	9.093	−1.990	−14.431	7.796	−1.851
P-FEM	−26.868	10.250	−2.621	−25.550	12.164	−2.100	−26.814	12.544	−2.138	−25.134	11.211	−2.242
STUDENTS	729.548	453.161	1.610	659.641	484.717	1.361	729.548	398.860	1.829	677.993	439.978	1.541
RESEARCH	−0.121	0.064	−1.880	−0.129	0.054	−2.387	−0.149	0.056	−2.681	−0.130	0.051	−2.558
MFF	0.138	0.064	2.159	0.122	0.069	1.761	0.152	0.070	2.163	0.111	0.064	1.715
λ				2.279	0.364	6.266	1.723	0.560	3.078			
μ/σ_u							−0.005	1.764	−0.003			
θ										0.202	0.030	6.806
σ_v^2	12.988			12.988			17.899			14.651		

Total cost	COLS			Half-normal			Truncated normal			Exponential		
	Coeff.	s.e.	t	Coeff.	s.e.	t	Coeff.	s.e.	t	Coeff.	s.e.	t
σ_u^2					67.485			53.162			24.587	
Log-likelihood					−724.673			−726.098			−721.917	
Adj. R^2		0.947										
Efficiency												
mean		0.694			0.874			0.883			0.903	
s.d.		0.134			0.092			0.833			0.08	
min.–max.	0.178–1.000			0.396–1.000			0.420–0.990			0.500–0.992		

Table 3.6. Correlations across total cost specifications

Total Cost	COLS	Half-normal	Exponential
Scores			
COLS	1.000		
Half-normal	0.893*	1.000	
Exponential	0.814*	0.981*	1.000
Ranks			
COLS	1.000		
Half-normal	0.887*	1.000	
Exponential	0.832*	0.990*	1.000

Note:
* Significant at 0.01 level.

Table 3.7. Correlations across average and total cost specifications

	TC COLS	TC Half-normal	TC Exponential
Scores			
AC COLS	0.523*	0.572*	0.549*
AC Half-normal	0.647*	0.778*	0.788*
AC Exponential	0.585*	0.743*	0.793*
Ranks			
AC COLS	0.588*	0.731*	0.711*
AC Half-normal	0.639*	0.836*	0.838*
AC Exponential	0.611*	0.839*	0.843*

Note:
* Significant at 0.01 level.

there are no overarching statistical or economic criteria on which to base the decision. In such cases, the appropriate strategy and the robustness of results to alternative choices may depend on the purpose of the analysis and the nature of the data.

Some of the problems confronting the analyst might be alleviated if more data were available, particularly if organisations were observed more than once. The advantages of panel data, and the techniques available to analyse these data in the context of efficiency measurement, are the subject of the next chapter.

4 | *Stochastic frontier analysis of panel data*

4.1 Introduction

THE previous chapter discussed econometric approaches to efficiency analysis when only cross-sectional data are available. Along with general issues of specifying the estimation model, particular attention was drawn to the interpretation placed on the residual and the assumptions required in order to extract estimates of efficiency. Some of the strong assumptions required for efficiency analysis based on cross-sectional data may be relaxed if longitudinal data are available, with organisations observed over several time periods. Repeated observations of the same organisation make it possible to control for unobservable organisation-specific attributes and, thereby, to extract more reliable parameter estimates, both of the explanatory variables and of the efficiency term. Specifically three shortcomings of cross-sectional analysis can be addressed (Schmidt and Lin 1984).

First, recall from the previous chapter that, when only a single observation is available per organisation, it is necessary, in order to partition the composite error term, to specify how inefficiency is distributed among organisations. Standard software allows analysts to choose truncated normal, half-normal, exponential and gamma distributions. However, there is no economic basis for selecting one distribution over another and the choice is somewhat arbitrary (Schmidt 1985). Repeated observations of the same organisation can substitute for distributional assumptions if the fixed-effects panel data estimator is used.

Second, under some formulations of the production model the inefficiency term, u_i, and the explanatory variables, x_i, are unlikely to be independent. For instance, it is quite likely that if an organisation knows its level of technical efficiency this will affect its choice of input levels. By the same reasoning, a firm may make its input choices in order to attain a specific level of efficiency. Again, use of the fixed-effects estimator makes it possible to avoid the assumption of independence.

69

Third, in cross-sections, only the entire residual, ε_i, can be estimated consistently, with the variance of the conditional distribution of u_i failing to become zero as the sample size approaches infinity. With panel data, adding more observations from the same organisation generates more information about each organisation so that u_i can be estimated consistently as the number of observations over time approaches infinity. That said, in many applications organisations are not observed frequently enough for the benefit of consistency to be realised (Kumbhakar and Lovell 2000).

The panel data model applied to a cost function takes the following general form:

$$C_{it} = \alpha + \beta x_{it} + u_{it} + v_{it}, \quad u_{it} \geq 0 \qquad (4.1)$$

where t indexes time, and u_{it} captures inefficiency. Two broad approaches have emerged in order to estimate this model, distinguished according to beliefs about whether or not efficiency varies across time periods. Naturally, estimation is simplified if efficiency can be assumed to be constant over time.

4.2 Time-invariant efficiency

In the presence of time-invariant efficiency, the model in (4.1) reduces to:

$$C_{it} = \alpha + \beta x_{it} + u_i + v_{it}, \quad u_i \geq 0 \qquad (4.2)$$

Three main methods have been used to estimate this model:

- fixed-effects, estimated using ordinary least squares;
- random-effects, estimated using generalised least squares;
- random-effects, estimated by maximum likelihood.

The fixed-effects (FE) estimator is equivalent to adding a dummy variable for all but one organisation, with this remaining organisation identified by the constant term. This procedure generates a set of organisation-specific intercepts, $\alpha_i = \alpha + u_i$ (Schmidt and Lin 1984). Analogously to the COLS approach in the cross-sectional context, the estimated frontier, $\hat{\alpha}$, is located by assuming that the organisation with the lowest intercept is fully efficient (in the case of the cost function), such that $\hat{\alpha} = \min_i(\alpha_i)$. Estimates of $\hat{u}_i$ are derived from $\hat{u}_i = \alpha_i - \min_i(\alpha_i)$. If the model is specified in natural units, organisation-specific estimates of technical efficiency, eff_i, are calculated as $eff_{it} = (\hat{\beta}x_{it} + \hat{u}_i)(\hat{\beta}x_{it})^{-1}$. For logarithmic models the calculation is $eff_i = \exp(\hat{u}_i)$ (Battese and Coelli 1988; Coelli and Perelman 1996).

The FE estimator is attractive because it does not require the imposition of distributional assumptions about u, nor is it necessary to assume that inefficiency is uncorrelated with the regressors. However, the estimator does require there to be variation within organisations over time in respect to the factors that explain the levels of cost or output. In other words, the value of x must vary for individual organisations from one period to the next. If not, the FE estimator is susceptible to two limitations, one common to all panel data applications, the other particularly important in the stochastic frontier context.

First is the problem of attenuation bias, whereby measurement error in the independent variables causes coefficient estimates to tend towards zero. This problem is exacerbated by the FE estimator because it eliminates a large amount of variation in the data. This can lead to FE estimates being interpreted as having little or no effect (McKinnish 2000). Second, at the extreme, if there are organisational factors that explain costs but which do not vary at all over time – such as the operating environment – their influence will be captured by the organisation-specific term, α_i. Thus, the FE estimator fails to distinguish between time-invariant heterogeneity and inefficiency. This confounding might be a serious shortcoming, with organisations being identified as more or less 'efficient' than they would be if the model was correctly specified.

If one wishes to include time-invariant regressors this can be achieved by using a random-effects (RE) estimator. Opting for the RE one in preference to the FE one comes at a price: it is necessary to impose distributional assumptions on u and to assume that there is no correlation between the regressors and the u_i's. If one can accept these assumptions (remembering that they were unavoidable in the cross-sectional context) the random-effects model can be estimated by either generalised least squares (GLS) or maximum likelihood estimation (MLE). These two estimators are both more efficient than the FE estimator, this informational advantage deriving from the distributional assumption imposed on u. Essentially, the random-effects model assumes that organisational effects are random draws from an underlying population. Accordingly, the RE estimator is able to utilise information about variation both within individual organ-isations over time (within-variation) – as for the FE estimator – and across different organisations in the sample (between-variation) – unlike the FE estimator.

The choice between the GLS and maximum likelihood RE estima-tors requires weighing further considerations, with the GLS estimator requiring fewer distributional assumptions, but at the cost of being less efficient than the maximum likelihood estimator.

Under GLS, the RE model to be estimated can be written as (Kumbhakar and Lovell 2000):

$$C_{it} = [\alpha + E(u_i)] + \beta x_{it} + [u_i - E(u_i)] + v_{it}$$
$$= \alpha^* + \beta x_{it} + u_i^* + v_{it}, \quad u_i \geq 0 \tag{4.3}$$

where $E(u_i)$ is the mean estimate of technical efficiency. The GLS estimator requires only weak assumptions about the shape and loca-tion of the u, namely that the u_i are randomly distributed with con-stant mean and variance (Kumbhakar and Lovell 2000). Estimation follows a two-step procedure in which ordinary least squares (OLS) is first applied to obtain parameter estimates, including variance com-ponents for v_{it} and u_i^*. The parameters are then re-estimated in a second stage by feasible GLS, using the OLS estimates as starting values. The u_i^* can then be recovered as estimates of the mean residual over time for organisation i:

$$\hat{u}_i^* = \frac{1}{T} \sum_t (C_{it} - \hat{\alpha}_i^* - \hat{\beta} x_{it}) \tag{4.4}$$

The estimates of u_i are then derived as $\hat{u}_i = \min_i(\hat{u}_i^*) + \hat{u}_i^*$, with tech-nical efficiency estimates obtained as previously described for the FE estimator. These estimates are consistent as the numbers of both organisations and time periods approach infinity.

The earliest application of stochastic frontier analysis in the panel data context employed the RE model estimated by maximum like-lihood (Pitt and Lee 1981). This requires stronger assumptions about the shape of the distribution of u than are needed for GLS estimation. Here the model takes the form (Greene 1993):

$$C_{it} = \alpha + \beta x_{it} + u_i + v_{it} \tag{4.5}$$

with u_i distributed as $u_i \sim N^+(\mu, \sigma_u^2)$. Choices about distributional shape have followed those made in the cross-sectional context, with

Pitt and Lee formulating a half-normal likelihood function (Pitt and Lee 1981) and Battese and Coelli generalising this to a truncated normal (Battese and Coelli 1988). Estimation requires specification of the likelihood function and derivation of the distribution of u conditional upon the composite error in order to obtain organisation-specific estimates of efficiency. Maximum likelihood estimates may be sensitive to the iterative process and updating methods and even rescaling the dependent variable can yield different parameter and efficiency estimates. Particular care must be taken in applying this technique to ensure that estimates reflect convergence to the global rather than to a local maximum.

The choice, then, among these various estimators is not straightforward and requires weighing a set of distinct advantages and disadvantages associated with each estimator, as summarised in Table 4.1. In some contexts and for some data sets it may be possible to make an unequivocal choice. The FE estimator is to be preferred if:

1. The analyst wishes to avoid imposing an assumption about how efficiency is distributed.
2. There is evidence of correlation between the regressors and the u_i. The Hausman test can be used to check this possibility (Hausman 1978).
3. There are no time-invariant regressors to be included in the model.
4. The purpose of the estimation process is to generate inferences about individual organisations. In such circumstances the assumption that the effects are random draws from a population may be unwarranted (Rice and Jones 1997).

4.2.1 Empirical application

In order to illustrate some of the models introduced in this chapter we use data for acute hospitals in England observed over four financial years from 1994/95 to 1997/98. The variables in the data set are described in the Appendix. As would be expected, not every model reviewed in the chapter can be applied: some are ruled out by the characteristics of these particular data. For simplicity the panel is balanced, with hospitals included only if data are available for all four years. Four years' worth of data is available for 185 hospitals, giving a total of 740 observations. These data are summarised in Table 4.2.

Table 4.1. *Summary of time-invariant SF panel data models*

Time-invariant efficiency	Assumptions	Advantages	Disadvantages
FE model	$u_i \geq 0$; $v_{it} \sim N(0, \sigma_v^2)$	No distributional assumptions required for u_i No need to assume that u_i independent of x_{it} and v_{it}	One organisation assumed 100 per cent efficient Can exacerbate attenuation bias Cannot include time-invariant regressors u_i captures technical efficiency and *all* time-invariant effects u_i consistency requires both $N \to +\infty$ and $T \to +\infty$
RE model GLS	$u_i \geq 0$; $v_{it} \sim N(0, \sigma_v^2)$ u_i constant mean and variance u_i uncorrelated with x_{it} and v_{it}	Weak distributional assumptions on u_i Allows time-invariant regressors Appropriate when N is large and T is small	Assume corr $(x, u) = 0$ u_i consistency requires both $N \to +\infty$ and $T \to +\infty$
RE model ML	$u_i \geq 0$; $u_i \sim N^+(\mu, \sigma_u^2)$; $v_{it} \sim N(0, \sigma_u^2)$. u_i uncorrelated with x_{it} and v_{it}	Most efficient because exploits most distributional information u_i consistency requires only $T \to +\infty$	Requires strong distributional assumption for u Assume corr $(x, u) = 0$ Estimates may reflect convergence to local rather than global maximum

Table 4.2. Descriptive statistics

Description		Mean	Std Dev.	Minimum	Maximum
Dependent variable					
C (£'000)	1994/95	52,047	24,969	9,294	156,999
	1995/96	55,053	26,491	10,944	166,176
	1996/97	57,496	27,483	10,822	175,736
	1997/98	59,835	28,926	11,919	182,184
Explanatory variables					
INPATIENTS	1994/95	40,064	20,074	1,647	144,616
	1995/96	40,278	18,641	4,477	110,569
	1996/97	40,465	19,138	4,668	104,045
	1997/98	41,711	20,276	3,469	107,242
OUTPATIENTS	1994/95	45,021	23,110	0	136,569
	1995/96	47,981	25,107	0	130,538
	1996/97	49,538	27,168	0	149,526
	1997/98	50,803	26,619	0	146,721
A&E	1994/95	48,601	27,745	0	137,865
	1995/96	48,098	28,396	0	157,042
	1996/97	46,941	29,876	0	160,136
	1997/98	48,473	31,285	0	165,145

For illustrative purposes fairly straightforward models have been specified, the intention being to maximise the amount of variation in the 'unexplained' part of the model. There are two components to the restrictive assumptions we have made. First, the dependent variable, total cost (in £'000), is not adjusted for inflation. In health care, a panel of only four years is likely to be too short to identify major shifts of the production function, so in order to give the appearance of temporal change we illustrate the estimation techniques using an undeflated cost series without including a time trend. This matter is important only for the models that allow for time-varying inefficiency.

Second, the model is estimated in linear form on a parsimonious set of regressors. Total undeflated costs are regressed on a set of variables capturing output (Y_S), with S being an output category. Only three types of output are included: the number of case mix weighted inpatient admissions; first outpatient attendances; and visits to Accident and Emergency (A&E). The other variables included in the cross-sectional model in the previous chapter are omitted from most of the examples considered in this chapter. These variables are considered exogenous to hospital control, and their omission implies that substantial heterogeneity among hospitals is not being accounted for. Their omission has implications for the estimation of the amount of efficiency considered present in the sample and, indeed, whether or not it is possible to estimate these models in the first place. We shall return to the issue of their omission later in the chapter.

Towards the end of the chapter we address the sensitivity of results to decisions about how the dependent variable is defined, function form, and the inclusion of additional explanatory variables.

Descriptive data for the four variables are presented in Table 4.2, with the mean values for each year plotted in Figure 4.1. Over the period, total undeflated costs in the average hospital increased by 15%. Activity also increased, but less rapidly. There was a 4% increase in hospital admissions and a 13% increase in outpatient attendances. Despite some year-on-year variation, visits to A&E were the same at the end as at the beginning of the period. We analyse the data in order to consider two questions:

- Was the increase in activity sufficient to offset the increase in costs? If not, we would expect mean efficiency to have declined over the period.
- Are estimates of the mean level of efficiency and the variation in efficiency among hospitals sensitive to model specification?

We start with the time-invariant FE model specified by Schmidt and Sickles (1984). Results are shown in the middle columns of Table 4.3. Parameter estimates suggest that, for the average hospital, an additional hospital episode increases total cost by £195, an outpatient attendance by £134 and an A&E visit by £9. These estimates are considerably different from the OLS estimates taken as starting values (£919, £296 and £41 respectively for the three activity categories). The discrepancies may suggest attenuation bias or be due to there being very little time variation (within-variation) in these data: 95% of the variation in the data arises from differences *between* hospitals

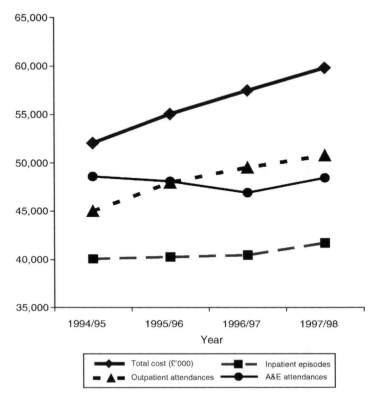

Figure 4.1. Mean changes in costs and activity over time.

not *within* them over time. This lack of temporal variation reduces the appeal of using the fixed-effects estimator.

Estimates of technical efficiency are shown at the foot of the table. Average efficiency for the period as a whole is estimated to be 61%, ranging from 24% to 100%. As this model is specified in natural units it is possible to calculate technical efficiency for each year to give an estimate of temporal change. However, temporal change is driven by changes in the value of the regressors *not* u_i, with technical efficiency being calculated as $eff_{it} = (\hat{\beta}x_{it} + \hat{u}_i)(\hat{\beta}x_{it})^{-1}$ when the model is calibrated in natural units. These estimates suggest that changes in activity were not sufficient to offset the cost increases, efficiency declining from 63.6% in 1994/95 to 59.5% in 1997/98 (see Table 4.6).

Table 4.3. Estimates from time-invariant SF models

Total cost	OLS			FE: Schmidt and Sickles			RE: Pitt and Lee		
	Coeff.	s.e.	t	Coeff.	s.e.	t	Coeff.	s.e.	t
CONSTANT	2,419,969	991,655	2.54	4,128,033	206,562	2.68	3,219,818	1,124,889	2.84
INPATIENTS	919	32	28.55	195	47	4.57	618	34	18.45
OUTPATIENTS	297	24	12.08	134	22	6.07	260	19	13.53
A&E	41	16	2.62	9	13	0.69	59	12	4.95
Log likelihood							−746.247		
Adj. R^2	0.846			0.834					
Efficiency									
mean				0.613			0.779		
s.d.				0.115			0.106		
min.–max.				0.239–1.000			0.410–0.979		

By way of comparison, we estimate the RE model of Pitt and Lee (Pitt and Lee 1981). There is a danger with the RE model that iteration may not be to a global maximum, and this appears to be the case here, as evidenced by the sensitivity of results to a change in the scale of the dependent variable. When costs are measured in a similar scale to the regressors (i.e. they are measured in £'000), mean efficiency is estimated to be 77.9%, with the model taking fifty-three iterations to converge. If costs remain in their original unit (£), the model converges after eleven iterations, with mean efficiency estimated to be 74.2%. In fact, for these data the RE model is inappropriate, with the Hausman test being significantly in favour of a fixed-effects specification ($\chi^2 = 245.84$, $p < 0.001$).

4.3 Time-varying efficiency

Perhaps the most critical drawback of the time-invariant estimators considered in the preceding sections is the assumption that organisational efficiency is constant over time. The assumption of a constant level of efficiency is not particularly appealing in contexts where data are observed over long periods or when there are expected to be external influences that affect the temporal pattern of efficiency, such as periodic regulatory initiatives. Indeed, the purpose of the analytical exercise often is to explore the impact of such initiatives on organisational efficiency. In such situations, allowing efficiency to vary over time is a necessary condition of analysis.

If efficiency is believed to vary over time, for whatever reason, the challenge is how best to model this. Two questions require consideration:

- What is the general pattern of efficiency change over time?
- Are individual organisations likely to experience different temporal patterns of efficiency change?

The simplest approach to modelling temporal changes in efficiency is to assume that the effect is the same for all organisations. There are a number of ways that the model can be adapted to accommodate this effect.

One possibility is to employ a two-way error components model, in which inefficiency is separated into two components, one specific to each organisation, u_i, the other industry-wide but particular to each period, γ_t:

$$u_{it} = u_i + \gamma_t \tag{4.6}$$

This formulation enriches the model only slightly, in that the temporal effect is assumed identical for each organisation (Greene 1993).

A less restrictive assumption would be for the temporal *pattern* of efficiency change to be the same for all organisations, but for the *magnitude* to differ among organisations. This is not an unrealistic scenario. In many contexts, the pattern of change may be common across the industry, perhaps because of technological and knowledge transfer among organisations. However, the pace of transfer may not be uniform, with organisations differing in how quickly they embrace such advances. The specification proposed by Lee and Schmidt captures this possibility (Lee and Schmidt 1993):

$$u_{it} = \gamma(t)u_i \tag{4.7}$$

This is equivalent to introducing a set of dummy variables for time interacted with the individual efficiency component. Lee and Schmidt outline how the model is amenable to use of the fixed-effects estimator and that a random-effects model can be estimated using GLS. If $\gamma_t = 1$, $\forall t$ efficiency is constant over time. The virtue of this formulation is that it is not necessary to impose any assumptions about how efficiency changes over time. This specification is particularly appropriate for short panels, but too many additional dummy variables are introduced for the formulation to be of use in longer panels.

Kumbhakar proposed a similar formulation to that of Lee and Schmidt, but rather than $\gamma(t)$ being represented by a set of dummy variables, a distribution was imposed on the evolution of efficiency, this being specified as an exponential function of time, $\gamma(t) = (1 + \exp(\phi_1 t + \phi_2 t^2))^{-1}$ (Kumbhakar 1990). This ensures that $0 \leq \gamma(t) \leq 1$ and, depending on the signs of ϕ_1 and ϕ_2, allows the function to increase or decrease in a monotonic fashion, or to be convex or concave.

A slightly different exponential specification was proposed by Battese and Coelli, such that $\gamma(t) = \exp(-\phi(t - T))$ (Battese and Coelli 1992). Simplicity comes at the cost of imposing less flexibility on the function, with interpretation of how efficiency changes over time being restricted to decreasing at an increasing rate if $\phi > 0$, increasing at an increasing rate if $\phi < 0$, and being time-invariant if $\phi = 0$. This model is estimated below.

An alternative approach, suitable when the number of time periods is large relative to the number of organisations, was proposed by Cornwell, Schmidt and Sickles (1990). Under their formulation it is necessary to specify how efficiency might be expected to evolve over time. Cornwell *et al.* propose a quadratic specification and describe a two-stage procedure for estimation of a fixed-effects model (although when the ratio of organisations to time periods is small it is possible to undertake estimation in a single stage). The first stage involves estimation of the production model, taking the form $c_{it} = \beta x_{it} + \varepsilon_{it}$. The residuals, $\hat{\varepsilon}_{it}$, from this equation are then regressed on time under the following formulation:

$$\hat{\varepsilon}_{it} = \gamma_{i1} + \gamma_{i2}t + \gamma_{i3}t^2 \tag{4.8}$$

This model requires estimation of an additional three parameters per organisation, which can be cumbersome with large samples. The fitted values from the above equation are interpreted as estimates of α_{it}. Analogously to a cost function estimated on cross-sectional data, in the panel data context, at time t, the frontier $\hat{\alpha}_t$ and firm-specific estimate of inefficiency, $\hat{u}_{it}$, are calculated respectively as $\hat{\alpha}_t = \min_i(\alpha_{it})$ and $\hat{u}_{it} = \alpha_{it} - \min_i(\alpha_{it})$. This formulation makes it possible to test assumptions about the nature of efficiency over time and across organisations. If, indeed, efficiency is time-invariant, this would imply that $\gamma_{i2}t = \gamma_{i3}t^2 = 0, \forall i$. If changes in efficiency – or technical changes – are common across all organisations this would imply that $\gamma_{i2} = \gamma_2, \forall i$ and $\gamma_{i3} = \gamma_3, \forall i$.

4.3.1 Empirical application

Estimates from the Battese and Coelli specification (Battese and Coelli 1992) are presented in Table 4.4. Parameter estimates suggest that, for the average hospital, an additional hospital episode increases total cost by £822, an outpatient attendance by £293 and an A&E visit by £88. While mean efficiency over the period as a whole is similar to that for the Schmidt and Sickles (1984) specification where u_i was assumed time-invariant, the temporal gradient is now considerably steeper because the values of both the regressors and u_i are allowed to vary over time. Average efficiency was estimated as being 65% in 1994/95. By 1997/98 this had fallen to 56%.

Table 4.4. Estimates from time-varying SF models

	Battese and Coelli			
Total cost	Coeff.	s.e.	t	
CONSTANT	−8,946,580	1,000,000	−894,653.00	
INPATIENTS	822	26	31.23	
OUTPATIENTS	293	19	15.67	
A&E	88	12	7.57	
ϕ	−0.123	0.012	−10.647	
Log likelihood		12,735		
Efficiency	mean	s.d.	min.	max.
1994/95	0.652	0.199	0.041	1.000
1995/96	0.624	0.225	0.037	1.000
1996/97	0.595	0.255	0.033	1.000
1997/98	0.565	0.288	0.029	1.000

4.4 Unobserved heterogeneity

One of the key benefits of using panel data is the ability to control for unobserved individual heterogeneity (Baltagi 2005). Organisations may face different external constraints that influence the costs of production but that are not within their control and that cannot be measured directly. Hospital location is an example. Hospitals might have higher costs because levels of sickness are greater among their local population or because there is poor integration of care among primary care providers. Often data on these location effects are poorly measured, or only weak proxies are available. Cross-sectional or time-series analyses are unable to control adequately for such factors and produce biased estimates (Baltagi 2005). Standard panel data models are able to overcome this deficiency, with unobserved organisation-specific characteristics being captured by the fixed or random effect.

When applied to stochastic frontiers, however, panel data models can no longer be considered 'standard'. The specifications described in the preceding sections of this chapter have lost this attractive feature of panel data estimators. This is because the fixed or random effect is interpreted as arising solely from inefficiency. As in cross-sectional efficiency analysis it has to be *assumed* that the stochastic frontier model is specified correctly and that all relevant factors have been observed accurately. In short, the specifications described previously in this chapter assume there to be no unobserved heterogeneity among organisations. If this assumption is false, the fixed or random effect will contain a mixture of inefficiency and unobserved heterogeneity.

Recent developments in the efficiency literature have sought to address this shortcoming, recognising that the assumption is a strong one. The general approach has been to specify separate expressions to capture efficiency and unobserved heterogeneity. Greene has pioneered this line of work, describing both fixed- and random-effects estimators that he describes as 'true' specifications of the stochastic frontier model (Greene 2004; Greene 2005).

The 'true' FE model includes organisational dummies as an additional set of explanatory variables (Polachek and Yoon 1996; Greene 2004), the resulting specification being written as:

$$C_{it} = \beta x_{it} + \alpha_i + u_{it} + v_{it}$$
$$u_{it} \sim |N(0, \sigma_u^2)|, \quad v_{it} \sim N(0, \sigma_v^2) \tag{4.9}$$

Under the Schmidt and Sickles formulation of the FE model with time-invariant inefficiency the fixed effects were interpreted as inefficiency (Schmidt and Sickles 1984). In Greene's 'true' FE model the fixed effects capture unobserved heterogeneity (Greene 2004). The drawback of this specification is the incidental parameters problem, whereby the number of parameters to be estimated increases with sample size (the same problem afflicts the other specifications in which the organisation is used to create a variable).

The 'true' RE model includes a random constant term, α_i, which is a time-invariant organisation-specific parameter that captures heterogeneity. Unlike the 'true' FE model it is necessary to specify the distribution of α_i which Greene considers to be i.i.d. normal (Greene 2004). It is also necessary to assume that the organisation-specific effects are uncorrelated with the regressors. In recognition of this limitation, Farsi, Filippini and Kuenzle have extended Greene's 'true' RE model using Mundlak's formulation of a 'within' estimator' to control for the possibility of correlation between α_i and the x_{it}'s (Farsi, Filippini and Kuenzle 2003).

4.4.1 Empirical application

Greene provides two 'true' fixed-effects specifications of the stochastic frontier in Limdep version 8.0, one of which assumes that efficiency is time-invariant, with the second relaxing this assumption (Greene 2002). The former is specified as:

$$C_{it} = \beta x_{it} + \alpha_i + u_i + v_{it}$$
$$u_i \sim |N(0, \sigma_u^2)|, \quad v_{it} \sim N(0, \sigma_v^2)$$

(4.10)

The latter is a two-way error components model, specified as:

$$C_{it} = \beta x_{it} + \alpha_i + u_i + \gamma_t + v_{it}$$
$$u_i \sim |N(0, \sigma_u^2)|, \quad v_{it} \sim N(0, \sigma_v^2)$$

(4.11)

Parameter and efficiency estimates for the two models are in Table 4.5. The final estimates are found after a large number of iterations, suggesting the lack of a global maximum. The parameter estimates are similar to those of the Battese and Coelli (1992) model.

The most striking change from previous models considered in this chapter, as might be expected, is in the estimate of efficiency. The mean level of efficiency was estimated to be around 60–75% in the preceding models but, as Greene points out, these estimates contain a mixture of inefficiency and unobserved heterogeneity. When this is taken into account, mean efficiency over the entire period is estimated as being 92%, declining from 93.3% in 1994/95 to 89.6% in 1997/98. This order of magnitude is similar to that reported when switching from a COLS to the stochastic frontier approach in the cross-sectional context. Given that the same argument applies in the panel data context, failure to account for unobserved heterogeneity must be considered a serious drawback.

That said, little reliance should be placed on these estimates, as both models are highly unstable for these data, with no global maximum being found. This is particularly a problem with the two-way error components model. The majority of observations are estimated as fully efficient, while a few are assessed as being located a great distance from the frontier, as illustrated by the unfeasible negative minimum values that have been produced, which influence the dramatic year-on-year changes in the estimate of mean efficiency. The inability to locate a global maximum may be due to the lack of variation in the data, itself implying that hospitals may be operating at similar levels of efficiency.

Table 4.5. Estimates from 'true' SF models

Total cost	Time-invariant 'true' FE model			Two-way error components 'true' FE model		
	Coeff.	s.e.	t	Coeff.	s.e.	t
INPATIENTS	881	0.001	1,158,640	885	0.001	836,225
OUTPATIENTS	250	0.001	317,350	250	0.001	294,957
A&E	15	0.001	27,131	−1	0.001	−2,333.74
λ	20.622	0.111	1,858,210	20.629	0.000	955,757
Period 1				−0.327	0.000	−6,209.83
Period 2				−0.046	0.000	−958.078
Period 3				−0.058	0.000	−1,132.98
Log likelihood	−4865.28			−19461.65		

Efficiency	mean	s.d.	min.	max.	mean	s.d.	min.	max.
1994/95	0.933	0.228	−0.491	1.000	0.768	0.373	−0.7	1.000
1995/96	0.937	0.201	−0.129	1.000	0.760	0.356	−0.598	1.000
1996/97	0.897	0.284	−1.143	1.000	0.989	0.089	0.141	1.000
1997/98	0.896	0.283	−1.026	1.000	0.720	0.397	−0.667	1.000

4.5 Summary and sensitivity analysis

For the purposes of illustration, this chapter has considered a simple model in which costs are regressed against three measures of activity. Two questions were posed of the data for 185 hospitals observed over four years:

1. Was the increase in activity sufficient to offset the increase in costs?
2. Are estimates of the mean level of efficiency and the variation in efficiency among hospitals sensitive to model specification?

Five competing models were applied to the data, three of which assume time-invariant efficiency, these being:

- the Schmidt and Sickles FE model (S&S) (Schmidt and Sickles 1984)
- the Pitt and Lee RE model (P&L) (Pitt and Lee 1981)
- the Greene time-invariant 'true' FE model (True FE) (Greene 2004)

and two of which allow time-varying efficiency, these being

- the Battese and Coelli model (B&C) (Battese and Coelli 1992)
- the Greene 'true' two-way error components model (Two-way) (Greene 2004)

These are not of equal suitability when applied to this data set. The Pitt and Lee specification is ruled out by the Hausman test; the two Greene models fail to converge to a global maximum.

The parameter and efficiency estimates from these five models are reproduced in Table 4.6. All but the two-way error components model suggest that efficiency declined over time. But even the mean efficiency estimates differ considerably, implying that results are sensitive to how efficiency is specified.

Various conditions have been imposed on the analysis so that these data can serve their illustrative purpose. Relaxation of some of these conditions in the ways which follow yields different conclusions:

- deflating costs;
- including additional regressors;
- estimating the model in logarithmic form.

First, the failure to deflate costs or to add a time trend gives the impression of more temporal variation in the dependent variable

Table 4.6. Comparison of estimates from different models

Coefficients	Time-invariant			Time-varying	
	S&S	P&L	True FE	B&C	Two-way
INPATIENTS	195	619	881	822	881
OUTPATIENTS	134	260	250	293	250
A&E	8	59	15	88	1
Mean efficiency					
Year 1	63.6		93.3	65.2	76.8
Year 2	61.9		93.7	62.4	76.0
Year 3	60.5		89.7	59.5	98.9
Year 4	59.5		89.6	56.5	72.0
Overall	61.3	77.9	91.6	60.7	80.9
Comments			iterations >100	iterations >100	iterations >100

than is in fact the case. This does not affect the models that assume time-invariant inefficiency or the estimates of relative efficiency within a particular year. However, for the time-varying models variation in costs over time due to inflation will be captured by the u_{it}. Thus the industry-wide inefficiency will be overestimated.

Second, the chosen model is parsimonious, including only three explanatory variables. Inclusion of additional variables, corresponding to those in the specification used for the cross-sectional analysis in the previous chapter, has a substantial effect, as shown in Table 4.7. For the Schmidt and Sickles specification, mean efficiency increases from around 61% to 74%. The other specifications fail to converge or the inefficiency term is wrongly skewed.

Finally, the original model with just three explanatory variables is estimated in logarithmic form. According to the FE model, mean efficiency is around 79%, substantially higher than when specifying the variables in natural units. The Greene true FE time-invariant model converges successfully, and suggests higher levels of efficiency than implied by the Schmidt and Sickles specification. This is to be expected given that the Greene model includes both α_i and u_i. Greene's

Table 4.7. Sensitivity analysis of mean efficiency

Deflated costs	Time-invariant			Time-varying	
	S&S	P&L	True FE	B&C	Two-way
Year 1	63.6		86.8	73.5	
Year 2	61.9		86.6	73	
Year 3	60.5		82.1	72.5	
Year 4	59.5		76.6	72	
Overall	61.4	74.6	83.0	73.1	
Comments			iterations >100	iterations >100	unable to converge

Additional regressors	Time-invariant			Time-varying	
	S&S	P&L	True FE	B&C	Two-way
Year 1	74.5			62.9	
Year 2	73.4			60.6	
Year 3	75			58.5	
Year 4	74.2			56.5	
Overall	74.3	72.6		59.6	
Comments			wrong skew	iterations >100	wrong skew

Logarithmic	Time-invariant			Time-varying	
	S&S	P&L	True FE	B&C	Two-way
Year 1			85	78.1	
Year 2			84.8	74.1	
Year 3			84.2	69.9	
Year 4			84.4	64.9	
Overall	79.3	53.8	84.6	71.8	
Comments					singular covariance matrix

two-way error components model cannot be estimated, however, because the covariance matrix is singular.

The Battese and Coelli model also converges when estimation is in logarithmic form, and suggests lower levels of efficiency than the alternative specifications, with a more steeply declining time trend.

We return to our two original questions. First, was the increase in activity sufficient to offset the increase in costs? With the exception of the Battese and Coelli model applied to logarithmic data, none of the time-varying models converged for these data. This failure may be due to there being little variation among hospitals in their levels of efficiency over time.

The second issue was whether estimates of the mean level of efficiency and the variation in efficiency among hospitals are sensitive to model specification. Indeed they are. The Schmidt and Sickles FE model proved the most appropriate for these data, with the models based on maximum likelihood failing to converge in many instances. Estimates are also sensitive to specification choices, such as the choice of explanatory variables and functional form.

4.6 Conclusions

In this and the preceding chapter we have discussed the key technical choices that have to be made when developing a stochastic frontier model. For many of these choices, the appropriate decision depends on the objective of the analysis and on the nature of the data. Some estimation decisions can be made on statistical grounds. However, the statistical criteria developed to evaluate econometric models are rarely suitable for assessing the suitability of stochastic frontier models, simply because the focus of the latter is on placing an interpretation on the residuals. In view of this, the analyst usually has to make recourse to sensitivity analysis of the modelling approach. If estimates – or, at least, rankings – of individual organisations are little affected by alternative technical choices, greater confidence can be placed in the results. Frequently, however, results are highly sensitive to the estimation decisions made, as was so for the case studies of the cross-sectional data considered in chapter 3 and of the panel data analysed in this chapter.

Given the challenges associated with model construction, such as specification of functional form and identification and extraction of efficiency estimates, an alternative strand of efficiency analysis has been developed which supposedly allow the 'data to speak for themselves'. Data envelopment analysis requires no prior specification of the functional form, with the efficiency frontier positioned and shaped by the data rather than by theoretical considerations. This non-parametric technique is the subject of the next chapter.

5 | Data envelopment analysis

5.1 Introduction

D ATA envelopment analysis (DEA) has become the dominant
approach to efficiency measurement in health care and in
many other sectors of the economy (Hollingsworth 2003).
While the parametric approach is guided by economic theory, DEA is
a data-driven approach. The location (and the shape) of the efficiency
frontier is determined by the data, using the simple notion that an
organisation that employs less input than another to produce the same
amount of output can be considered more efficient. Those observations
with the highest ratios of output to input are considered efficient, and
the efficiency frontier is constructed by joining these observations up in
the input-output space. The frontier thus comprises a series of linear
segments connecting one efficient observation to another. The construction of the frontier is based on 'best observed practice' and is therefore
only an approximation to the true, unobserved efficiency frontier.

Inefficient organisations are 'enveloped' by the efficiency frontier in
DEA. The inefficiency of the organisations within the frontier boundary is calculated relative to this surface (Grosskopf and Valdmanis
1987; Charnes *et al.* 1994; Cooper, Seiford and Tone 2000). This
chapter outlines the distinctive features of the DEA methodology, along
with key issues in specifying and judging the quality of a DEA model.

5.2 The DEA methodology

DEA literature traditionally uses the terminology of a decision-
making unit (DMU) for each of the units of analysis under scrutiny,
a term coined by Charnes, Cooper and Rhodes (1978) in their
seminal paper which introduced DEA. The DMU can reflect a whole
range of different levels in health care settings, including the entire
health care system (comparing countries) (Puig-Junoy 1998a), health

regions or health districts (Ozcan and Cotter 1994; Gerdtham, Rehnberg and Tambour 1999), hospitals (Grosskopf and Valdmanis
1987), specific services or departments (Puig-Junoy 1998b; Hollingsworth and Parkin 2001), and individual physicians (Chilingerian
1994). In this chapter, the choice of unit of analysis is taken as given,
and the methodology is described in relation to comparing a given set
of similar DMUs.

In this section, we examine within the context of DEA the various
notions of efficiency assuming a constant returns to scale production
technology. In section 5.3 we shall introduce the concept of variable
returns to scale and the notion of *scale efficiency*. In DEA we can
examine the efficiency of DMUs using either an input or an output
orientation. *Input-oriented technical efficiency measures* keep output
fixed and explore the proportional reduction in input usage which is
possible, while *output-oriented technical efficiency measures* keep
input constant and explore the proportional expansion in output
quantities that are possible. We now illustrate efficiency measurement
for DEA under each of these possibilities.

5.2.1 *Input-oriented efficiency*

Suppose a DMU uses two inputs (x_1 and x_2) to produce a single output
(y) as depicted in Figure 5.1. In the health care setting, we could for
example depict a hospital using two inputs (doctors and nurses) to
produce a single output (patients treated). Assuming diminishing marginal factor productivity, isoquants can be constructed that are convex
to the origin. Thus, along the frontier, reduced use of one input, say x_1
(doctors), necessitates an increase (or no decrease) in the use of the
other input, x_2 (nurses), in order to maintain the level of treatment
provided.

Assume that the curve ZZ' represents the production frontier. All
DMUs lie on the production frontier (if they are efficient) or above it
(if they are inefficient). Using the input-orientation, DMUs which lie
above the production frontier could proportionally reduce their input
usage (x_1 and x_2) for a given output level (y). Thus hospital A could
proportionally reduce its use of doctors and nurses, given the amount of
treatment it provides, and move to a feasible and technically efficient
production point such as that adopted by hospital B.

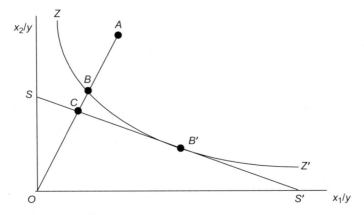

Figure 5.1. Technical and allocative efficiency under an input orientation.

SS' is a budget line, or isocost line, which reflects the ratio of prices of the inputs (x_1 and x_2), in this case the relative price of labour. The cost-efficient point of production is B' where the marginal rate of substitution of x_1 for x_2 is equal to the price ratio. Hospital A's production is currently above the production frontier which is clearly inefficient (more inputs are required to produce the output at A than if it were to move to a point such as B or B'). In DEA, technical inefficiency is usually measured using the notion of the *radial* measure of inefficiency, by comparing where the hospital is located in relation to the production function (distance BA) with where it is located in relation to the origin (distance OA). The distance BA is the amount by which all inputs (doctors and nurses) could be proportionally reduced without a reduction in hospital admissions. This is expressed in percentage terms by the ratio BA/OA. The *technical efficiency* (TE_{IN}) of hospital A is then expressed as follows:

$$TE_{IN} = \frac{OB}{OA} \tag{5.1}$$

which is equal to $1 - BA/OA$, and where the IN subscript denotes the input orientation. Pure *technical efficiency (TE)* shows the deviation from the production frontier ZZ'. This value lies between 0 and 1 with a value of 1 indicating full technical efficiency (if hospital A produced at a point such as B).

If the isocost can be specified – because input prices are known – it can be used to calculate the *allocative efficiency* (AE_{IN}) of the hospital operating at point A by the following ratio:

$$AE_{IN} = \frac{OC}{OB} \qquad (5.2)$$

where the distance CB is the reduction in production costs that would occur if production were to take place at the allocatively (and technically) efficient point B' instead of at the technically efficient, but allocatively inefficient, point B. It thus represents the deviation from the price-efficient point.

The extent to which a DMU incurs expenditure in excess of the minimum feasible therefore comprises two components: *technical efficiency*, which reflects the ability of a DMU to produce the maximum amount of output given a set of inputs, and *allocative efficiency*, which reflects the ability of a DMU to use inputs in optimal proportions given their respective prices. The product of these measures can be combined to give a measure of total *economic efficiency* (EE_{IN}) such that:

$$EE_{IN} = TE_{IN} \times AE_{IN}$$
$$= \frac{OB}{OA} \times \frac{OC}{OB} = \frac{OC}{OA} \qquad (5.3)$$

5.2.2 Output-oriented efficiency

An alternative exposition would be to examine efficiency measurement under an output orientation. Suppose a hospital produces two outputs (y_1 and y_2), for example inpatient treatments and outpatient visits, from a single input (x), hospital staff, as depicted in Figure 5.2.

In this case ZZ' represents the production possibility curve, the upper bound of all the technically feasible production possibilities. All hospitals lie on the production frontier (if they are efficient) or below it (if they are inefficient). Using the output orientation, hospitals which lie below the production frontier, such as hospital A, could proportionally expand their output quantities (y_1 and y_2) of inpatient treatments and outpatient visits, holding their level of input use (x), hospital staff, constant. Under the existing technology, they could do this up to a point such as B which is located on the production boundary.

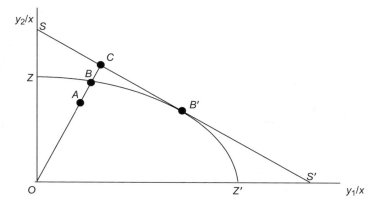

Figure 5.2. Technical and allocative efficiency under an output orientation.

If we had information about the relative value of the two outputs it would be possible to construct the equivalent of an iso-revenue line, shown here as SS', which reflects the market value of the two outputs (y_1 and y_2). The efficient point of production is B' where ZZ' is tangential to the iso-revenue line.

The *technical efficiency (TE_{OUT})* of hospital A is expressed as:

$$TE_{OUT} = \frac{OA}{OB} \qquad (5.4)$$

where the OUT subscript denotes the output orientation. The *allocative efficiency (AE_{OUT})* of the hospital is expressed as:

$$AE_{OUT} = \frac{OB}{OC} \qquad (5.5)$$

Total *economic efficiency (EE_{OUT})* is given by:

$$EE_{OUT} = TE_{OUT} \times AE_{OUT}$$
$$= \frac{OA}{OB} \times \frac{OB}{OC} = \frac{OA}{OC} \qquad (5.6)$$

In health care, output prices are seldom available, and so most studies restrict the analysis to the calculation of *technical efficiency* and not total *economic efficiency*.

All these measures of efficiency (technical, allocative and economic efficiency) are bounded by 0 and 1. Because they are measured along a ray from the origin to the observed production point, they hold relative proportions of inputs (or outputs) constant. These radial efficiency measures are *units-invariant* in the sense that changing the units of measurement will not change the value of the efficiency measure. Thus, for example, the results are invariant to whether the input of nursing staff is measured in hours worked or months worked.

5.2.3 DEA formulation

The efficiency measures discussed above assume the production function of the fully efficient organisation is known. In practice this is not the case and the efficient isoquant must be estimated from the data.

DEA assesses efficiency in two stages. First, a frontier is identified based on either those organisations using the lowest input mix to produce their outputs or those achieving the highest output mix given their inputs (i.e. the input or output orientation). Second, each organisation is assigned an efficiency score by comparing its output/input ratio to that of efficient organisations that form a piecewise linear 'envelope' of surfaces in multidimensional space. If there are M inputs and S outputs, then the production frontier becomes a surface in $(M+S)$ dimensional space. The efficiency of a DMU is the distance it lies from this surface – the maximum extent by which it could improve its outputs given its current level of inputs (or reduce its inputs given its current level of outputs).

Efficiency in DEA is therefore defined as the ratio of a weighted sum of outputs of a DMU divided by a weighted sum of its inputs, therefore corresponding closely to the notion of efficiency developed in chapter 2. Technical efficiency (*TE*) is computed by solving for each DMU the following mathematical programme:

$$\max \left(\frac{\sum_{s=1}^{S} u_s \times y_{s0}}{\sum_{m=1}^{M} v_m \times x_{m0}} \right) \tag{5.7}$$

subject to:

$$\frac{\sum_{s=1}^{S} u_s \times y_{si}}{\sum_{m=1}^{M} v_m \times x_{mi}} \leq 1 \qquad i = 1, \ldots, I$$

where:

$$y_{s0} = \text{quantity of output } s \text{ for DMU}_0$$
$$u_s = \text{weight attached to output } s, \; u_s > 0, \; s = 1, ..., S$$
$$y_{s0} = \text{quantity of input } m \text{ for DMU}_0$$
$$v_m = \text{weight attached to input } m, v_m > 0, \; m = 1, ..., M$$

This mathematical programme seeks out for DMU$_0$ the set of output weights u_s and input weights v_m that maximises the efficiency of DMU$_0$, subject to the important constraint that – when they are applied to all other DMUs – none can have an efficiency greater than 1. The weights can take any non-negative value, and in general a different set of weights is computed for each DMU. Thus, the weights u_s and v_m are a central feature of DEA. They are chosen to cast the DMU in the 'best possible light', in the sense that no other set of weights will yield a higher level of efficiency.

Equation 5.7 can be rewritten more succinctly as:

$$\max_{u,v}(u'y_0/v'x_0) \tag{5.8}$$

subject to:

$$u'y_i/v'x_i \leq 1 \; i = 1, \ldots, I$$
$$u, v \geq 0$$

where u' and v' are vectors of output and input weights respectively.

In order to select the optimal weights, we estimate this equation as a linear programming problem. This entails converting equation 5.8 into a system of linear equations, set up such that a linear objective function can be maximised subject to a set of linear constraints. The linear programme seeks out values for u and v that maximise the efficiency measure of the ith DMU, subject to the constraint that all efficiency measures are no greater than 1. But this ratio formulation has an infinite number of solutions, because if (u^*, v^*) is a solution, then so too is $(\alpha u^*, \alpha v^*)$ (Coelli, Rao and Battese 1998). We therefore impose an additional constraint that either the numerator or the denominator of the efficiency ratio be equal to 1 (e.g. $v'x = 1$). The problem then becomes one of either maximising weighted output subject to weighted input being equal to 1 or of minimising weighted input subject to weighted output being equal to 1 (Parkin and Hollingsworth 1997). We can therefore rewrite equation 5.8 in the multiplier form to reflect this transformation by adding a constraint as follows:

$$\max_{\mu,\nu}(\mu' y_0) \tag{5.9}$$

subject to:

$$v' x_i = 1$$
$$\mu' y_i - v' x_i \leq 0 \quad i = 1, ..., I$$
$$\mu, v \geq 0$$

This maximisation problem can also be expressed as an equivalent minimisation problem, the advantage being that it involves fewer constraints (Coelli, Rao and Battese 1998):

$$\min_{\theta,\lambda} \theta_0 \tag{5.10}$$

subject to:

$$-y_i + Y\lambda \geq 0$$
$$\theta x_i - X\lambda \geq 0$$
$$\lambda \geq 0$$

where x_i and y_i are column vectors of inputs and outputs for each of the I DMUs, X and Y are input and output matrices representing the data for all the I DMUs, θ is a scalar and λ is a $n \times 1$ vector of constants. The value of θ obtained will be the efficiency score for DMU_0 and satisfies $\theta \leq 1$, with a value of 1 indicating a point on the frontier and hence a technically efficient DMU. The linear programming problem must be solved separately for each DMU in the sample in order to obtain a value of θ for each DMU (Coelli, Rao and Battese 1998). The objective of the linear programme is therefore to seek the minimum θ that reduces the input vector x_i to θx_i while guaranteeing at least the output level y_i.

This formulation of DEA yields weights λ that are specific to each unit. However, under this formulation the value λ_i now reflects the weight to be attached to DMU_i in forming the efficient benchmark for DMU_0. Effectively, the point on the frontier with which DMU_0 is compared is formed by creating a composite 'peer' DMU comprising a linear combination of all other DMUs, weighted in accordance with the elements of λ. Of course, only efficient DMUs will be assigned a non-zero weight in the peer group. Those DMUs with a non-zero weight are referred to as the efficient peers or comparators of DMU_0.

In creating the efficient frontier, DEA yields specific input or output targets for each DMU, depending on whether the input or output orientation has been used. For example, under input orientation, these indicate the specific amounts by which a particular DMU should be able to reduce its consumption of particular inputs without reducing output. The input-output levels (x_i^P, y_i^P) on the estimated frontier are the co-ordinates of the point used as a benchmark for evaluating DMU $_i$, yielding the 'targets' for DMU $_i$. In principle, one could project an inefficient DMU onto any part of the efficient frontier. In practice, the usual approach is to calculate (x_i^P, y_i^P) by undertaking radial contraction of input levels (if the input orientation is used) or radial expansion of output levels (if the output orientation is used) of DMU $_i$. This approach preserves the input-output mix of DMU$_i$, which is therefore compared to a set of efficient peers that use similar or identical input-output ratios, but at more efficient levels. Box 5.1 gives an example of how efficiency is measured as the distance of the DMU to the piecewise linear surface, how inefficient DMUs are compared to linear combinations of efficient benchmark DMUs, and how targets can be set.

Box 5.1. An example of DEA

Assume there are five DMUs using one input to produce two outputs, as shown in the table below. Note that they are operating under different scales, so any attempt to draw the DEA isoquants can only be undertaken after rescaling outputs to be output per unit of input (for example by dividing each output by the level of input or as we do in this example normalising outputs to 10 inputs).

DMU	Input	Output 1	Output 2
A	5	2	1
B	30	6	9
C	10	3	2
D	20	2	8
E	20	6	6

We can represent this diagrammatically, as in the figure below. This shows the outputs produced from 10 units of input for each DMU. The efficient frontier is the piecewise series of linear segments with the associated vertical and horizontal extensions.

Box 5.1. (*continued*)

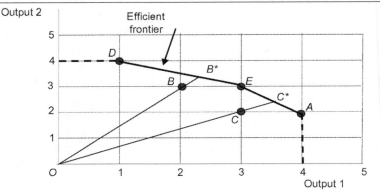

The DEA linear program is run for each DMU in turn, with inputs held constant. It is verified that DMUs *A*, *D* and *E* are efficient. However, *B* has an efficiency of 88.9%, indicated by the ratio OB/OB^*. Its efficient comparators are DMUs *D* and *E*, and its composite benchmark comprises a weighted mix of 0.56 of DMU D and 0.94 of DMU E, represented by the point B^*. Similarly, the other inefficient DMU is *C*, the benchmark for which comprises 1.20 of DMU A and 0.20 of DMU E. The table below shows the outputs that the two inefficient units should be able to achieve if they were to emulate their composite benchmark (after rescaling the outputs back up to their original values of input).

DMU	Input	Output 1	Output 2
Actual B	30	6	9
Target B	30	6.75	10.13
Actual C	10	3	2
Target C	10	3.60	2.40

5.3 Considerations in data envelopment analysis

There are a number of considerations in estimating a DEA model:

- whether to assume constant or variable returns to scale;
- whether to assume an input or an output orientation;
- whether to apply weight restrictions;
- dealing with 'slacks';

- model specification and judging the quality of a DEA model;
- how to adjust for environmental factors.

We consider these in turn.

5.3.1 Whether to assume constant or variable returns to scale

Thus far we have considered various measures of efficiency under constant returns to scale (CRS), as assumed in the original DEA paper (Charnes, Cooper and Rhodes 1978). Banker, Charnes and Cooper (1984) extended this to accommodate a more flexible variable returns to scale (VRS) model which may be appropriate when not all DMUs can be considered to be operating at an optimal scale. In the health care sector imperfect competition, constraints on finance, and regulatory constraints on entry, mergers and exits may often result in organisations operating at an inefficient scale. The choice of CRS or VRS is therefore an important decision and relies on the analyst's understanding of the market constraints facing firms within a particular sector. If the CRS technology is inappropriately applied when, say, all hospitals are operating at a sub-optimal scale, then the estimates of technical efficiency will be confounded by *scale efficiency effects*.

The CRS linear programming problem is easily extended to account for VRS by adding to the convexity constraint in equation 5.10 (the $n \times 1$ vector $\lambda \geq 0$) the further constraint:

$$\sum_{i=1}^{I} \lambda_i = 1 \qquad (5.11)$$

To calculate scale inefficiency, both the CRS and VRS DEA models are run on the same data, and any change in measured efficiency can be attributed to the presence of scale inefficiency. This is illustrated in the following example. Assume DMU_A produces a single output (y), for example hospital treatments, from a single input (x), hospital staff, as depicted in Figure 5.3. This figure highlights the difference between the two production frontiers (adapted from Coelli, Rao and Battese, 1998). The line from the origin OE depicts the CRS frontier whereas the segmented line $FGHIJ$ is the VRS frontier. Assuming an input orientation, implying a reduction of input (x) in the horizontal plane, the *technical efficiency* $(TE_{IN,CRS})$ of DMU_A with respect to the constant returns to scale technology is then expressed as:

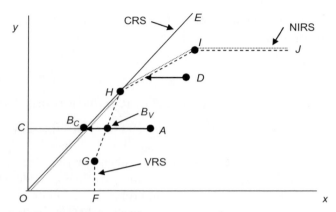

Figure 5.3. Constant and variable returns to scale

$$TE_{IN,CRS} = \frac{CB_C}{CA} \qquad (5.12)$$

where the *IN* subscript denotes the input orientation and the *CRS* subscript denotes the constant returns to scale technology.

In contrast, the *technical efficiency (TE$_{IN,VRS}$)* of DMU$_A$ with respect to the variable returns to scale technology is expressed as:

$$TE_{IN,VRS} = \frac{CB_V}{CA} \qquad (5.13)$$

where the *VRS* subscript denotes the variable returns to scale technology.

Scale efficiency is then measured as the distance between the CRS and VRS technologies, or:

$$SE_{IN} = \frac{CB_C}{CB_V} \qquad (5.14)$$

and therefore:

$$TE_{IN,CRS} = TE_{IN,VRS} \times SE_{IN} \qquad (5.15)$$

Again, all these efficiency measures are bounded by 0 and 1.

If we imagine Figure 5.3 in multidimensional space, the VRS technology forms a convex hull of intersecting planes which envelop the data points, such as *A* and *D*, more tightly than the CRS approach, where the frontier would extend from the origin. Thus, by introducing an additional constraint, VRS produces technical efficiency scores which are greater than or equal to those obtained using CRS (Coelli 1996b; Parkin and Hollingsworth 1997).

The convexity constraint in equation 5.11 ensures that an inefficient DMU will usually be compared only with DMUs of a roughly similar size. Thus the projected point for DMU_A on the DEA frontier will be a convex combination of other DMUs, such as G and H. This convexity restriction implies that the efficient frontier is formed only by interpolation between DMUs, and precludes extrapolation of performance at one scale to a different scale. In contrast, the CRS case permits extrapolation, with the result that DMUs may be compared with others operating at substantially different scales. Thus under CRS the λ weights may sum to a value greater than (or less than) 1.

In order to obtain an indication of whether a DMU is operating in the area of increasing, or the area of decreasing, returns to scale, a non-increasing returns to scale (NIRS) constraint can be added by altering the convexity constraint in equation 5.11 to:

$$\sum_{i=1}^{I} \lambda_i \leq 1 \tag{5.16}$$

In Figure 5.3 the NIRS frontier runs from the origin O to H and then follows the VRS frontier HIJ. Scale inefficiencies can then be determined (whether increasing or decreasing returns to scale) by comparing the DMU's technical efficiency score under the NIRS constraint (equation 5.11) to their technical efficiency score under the NIRs constraint (equation 5.16). If they are not equal, increasing returns to scale exist; if they are equal, then decreasing returns to scale apply (Coelli, Rao and Battese 1998). DMUs between F and H such as DMU_A have increasing returns to scale whereas DMUs between H and J such as DMU_D have decreasing returns to scale. A DMU at point C is scale-efficient under both CRS and VRS. More DMUs are therefore likely to be found efficient under VRS than CRS.

The choice of CRS or VRS will usually depend on the context and purpose of the analysis, or whether short-run or long-run efficiency is under scrutiny. For example, from a societal perspective, interest may be in productivity regardless of the scale of operations, so CRS may be more appropriate. From a managerial perspective, interest may be focused on the extent to which the scale of operations affects productivity, so VRS may be preferred, particularly if it is believed that DMUs are not operating at the optimal scale because of the time-scale of operations or their location on a certain range of the production function.

If the incorrect scale assumption is invoked in the modelling, it is likely to have the greatest effect on efficiency estimates when sample sizes are small, as with larger sample sizes there is a greater probability of being able to form a comparison group with weights which conform to equation 5.11 and which exhibit efficiency which is close to that of the unconstrained comparison group (Smith 1997). Thus with smaller sample sizes, the choice of VRS or CRS becomes more important.

A complication to the choice of CRS or VRS is that often data take the form of ratios rather than absolute numbers as measures of inputs and outputs in DEA. This is very common in health care. For example, mortality rates, discharge rates, doctors per head of population, nurses per occupied bed, proportion of expenditure on clinical supplies from total expenditure, proportion of theatre time for hip replacement operations from total theatre time are commonly used measures of input or output. The essential point to note is that the use of such data automatically implies an assumption of constant returns to scale, because the creation of the ratio removes any information about the size of the organisation.

Where a decision is made to use ratio data, Hollingsworth and Smith (2003) show why it is essential to use the Banker, Charnes and Cooper (1984) formulation of DEA, even though the ratio data used implicitly assume constant returns to scale. The technical reasoning is as follows. If a ratio variable y_{si} for DMU$_i$ is calculated with numerator p_{si} and denominator q_{si} (i.e. $y_{si} = p_{si}/q_{si}$) then combining the ratios for I DMUs should be achieved by computing the weighted average :

$$y_s^* = \frac{\sum_{i=1}^{I} w_i p_{si}}{\sum_{i=1}^{I} w_i q_{si}} \qquad (5.17)$$

where w_i are the weights on DMU$_i$ in creating the weighted average. Thus the weights apply to both the numerator and the denominator.

When DEA combines the ratios of I DMUs it creates the composite ratio:

$$y_s^d = \sum_{i=1}^{I} \lambda_i \frac{p_{si}}{q_{si}} \qquad (5.18)$$

For equations 5.17 and 5.18 to be equivalent, or for y_s^* to equal y_s^d, the coefficients of p_{si} in each of the combined ratios should be equal, therefore:

$$\frac{w_i}{\sum_{i=1}^{I} w_i p_{si}} = \frac{\lambda_i}{p_{si}} \qquad \text{for all } i \qquad (5.19)$$

This amounts to the Banker, Charnes and Cooper (1984) formulation of equation 5.11:

$$\sum_{i=1}^{I} \lambda_i = 1.$$

5.3.2 Whether to assume an input or an output orientation

Under CRS, the DEA results are the same whether an input orientation or an output orientation is specified. However, under VRS the two are not in general equivalent. The difference is illustrated in Figure 5.4, using one input x and one output y with an inefficient DMU operating at point C. Under VRS the technical efficiency measure for DMU C in the input-orientation specification depends on the horizontal distance from the frontier, and in the output-orientation specification on the vertical distance from the frontier.

In algebraic terms, from Figure 5.4:

$$TE_{IN,CRS} = \frac{AB}{AC} = \frac{DC}{DE} = TE_{OUT,CRS} \qquad (5.20)$$

where the *IN* and *OUT* subscripts denote, respectively, the input and output orientation under CRS.

But:

$$TE_{IN,VRS} = \frac{AB}{AC} \neq \frac{DC}{DF} = TE_{OUT,VRS} \qquad (5.21)$$

The choice of orientation does not affect which observations are identified as fully efficient, since the models will estimate exactly the

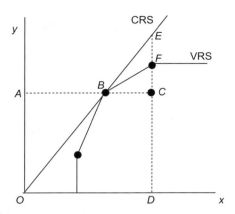

Figure 5.4. Input and output orientation.

same frontier (Coelli 1996b). The difference lies in the part of the frontier to which the inefficient DMU is projected. Therefore, under VRS, the choice of input or output orientation may be an important consideration that will be affected by the analyst's view on which parameters managers are able to control. For instance, hospital specialities may face a fixed quantity of inputs in any given period. Subject to this resource constraint, managers must decide how many patients to treat. This would imply that technical inefficiency is measured by considering the extent to which outputs can be expanded proportionately without altering the quantity of inputs. This suggests an output-oriented measure of efficiency. On the other hand, contractual arrangements with a hospital (say) may be specified in terms of a target number of patients treated. The managerial problem might then be better formulated by considering how much input quantities could be reduced while still maintaining the output target. This would imply an input-orientation to the problem.

5.3.3 Whether to apply weight restrictions

As discussed in Chapter 2, efficiency measurement requires the specification of a set of weights to the inputs and outputs, and in principle we could *a priori* assign fixed weights to our inputs and outputs. For example, let us assume we are evaluating the efficiency of hospitals, producing two outputs (inpatients and outpatients), with the use of two inputs (doctors and nurses). Suppose we impose fixed weights to generate efficiency ratios, such as the following:

v_1 (weight for doctors) : v_2 (weight for nurses) = 5 : 1

u_1 (weight for outpatients) : u_2 (weight for inpatients) = 1 : 3

This fixed weights approach makes the efficiency calculations trivial, and renders DEA unnecessary (Cooper, Seiford and Tone 2000). It is, however, generally infeasible to assign fixed weights in health care where many crucial values are unknown. Moreover, we may not know how much of the estimated inefficiency reflects factors beyond the hospitals' control, an issue to which we return in sub-section 5.3.6.

In contrast to this fixed weights approach, conventional DEA allows total flexibility in weights. The weights, which are specific to each DMU, are chosen so that they place each DMU in the best possible light. This means that the input-output ratio for each DMU is maximised relative to that for all other DMUs. Therefore, if we were to compare the results from our example above with fixed weights (say the ratios of 5:1 and 1:3 for inputs and outputs) to that of variable weights under DEA, we would find that DEA will assign efficiency scores greater than or equal to those using fixed weights (Cooper, Seiford and Tone 2000).

DEA will allow a DMU on the frontier to assign very high weights to the inputs and outputs for which the unit is particularly efficient and very low weights to the other inputs and outputs. Indeed, one can find in an unconstrained DEA that the highest efficiency score for a DMU can be obtained only by assigning a zero weight to one or more outputs on which it performs poorly. Extreme DMUs that excel at one particular aspect of performance will be classified as efficient, irrespective of how they perform on other tasks they undertake (Doyle and Green 1994). Thus if DEA is allowed complete freedom to choose the weights for DMUs, factors of secondary importance may dominate a DMU's efficiency assessment or, alternatively, important factors may be ignored in the analysis.

This consideration has led to various approaches to limit the flexibility of the choice of weights on inputs and outputs in DEA. By placing constraints on the weights, the region of search for those weights is reduced and so a DMU's efficiency cannot increase, and may decrease, compared to the value obtained using unconstrained DEA. Various authors have suggested ways of imposing restrictions on the weights, including Charnes *et al.* (1989); Thompson *et al.* (1990),

Wong and Beasley (1990), and Roll, Cook and Golany (1991). How-ever, most of the effort has focused on the technical considerations of weight restrictions rather than the economic theory underpinning the rationale for such restrictions.

The degree of weight flexibility to be allowed depends on consid-erations such as the extent to which DMUs are considered homoge-neous. On the one hand, they may face the same input prices, produce similar outputs and employ the same technologies (implying very limited weight flexibility). On the other, they may enjoy the freedom to vary local priorities, or there may be considerable uncertainty about the appropriate weights, implying a need for greater weight flexibility.

The use of weight restrictions requires value judgements about the relative importance of different outputs and about the relative oppor-tunity cost of the inputs used. Thus weight restrictions can be criti-cised on the grounds that they compromise some of the objectivity implicit in the unrestricted DEA. However, there are many other value judgements that go into the construction of a DEA model, including the choice of inputs and outputs and the assumption that the implicit weights chosen by DEA are acceptable (Allen *et al.* 1997; Pedraja-Chaparro, Salinas-Jiménez and Smith 1997). We consider these issues further in chapter 8.

A possible approach towards examining sensitivity to weight selec-tion is the calculation of 'cross-efficiencies' (Doyle and Green 1994). Once the unconstrained DEA set of weights has been chosen for a particular DMU, that set is used to weight the inputs and outputs for each of the other DMUs, yielding for each DMU a set of I efficiency scores. This procedure is repeated for all DMUs, yielding a matrix of cross-efficiencies. The usual DEA efficiency measurements for each DMU are given along the leading diagonal of the matrix.

It is then possible to examine the range of efficiency scores secured for each DMU, using all other DMU weights, and this offers some indication of the robustness of the initial DEA efficiency estimate to realistic changes in the weights, as adopted by other DMUs. However, it should be noted that the set of weights that DEA selects to maximise a DMU's efficiency may not be unique, and thus the evaluation of the other DMUs may depend to some extent on which of the solutions the linear programme generates with the chosen software (Doyle and Green 1994).

5.3.4 Dealing with 'slacks'

The optimal solution linear programme (equation 5.10) can include what are termed 'slacks' in either the input or output constraints. For constraints with non-zero slacks, the performance of the peer group suggests that the DMU under scrutiny can improve beyond the level implied by the overall efficiency estimate θ. For such inputs (or outputs) the estimated frontier effectively runs parallel to the relevant input or output axis in multidimensional space. To illustrate, suppose we have two inputs (x_1 and x_2) to produce a single output (y). Figure 5.5 shows four DMUs, where A and B represent inefficient production units and C and D are efficient, forming the frontier. Thus the inefficiency of units A and B is calculated as OB'/OB and OA'/OA respectively. However, the radial projection for A does not encounter the frontier interpolated between C and D, so is not naturally enveloped because the frontier is incomplete. Whether point A' is an efficient point is questionable, because one could still reduce the amount of input x_2 by the amount $A'C$. Any point along such artificial frontier extensions (the broken lines in Figure 5.5) is always dominated by a point on the edge of the frontier. For inefficient DMU $_A$, the difference in input x_2 between these two points (A' on the extension and C on the frontier) is the slack associated with that input (Tofallis 2001).

We can envisage a similar situation in Figure 5.6 where we have two outputs (y_1 and y_2) and a single input (x). DMUs A and B represent inefficient production units and C, D and E are efficient, forming the frontier. Thus the inefficiency of units A and B is calculated as OA/OA' and OB/OB' respectively. $A'C$ represents the 'output slack' or the amount by which output y_1 can still be expanded.

Point A' in both Figures 5.5 and 5.6 represents the Farrell (1957) definition of efficiency, or the radial reduction in inputs (Figure 5.5) or radial expansion in outputs (Figure 5.6) which is possible. A stricter definition of efficiency is supplied by Koopmans (1951) who argues that points such as A' are not efficient. According to the Koopmans definition, DMUs are technically efficient only if they operate on the frontier (such as DMUs C and D) and all associated slacks are zero.

Failure to account for slack will result in an overestimation of technical efficiency (using Farrell estimates) for those DMUs operating with slack (such as DMU A). Furthermore, if the targets calculated for inefficient DMUs (such as A) include the slack values, they may imply

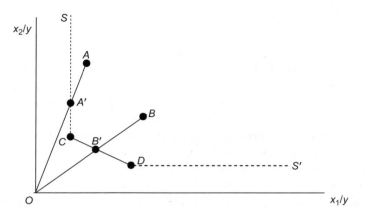

Figure 5.5. Efficiency measurement and input slacks.

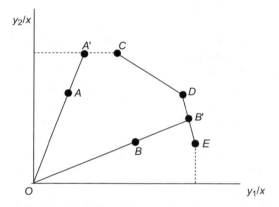

Figure 5.6. Efficiency measurement and output slacks.

a significant change in the input/output mix (moving from a point A' to C) which may then result in the targets not being helpful or practicable. In assessing how to deal with slacks, some commentators have argued that DEA should not be used for ranking DMUs or for target-setting (Tofallis 2001).

Other authors have proposed various ways of dealing technically with slacks (Bessent *et al.* 1988; Torgerson, Forsund and Kittelesen 1996; Tofallis 2001). Ali and Seiford (1993) have proposed deriving Koopmans, technical efficiency by means of a second-stage DEA linear programming problem which can be run to move from a point such as A' (Farrell-efficient) to C (Koopmans-efficient) on the frontier. This is done by taking the θ-value from the first-stage linear programming problem and running a second-stage linear programming problem and setting the input and output slacks to zero. However, there is a potential problem with this two-stage approach, namely that one loses the *units-invariant* nature of the radial efficiency measures in the second stage (thus changing the units of measurement of the inputs or outputs will change the value of the efficiency measure). *Units invariance* is one of the desirable properties of DEA.

Coelli (1998) has proposed a multistage DEA which involves the solution of a sequence of radial linear programming problems to identify efficient projected points which have an input/output mix as close as possible to those inefficient points (such as A). The resultant efficiency measures are also *units-invariant*.

While some authors have argued that Farrell efficiency measures should be reported alongside non-zero input or output slacks to give an accurate picture of efficiency, others have argued that slacks should essentially be viewed as allocative inefficiency (Ferrier and Lovell 1990) and obtaining the Koopmans-efficient points is not important. Coelli, Rao and Battese (1998) argue that slacks are an artefact of the frontier construction method and conclude that an analysis of technical efficiency can reasonably use the Farrell radial efficiency scores. The choice of dealing with slacks remains an unresolved issue.

5.3.5 Model specification and judging the quality of a DEA model

Being a non-parametric technique, DEA has the advantage of requiring no assumptions about the functional form of the production or cost frontier. While this reduces the need for a theoretical exposition of model specification, it does not avoid the problem of how to assess the quality of a DEA model – or how well it reflects reality. There are several considerations, each of which is discussed in detail in this sub-section:

- DEA assumes no random noise or measurement error;
- results are sensitive to small samples and outlier observations;
- the inclusion or exclusion of certain variables can bias efficiency estimates;

- the more variables are included the less discriminating between
  DMUs the model becomes;
- caution needs to be exercised with zero input output levels;
- sensitivity analysis may help to refine model specification.

We consider these in turn.

First, DEA is deterministic, which means there is no way to take account of statistical error, random shocks or noise. Given that the method is based on outlier observations, measurement error is a potentially serious source of bias. The approach presupposes that all variables are measured accurately and that any shortfall between a DMU's input-output ratio and the maximum predicted by the frontier is attributable solely to inefficiency. Measurement error can have an impact which is dependent on whether a DMU is incorrectly assigned as efficient or inefficient. If the 'incorrectly measured DMU' is incorrectly assigned as efficient, the efficiencies of other DMUs for which it is an efficient peer may be underestimated. On the other hand, if the 'incorrectly measured DMU' is incorrectly assigned as inefficient, the DMUs which would otherwise have had the 'incorrectly measured DMU' as their efficient peer, may have their efficiency ratings over-estimated (Thanassoulis 2001).

There have been several applications of DEA using hospital data where outputs are expressed in fairly crude terms, such as the number of patients treated in medical or surgical specialities. Case mix within these groupings may vary systematically across hospitals. Hospitals with a more complex case mix will be estimated as being less efficient than they would be if case mix were adequately accounted for. Given that the DEA inefficiency score is likely to contain measurement error, it may be best to consider it as an equivalent to the residual ϵ_i from the COLS model, introduced in chapter 3.

Second, results are sensitive to model specification, particularly in small samples (Smith 1997). DEA generates efficiency scores for each individual organisation by comparing it to peers that produce a comparable mix of outputs. If any output is unique to an organisation, it will have no peers with which to make a comparison, irrespective of the fact that it may produce other outputs in common. An absence of peers results in the automatic assignation of full efficiency to the DMU under consideration. Consequently, caution should be exercised in accepting that DMUs classified as fully efficient actually are so.

By the same token, individual efficiency scores may not be robust in the presence of outlier observations and atypical input/output combinations.

Some criteria do exist, however, for detecting especially influential observations in DEA. One such is the 'super-efficiency' measure which indicates the extent to which an efficient DMU lies beyond the frontier that would have been estimated in its absence (Pedraja-Chaparro, Salinas-Jiménez and Smith 1999).

Third, it is critical to be clear about what variables should be classified and included as inputs to, or outputs from, the production process. There is no agreed method of determining whether or not a variable should be included in the model. Generally, the criteria of *exclusivity* and *exhaustiveness* should hold for the choice of inputs and outputs in a DEA model (Thanassoulis 2001). In other words, the inputs alone must influence the outputs (*exclusivity*), and only those outputs used in the model (*exhaustiveness*). The inputs and outputs need, therefore, to be chosen such that the inputs capture all the resources and the outputs capture all the activities or outcomes deemed relevant for the particular efficiency analysis, subject to the rule of exclusivity and exhaustiveness. In practice this may be quite difficult to achieve and the implications of model misspecification may be substantial.

For example, the exclusion of an important input or output can result in severely biased results and an underestimate of efficiency, because it may fail to recognise input constraints faced by some DMUs (Smith 1997). Conversely, the addition of extraneous inputs or outputs in DEA will tend to lead to overestimates of efficiency scores, because an unnecessary constraint has been added into the linear programme. The bias, however, tends to be much more modest when including an extraneous variable than omitting a relevant variable (Smith 1997). This consideration suggests that the criterion of seeking a parsimonious model, often adopted in econometrics, is less relevant for DEA. It may be safer to err on the side of inclusion of irrelevant variables, rather than exclusion of important variables.

Fourth, not only the choice of but also the number of inputs and outputs relative to the number of DMUs will affect efficiency evaluations. The more variables are included, the less discriminating the model becomes. The larger the number of input and output variables used in relation to the number of DMUs in the model, the more DMUs will be assigned as fully efficient and hence the less discriminating the DEA model will be. Banker *et al.* (1989) suggest as a rule of thumb that the number of DMUs should be at least three times the number of factors (inputs and outputs) in any DEA application, although there is no analytic support for this rule (Pedraja-Chaparro, Salinas-Jiménez and Smith, 1999).

Fifth, it is of course axiomatic that inputs and outputs in DEA should be 'isotonic', in the sense that increased inputs should reduce efficiency, whereas increased outputs increase efficiency, other things being equal. If this is not the case, the analyst must first transform the data so that they are isotonic. For example, 'bad' outputs such as mortality rates or readmission rates might be transformed either by inversion, or by subtracting the value of the variable from a large positive number (Scheel 2001; Lewis and Sexton 2004).

Special caution needs to be exercised when zero input or output levels are observed for some DMUs. For instance, if hospital activity in a sample is measured using as one of the outputs Accident and Emergency (A&E) attendances, but some hospitals in the sample do not run A&E departments, then they will artificially be deemed less efficient than those DMUs which do have A&E activity. Similarly, DMUs using zero levels of some inputs may be artificially shown as more efficient than they really are. There is no clear protocol for dealing with this problem. Some users add a positive constant to the zero input/output levels to make them positive, but results are sensitive to the choice of constant (Thanassoulis 2001). Cooper, Seiford and Tone (2000) describe a translation-invariant DEA model for use in such cases where adding a constant to input or output levels will not influence efficiency results.

Finally, sensitivity analysis may help to refine the model specification. DEA offers no diagnostic statistics with which to judge whether a model is misspecified. Analysts should therefore test a variety of model specifications using sensitivity analysis to ascertain the robustness of results, and construct data ranges within which results remain unchanged. Bootstrapping may be a useful way to obtain an assessment of the degree of certainty that exists around efficiency estimates (Salinas-Jiménez, Pedraja-Chaparro and Smith 2003).

No clear protocol exists for what action should be taken if results are found to be sensitive, other than appealing to the judgement of the analyst. Ultimately the central concern when judging the quality of a DEA model is that it should be formulated in light of the purpose for which the results will be used. The higher the regulatory stakes (in the form of the expected cost of incorrect inferences), the more caution and circumspection should be exercised.

5.3.6 *How to adjust for environmental factors*

Environmental variables describe factors which could influence the efficiency of a DMU, but are not traditional inputs to the production process and are assumed outside the control of the manager. They may include various characteristics of health care organisations, such as differences in ownership, location, the health needs of their patient populations, the local health economy and community and primary care services, or institutional constraints such as access to capital resources.

Inadequately accounting for the environment in which DMUs operate may lead to seriously faulty conclusions. However, there remains an active and unresolved debate about how to incorporate such environmental variables into DEA (Fried *et al.* 2002). If the sample can be divided into sub-samples on the basis of the environmental variable (e.g. public versus private hospitals), then an approach proposed by Charnes, Cooper and Rhodes (1981) can be used. DEA is undertaken for each sub-sample, and all observed data points are projected onto their respective frontiers. A single DEA is then undertaken using the projected points to assess any difference in the mean efficiency of the two sub-samples.

However, environmental variables are not in general categorical. An alternative approach is therefore to include an environmental variable (either categorical or continuous) as one of the inputs in the production model (using the Banker, Charnes and Cooper (BCC) formulation) (Lovell 2000). In DEA this means that DMUs will only be compared with other DMUs operating in identical or more adverse environments. Those operating in the most adverse environments will automatically be deemed efficient (Banker and Morey 1986; Coelli, Rao and Battese 1998).

A third approach involves a two-stage analysis, whereby DEA is solved using the traditional inputs and outputs, and the efficiency scores from the first stage are then regressed on the environmental variables (Ferrier and Valdmanis 1996). The DEA efficiency scores are then used as the dependent variable in a regression analysis. A censored Tobit regression model is often considered appropriate for these data, as they are bounded at both ends of the 0–1 distribution.

Many analyses then 'correct' the efficiency scores by using the estimated regression coefficients to adjust the efficiency scores for the environmental factors (Bhattacharyya, Lovell and Sahay 1997) so that the efficiency scores all correspond to a common level of environment, say the sample means. This approach is, however, problematic because the efficiency scores used as the dependent variable are serially correlated, and so the classical regression assumption of variables being independent and identically distributed is violated, thereby invalidating standard approaches to inference (Simar and Wilson 2004). It is therefore inadvisable to draw firm conclusions using conventional statistical tests from this analysis. Rather it might be considered exploratory, indicating which environmental variables appear to have the most influence on performance. This information could then be used to formulate a single-stage DEA model where the environmental variable is included in the DEA model as an input or an output (Coelli, Rao and Battese 1998).

Further suggested developments include a three-stage approach to account for environmental effects (Fried, Schmidt and Yaisawarng 1999; Blank and Valdmanis 2005). The two-stage approach is extended by following the second stage Tobit regression with another DEA evaluation in which the original data are adjusted to take account of the environmental impacts. There have been a number of baroque refinements to these approaches, for instance running a double DEA model (Lozano-Vivas, Pastor and Pastor 2002), running a second-stage seemingly unrelated regression model to take account of radial slacks and not just radial efficiency measures (Fried, Lovell and vanden Eeckaut 1993), and running a second-stage SFA model followed by a third-stage DEA model, to additionally take account of stochastic noise (Fried *et al.* 2002).

The complexity of these recommendations, and the fierce demands they make on data, are indicative of the complexity of the environmental variable problem. There is no generally accepted method for taking into account environmental variables in DEA models or for testing whether an environmental variable has a significant influence on the production process and the resultant efficiency estimation. For health care, the issue is often likely to be the single biggest source of technical and policy debate, and it must therefore be treated with great caution.

5.4 Application to acute hospitals in England

5.4.1 The methods and data

The considerations discussed above in estimating a DEA model are illustrated using a sub-set of the cross-sectional data used in chapter 3. Data for 171 hospitals with accident and emergency (A&E) departments are analysed in this chapter. The reason for excluding those hospitals without A&E departments is that DEA cannot easily cope with DMUs that produce zero amounts of some types of output.

We use total cost as the input and calculate technical efficiency scores for hospitals. A range of outputs are considered, including inpatient episodes, outpatient visits, A&E attendances, teaching, and research. Since no information is available on the relative importance of certain outputs, no weight restrictions are applied in the analysis. We also used the multistage DEA (Coelli 1998) to obtain Koopmans efficiency estimates with zero slacks. We use an input orientation, thus addressing the question: 'By how much can expenditure be proportionally reduced without changing the output quantities?'

We employ the Banker, Charnes and Cooper (BCC) (1984) formulation of the DEA model since we have ratio data for several variables. Non-ratio variables when included in the DEA model effectively mean that hospitals are compared only to other hospitals with the same value for the variable in question.

In addition, one of the variables is non-isotonic, namely transfers out of hospital. If patients end their care in one hospital with a transfer to another hospital it is assumed that this represents an inability on the part of the first hospital to meet the patient's treatment needs. Transfers into a hospital are likely to represent complex patients referred from less capable institutions. These variables capture an aspect of case mix and patient severity. In order to ensure that incentives remain in place for hospitals not to 'cream-skim' low severity patients by transferring them to other providers, we transform transfers out of hospital so that both these variables move in the same direction. This will encourage hospitals to increase efficiency whilst still managing more complex cases. In this example, we chose unity as the positive reference number from which to subtract transfers out of hospital.

Table 5.1 shows the descriptive statistics for the variables used in the DEA models.

5.4.2 Model specifications

Five model specifications are considered. The different specifications serve as a sensitivity analysis, to test whether the efficiency scores and ranks remain stable when variables are removed or added. However, while these specifications may have some intuitive appeal, they have been chosen purely for illustrative purposes. In practice, if we were to use this analysis for any purpose other than to illustrate the methodology, we would need to estimate more model specifications and examine carefully the impact of the inclusion and exclusion of additional variables. The five specifications are shown in Table 5.2.

Model 1 simply uses the three main treatment-related activities of hospitals, while Model 2 adds teaching and research activity. Model 3 includes the full set of outputs over which hospital managers potentially have control, at least in the short run. Model 4 is virtually identical, except that it includes the 'market forces factor', a variable that captures differences in factor prices across the country. We include this model to show an example of various ways of dealing with this environmental factor. Finally Model 5 includes all available output variables and environmental adjusters, including variables that capture the configuration of the hospital. Arguably hospitals may be able to alter these configuration factors in the long run, but it is unlikely that managers may have much control over hospital size and specialisation in the short term.

5.4.3 Results

Summary results from each of the five specifications are presented in Table 5.3. As progressively more variables are added to the model, a number of things happen: (i) more hospitals are assigned to the frontier; (ii) mean sample efficiency increases; and (iii) the variance in efficiency scores decreases. Two facets of the analytical technique drive these results. First, progressively more of the heterogeneity among hospitals is incorporated into the model, leaving less to be

Table 5.1. DEA model variables, 1997/98

Variable	Description	Mean	Std Dev.	Min.	Max.
TOTCOST	Total cost or total revenue expenditure (£m)	61.553	28.637	15.533	182.184
Main activities					
INPATIENTS	Total inpatient episodes weighted by HRG case mix index	0.043	0.020	0.003	0.107
OUTPATIENTS	Total first outpatient attendances	0.053	0.026	0.004	0.147
A&E	Total A & E attendances	0.058	0.024	0.002	0.165
Additional activities					
STUDENTS	Student whole-time teaching equivalents per inpatient spell	0.649	1.218	0.000	6.329
RESEARCH	Percentage of total revenue spent on research	1.189	2.356	0.002	15.430
Other outputs					
FCE	Finished consultant episode inter-speciality transfers per spell	0.079	0.049	0.000	0.302
EP_SPELL	Episodes per spell	1.085	0.385	0.463	5.844
TRANS-IN	Transfers in to hospital per spell	0.022	0.017	0.000	0.175
1−TRANS-OUT	1−Transfers out of hospital per spell	0.988	0.018	0.868	1.000
EMERGENCY	Emergency admissions per spell	0.363	0.062	0.133	0.582
FU-OUTPTS	Follow-up outpatient attendances per inpatient spell	2.915	0.881	1.270	8.053

Table 5.1. (continued)

Variable	Description	Mean	Std Dev.	Min.	Max.
EMERINDX	Standardised index of unexpected emergency admissions/total emergency admissions	0.020	0.014	0.005	0.098
P-15	Proportion of patients under 15 years of age	0.166	0.113	0.000	0.950
P-60	Proportion of patients 60 years or older	0.351	0.078	0.000	0.610
P-FEM	Proportion of female patients	0.574	0.053	0.363	0.999
Environmental adjusters					
MFF	Market forces factor – weighted average of staff, land, buildings and London weighting factors	86.495	9.341	75.817	131.217
HERF15	Herfindahl concentration/ competition index, 15-mile radius	0.364	0.308	0.040	1.000
AVBEDS	Average available beds	579	190	56	998
HEATBED	Heated volume per bed	3.689	1.164	1.749	8.209
SITES50B	Sites with more than 50 beds	1.854	1.021	1	8
ITINDX	Scope/specialisation index, information theory index	0.362	0.425	0.089	3.344

Table 5.2. *DEA model specifications*

Model	Variable names	Outputs included
1	INPATIENTS, OUTPATIENTS, A&E	Inpatient episodes; outpatient attendances; A&E attendances
2	As for model 1 plus STUDENTS and RESEARCH	Inpatient episodes; outpatient attendances; A&E attendances; teaching; research
3	As for model 2 plus TRANS-IN, 1–TRANS-OUT, FCE, EMERINDX, P-15, P-60, P-FEM, EP_SPELL, FU-OUTPTS and EMERGENCY	Inpatient episodes; outpatient attendances; A&E attendances; teaching; research; transfers in; transfers out; inter-speciality transfers; emergency index; proportions of young, old and female patients; episodes, outpatients and emergencies per spell
4	As for model 3 plus MFF	Inpatient episodes; outpatient attendances; A&E attendances; teaching; research; transfers in; transfers out; inter-speciality transfers; emergency index; proportions of young, old and female patients; episodes, outpatients and emergencies per spell; market forces factor
5	As for model 4 plus AVBEDS, HEATBED, SITES50B, ITINDX and HERF15	All outputs and environmental adjusters

Table 5.3. DEA model specifications and efficiency results

	Model 1	Model 2	Model 3	Model 4	Model 5
Efficient	14	27	97	100	150
>90%	26	42	121	126	163
<50%	5	2	0	0	0
Mean	0.744	0.787	0.932	0.938	0.988
Std dev.	0.136	0.137	0.098	0.092	0.038
Min.	0.419	0.437	0.651	0.651	0.769
Max.	1.000	1.000	1.000	1.000	1.000

labelled as 'inefficiency'. Second, as more variables are added, there is an increased chance that previously 'inefficient' hospitals will dominate on the added dimension and be promoted to the frontier (Nunamaker 1985).

The results for Models 1 and 2 and for Models 3 and 4 are in close agreement, unsurprisingly given the similarities of these two sets of specifications. Figure 5.7 shows the distribution of efficiency scores under each of the five specifications, with the distributions for Models 1 and 2 tracking each other closely, as do those for Models 3 and 4. The distribution for the most comprehensive model (Model 5) is clearly different, with most hospitals on the frontier and the remainder not far off it. This illustrates that great care should be taken in interpreting DEA results.

Alterations to model specification can impact not only on mean sample estimates of efficiency but also on how DMUs compare with one another. One way to consider this is by looking at how efficiency scores are correlated across specifications. Table 5.4 shows the correlation matrix between the efficiency scores from the five models. The correlations between Models 1 and 2, and between 3 and 4, are relatively high. But all correlate relatively poorly with Model 5, suggesting that the inclusion of the additional explanatory variables has a profound effect on the results.

We are also, however, interested in how the change in efficiency scores impacts on the individual rankings of hospitals. Table 5.5 shows the correlations between the rankings of hospitals obtained from the efficiency scores. These are generally lower than the correlations for

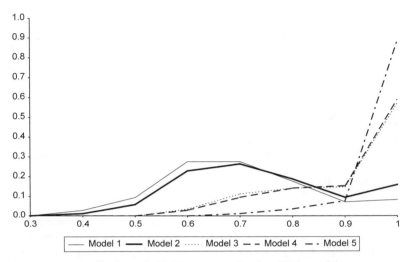

Figure 5.7. Distribution of efficiency scores for five DEA models.

Table 5.4. Correlations between efficiency scores

	Model 1	Model 2	Model 3	Model 4	Model 5
Model 1	1				
Model 2	0.7852	1			
Model 3	0.4572	0.5490	1		
Model 4	0.4244	0.5260	0.9698*	1	
Model 5	0.2311	0.2327	0.5180	0.5448	1

Note:
* Significant at 0.01 level.

the efficiency scores and show that individual hospitals can jump significantly depending on the specification choice.

While there are fourteen hospitals that remain on the frontier across all five specifications, there are also fourteen hospitals whose maximum change in ranking across the five specifications is more than 160 places (out of 171). In other words, for this latter group, such is their sensitivity to the choice of specification that they shift from one end of the 'league table' to the other. Table 5.6 illustrates sensitivity to

Table 5.5. Correlations between efficiency ranks

	Model 1	Model 2	Model 3	Model 4	Model 5
Model 1	1				
Model 2	0.7762*	1			
Model 3	0.3909	0.5350	1		
Model 4	0.3735	0.5141	0.9710*	1	
Model 5	0.1812	0.2233	0.4879	0.5006	1

Note:
* Significant at 0.01 level.

specification for a selection of hospitals. Hospital A remains efficient across all five specifications. In Model 2 when teaching and research is included, both Hospitals B and C are assessed as being fully efficient. Hospital D achieves relatively good rankings across all five specifications, but when the larger number of outputs is introduced in Model 3, it also moves onto the frontier. A similar pattern is evident for Hospitals E and F. Hospital G, presumably, is in an area where factor prices are high: when this is taken into account (through the market forces factor), the hospital gets a high efficiency score. Hospital H performs relatively well on the main hospital activities, but when the additional variables are included, while its efficiency score improves, its ranking relative to other hospitals declines. Hospital I's pattern of performance is similar, but it is always relatively poorer than H. Both hospitals, however, move to the frontier when all the hospital adjusters are included in Model 5. Hospital J remains inefficient across all specifications.

It is clear that the efficiency scores or ranks are not consistent across the different specifications. It is important for the analyst to have a clear understanding of the health care market under analysis and the rationale for including or excluding certain variables. In order to illustrate how these changes in efficiency scores and ranks come about, we examine in more detail the data underlying Models 1 and 2 for the above ten hospitals, as shown in Table 5.7. Recall Model 1 includes the three treatment-related activities, whereas Model 2 also includes teaching and research activities.

While Hospital A's costs are higher than the sample average, its outputs are also (apart from A&E) above average. Moreover, it clearly

Table 5.6. Individual hospital scores and rankings under various specifications

Hospital	DEA-1		DEA-2		DEA-3		DEA-4		DEA-5	
	Score	Rank	Score	Rank	Score	Rank	Score	Rank	Score	Rank
A	1.000	1	1.000	1	1.000	1	1.000	1	1.000	1
B	0.934	21	1.000	1	1.000	1	1.000	1	1.000	1
C	0.576	156	1.000	1	1.000	1	1.000	1	1.000	1
D	0.978	17	0.976	28	1.000	1	1.000	1	1.000	1
E	0.636	137	0.641	148	1.000	1	1.000	1	1.000	1
F	0.572	157	0.572	166	1.000	1	1.000	1	1.000	1
G	0.759	68	0.788	79	0.991	98	1.000	1	1.000	1
H	0.895	27	0.886	47	0.954	106	0.954	108	1.000	1
I	0.643	132	0.653	141	0.688	167	0.688	168	1.000	1
J	0.595	151	0.610	159	0.777	153	0.824	148	0.932	159

Table 5.7. Data for Models 1 and 2 of DEA specifications for ten hospitals

Hospital	TOTCOST	INPATIENTS	OUTPATIENTS	A&E	STUDENTS	RESEARCH
	Input	Model 1			Model 1 and 2	
A	113.524	0.090	0.147	0.018	2.757	3.610
B	44.258	0.033	0.042	0.073	0.918	2.650
C	66.503	0.042	0.052	0.054	3.714	3.295
D	108.679	0.092	0.105	0.057	0.088	0.491
E	110.669	0.073	0.072	0.087	0.413	0.450
F	83.237	0.049	0.081	0.061	0.056	0.034
G	37.077	0.029	0.036	0.038	0.456	0.188
H	108.908	0.087	0.102	0.079	0.000	0.759
I	67.643	0.037	0.043	0.074	0.328	0.082
J	85.284	0.050	0.053	0.076	0.453	0.078
Sample mean	61.553	0.043	0.053	0.058	0.649	1.189

Table 5.8. Tobit model of DEA efficiency scores regressed against a single environmental factor

	Number of obs. = 171
Tobit estimates	L.R. $\chi^2(1) = 0.24$
Log likelihood =	Prob. $> \chi^2 = 0.6241$
−44.4534	Pseudo $R^2 = 0.0027$

Model 3 efficiency scores					
	Coeff.	Std Err.	t	P > |t|	[95% conf. interval]
MFF	0.0009	0.0019	0.49	0.627	−0.003, 0.005
Constant	0.9438	0.1642	5.75	0.000	0.620, 1.268
Std err.	0.1901	0.0179	(Ancillary parameter)		
Obs. summary: 97 right-censored observations at Model 3 >= 1					

outperforms most other hospitals on the outputs of teaching and research. Hospital B performs better than Hospital C on Model 1 because its three outputs are very similar, but its costs are lower. However, in Model 2 both Hospitals B and C move onto the frontier because they excel at either research or both teaching and research.

We now examine the influence of the environmental factors on the efficiency scores in DEA, by regressing the efficiency scores produced by Model 3 against MFF, the market forces factor, as shown in Table 5.8. The variable appears to be statistically insignificant, and some would argue for its exclusion from the DEA analysis on this basis. But because standard errors are biased, the statistical significance may be incorrectly estimated – the omission would be equivalent to committing a Type I statistical error. Moreover, we know from Table 5.6 that the inclusion of the market forces factor, though perhaps not significant for the sample in general, can be highly material for particular hospitals, such as Hospital G. This cautions against the use of second-stage analysis to infer the importance of variables for individual DMUs in DEA.

5.5 Conclusions

This chapter has outlined the main issues involved in specifying a DEA model to assess efficiency using cross-sectional data. The analyst faces a number of decisions regarding the choice of inputs and outputs, whether to assume constant or variable returns to scale, an input or an output orientation, whether to apply weight restrictions, or control for slacks, whether and how to adjust for environmental factors and how to judge the quality of a DEA model. There are no statistical criteria with which to discriminate in many of these choices and the appropriate strategy may depend on the purpose of the analysis and the nature of the data.

In summary:

- The most important role of DEA may be as a simple exploratory analytic tool rather than as an instrument with which to extract precise estimates of organisational efficiency.
- The principal technical virtues of DEA (compared to regression methods) are its flexibility and its freedom from parametric assumptions.
- The principal drawback is that it offers little guidance on the quality of the results it yields, so there is always room for disagreement on the most appropriate DEA model.

6 | The Malmquist index

6.1 Introduction

W HEN longitudinal data or panel data are available, the most common approach in the data envelopment analysis literature is to apply a Malmquist index of the change in total factor productivity (TFP). This chapter outlines the distinctive features of the Malmquist index, along with key issues in specifying a Malmquist DEA model. We describe some of the applications of the Malmquist index in the health care sector, provide a graphical illustration of the Malmquist methodology, and outline some considerations when applying the Malmquist model, before turning to a case study of acute hospitals in England.

Index numbers are used to measure the change in TFP and involve the measurement of changes in the levels of output produced and input used. The most popular indices are the Laspeyres, Paasche, Fisher and Törnqvist (Laspeyres 1871; Paasche 1874; Fisher 1922; Törnqvist 1936). All index numbers measure the changes in the levels of a set of variables between a base period and the current period. The Laspeyres index uses the base period quantities or prices as weights, whereas the Paasche index uses the current period weights. The Fisher index is the geometric mean of these two indices. The Törnqvist index is often presented in a log-change form and represents the weighted average change in the log of the price or quantity of a particular commodity. In order to use these indices in productivity measurement, they are usually linked together to make annual comparisons of consecutive years to measure productivity over a given period in what is called a *chain index* (Coelli, Rao and Battese 1998).

Measuring productivity change by the Laspeyres, Paasche, Fisher or Törnqvist indices requires quantity and price information as well as assumptions about the structure of technology and the behaviour of producers.

Alternatively, change can be measured using a Malmquist productivity index (Malmquist 1953). This index was introduced into the DEA literature by Caves, Christensen and Diewert (1982) and is based on Malmquist's proposal to construct quantity indices as ratios of distance functions for use in consumption analysis. Distance functions are representations of multi-output multi-input technologies which require data only on input and output quantities (Färe *et al.* 1994).

The advantage of the Malmquist index over other TFP indices is that the former does not require information on the prices of inputs and outputs or technological and behavioural assumptions. This makes the Malmquist index a particularly suitable tool for the analysis of productivity change in the public sector, where output prices are not in general available (Coelli, Rao and Battese 1998).

Unlike the other indices, however, the Malmquist index does require the estimation of a representation of the production technology (Coelli, Rao and Battese 1998; Kumbhakar and Lovell 2000). This production technology may be a production frontier, or its dual, the cost frontier. The choice of perspective depends on the problem to be analysed.

A further advantage of the Malmquist approach is that, once the production technology is estimated, one can decompose TFP change into its component parts: efficiency change and technical change.

Malmquist indices can be calculated using either parametric methods (Nishimizu and Page 1982) or linear-programming DEA-type methods. The methodology proposed by Färe *et al.* (1994) makes operational the principles of the Malmquist index with non-parametric methods. This method uses DEA to calculate distance functions to produce the Malmquist TFP index and then decomposes this into technical change and technical efficiency change components. This is the approach described in this chapter and is the one which has been most widely applied in the literature.

6.2 The Malmquist methodology

6.2.1 A graphical illustration

Assume a decision-making unit (DMU) uses a single type of input (x) to produce a single type of output (y), as depicted in Figure 6.1. In the

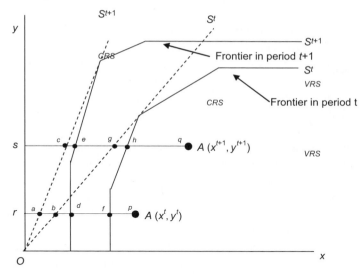

Figure 6.1. Illustration of productivity change with one input and one output.

health care setting, we could for example depict Hospital A using a single input (staff) to produce a single output (patients treated). We measure the productivity change of Hospital A by examining its efficiency in two time periods, t and $t+1$, and also the technology shift from t to $t+1$. This is illustrated graphically in Figure 6.1, which seeks to explain the Malmquist indices in intuitive form. In principle, one can calculate a Malmquist index relative to either variable returns to scale (VRS) or constant returns to scale (CRS) technology. The VRS technology estimated by DEA in period t is represented by the frontier S^t_{VRS}, while the CRS technology is indicated by the line S^t_{CRS}. Hospital A consumes input x^t and produces output y^t in period t. Hospital A moves to point (x^{t+1}, y^{t+1}) in period $t+1$. The VRS technology in period $t+1$ is estimated by S^{t+1}_{VRS}, while the constant returns to scale technology is indicated by the line S^{t+1}_{CRS}.

As mentioned, the Malmquist index is defined using distance functions. Inefficiency is measured by the distance from the origin O, this being the *radial* measure of inefficiency. For Hospital A, the distance fp represents the technical inefficiency of the hospital relative to the VRS technology in period t. Using an input orientation, this is the amount by which input (staff) could be proportionally reduced without a reduction in patients treated. This is expressed in percentage terms by the ratio *rf/rp*.

DEA is used to estimate an overall hospital industry frontier S^t based on the data from all hospitals in the sample. Each hospital is then compared to this frontier. However, this overall frontier also shifts over time, on account of technological change and innovation, to S^{t+1}. The productivity change therefore measures how much closer a hospital gets to the industry frontier (its efficiency change), as well as how much the industry frontier shifts given each hospital's input use (its technical change). The Malmquist is therefore constructed by measuring the change for Hospital A from point (x^t, y^t) to point (x^{t+1}, y^{t+1}) measured with respect to the CRS and VRS technologies using distance functions.

We can thus examine the Malmquist index, M, as comprising two main elements, $M = E \times T$, where E is the technical efficiency change and T the technical change. E can be further decomposed as follows: $M = (P \times S) \times T$, where P is the pure efficiency change, and S the scale efficiency change.

The pure efficiency change P for Hospital A between periods t and $t+1$ is given by the ratio:

$$P = \frac{(se/sq)}{(rd/rp)} \qquad (6.1)$$

This simply indicates the change in the hospital's distance from the current technically efficient frontier (under VRS) from one period to the next.

The change in scale efficiency S is given by calculating the efficiency of Hospital A relative to the CRS and VRS technology in each period, as follows:

$$S = \frac{(sc/sq)}{(se/sq)} \Big/ \frac{(rb/rp)}{(rf/rp)} \qquad (6.2)$$

The technical efficiency change term E $(E = P \times S)$ refers to efficiency change calculated under CRS, while P is efficiency change calculated under VRS. S captures the change in the deviation between the VRS and CRS technologies.

The change in the scale-efficient technology indicated by the CRS frontiers is estimated by:

$$T = \sqrt{\left[\frac{(sg/sq)}{(sc/sq)} \times \frac{(rb/rp)}{(ra/rp)}\right]} \tag{6.3}$$

Note that while P was calculated relative to the VRS technology, the frontier shift in T is measured relative to the constant returns to scale technology.

The Malmquist index is constructed using these radial distance functions. The Malmquist index is then given by:

$$M = \frac{(se/sq)}{(rd/rp)} \frac{\left[\frac{(sc/sq)}{(se/sq)} \Big/ \frac{(rb/rp)}{(rf/rp)}\right]}{\sqrt{\left[\frac{(sg/sq)}{(sc/sq)} \times \frac{(rb/rp)}{(ra/rp)}\right]}} \tag{6.4}$$

or $M = (P \times S) \times T$. That is, Hospital A's productivity change is expressed as the product of pure efficiency change, scale efficiency change, and the change in technology.

6.2.2 The general form of the Malmquist index

The Malmquist index can be computed in either the input orientation, as above (controlling for output use and measuring changes in input use), or the output orientation (controlling for input use and measuring changes in output levels) (Thanassoulis 2001). Following from the previous concepts, Färe *et al.* (1994) define an output-oriented Malmquist TFP change index M_O^{t+1}:

$$
M_O^{t+1}(X^{t+1}, Y^{t+1}, X^t, Y^t)
$$
$$
= \left[\frac{D_O^t(X^{t+1}, Y^{t+1})}{D_O^t(X^t, Y^t)} \frac{D_O^{t+1}(X^{t+1}, Y^{t+1})}{D_O^{t+1}(X^t, Y^t)}\right]^{1/2} \tag{6.5}
$$

where D_O represents the component output distance functions in periods t and $t+1$. Equation 6.5 is the geometric mean of two Malmquist productivity indices for periods t and $t+1$. The first uses reference technology corresponding to period t, whereas the second does the same for period $t+1$. This approach makes it unnecessary to adopt an arbitrary choice of one or other period as the reference base.

The most common way of formulating the Malmquist index is:

$$M_O^{t+1}(X^{t+1}, Y^{t+1}, X^t, Y^t) = \frac{D_O^{t+1}(X^{t+1}, Y^{t+1})}{D_O^t(X^t, Y^t)}$$

$$\left[\frac{D_O^t(X^{t+1}, Y^{t+1})}{D_O^{t+1}(X^{t+1}, Y^{t+1})} \frac{D_O^t(X^t, Y^t)}{D_O^{t+1}(X^t, Y^t)} \right]^{1/2} \quad (6.6)$$

$$\text{or } M = E \times T$$

A value for equation 6.6 of M_O greater than 1 indicates positive TFP growth from period t to period $t+1$. A value for M_0 of less than 1 indicates TFP decline between the two periods.

E (the ratio outside the brackets) represents the change in the output-oriented Farrell technical efficiency levels between periods t and $t+1$:

$$E = \frac{D_O^{t+1}(X^{t+1}, Y^{t+1})}{D_O^t(X^t, Y^t)} \quad (6.7)$$

A value of 1 for E means the hospital has the same distance from the frontier in both periods. A value greater than 1 means the hospital has improved its efficiency in period $t+1$ compared to period t in that it has moved closer to the frontier. When the value is less than 1 the hospital has moved further away from the frontier.

T reflects the changes in productivity levels due to technical progress for the hospital sector. It is the geometric mean of the shift in technology between the two periods, evaluated at X^{t+1} and X^t:

$$T = \left[\frac{D_O^t(X^{t+1}, Y^{t+1})}{D_O^{t+1}(X^{t+1}, Y^{t+1})} \frac{D_O^t(X^t, Y^t)}{D_O^{t+1}(X^t, Y^t)} \right]^{1/2} \quad (6.8)$$

A value of greater than 1 for T means the industry produces more outputs in period $t+1$ compared to period t, controlling for input levels (given that the output orientation is being used). In other words, the hospital sector has experienced productivity gains over time. A frontier shift of less than 1 would equivalently represent productivity loss by the industry. When $T = 1$ the industry has made neither a productivity gain nor a loss.

Note that these distance metrics all measure Farrell radial efficiency and ignore any slacks. Thus any gain or loss which is not captured by the radial efficiency measures will not be captured by the Malmquist index (Thanassoulis 2001). This has led to some criticisms of the Malmquist, but to date there has been no widely accepted solution to this problem.

Where variable returns to scale (VRS) exist, it is possible to further decompose the change in efficiency levels into two elements: that due to pure technical efficiency change (P), and that due to scale efficiency change (S). This is made operational by expressing equation 6.7 as follows:

$$E = \frac{D_O^{t+1}(X^{t+1}, Y^{t+1})}{D_O^t(X^t, Y^t)} = \frac{D_{VRS}^{t+1}(X^{t+1}, Y^{t+1})}{D_{VRS}^t(X^t, Y^t)} \frac{\dfrac{D_{CRS}^{t+1}(X^{t+1}, Y^{t+1})}{D_{VRS}^{t+1}(X^{t+1}, Y^{t+1})}}{\dfrac{D_{CRS}^t(X^t, Y^t)}{D_{VRS}^t(X^t, Y^t)}},$$

or $E = P \times S$,

(6.9)

where the first expression reflects the change in efficiency relative to the 'true' VRS frontier, and the second reflects the extent to which the distance from the scale-efficient point on the VRS frontier (relative to the notional CRS frontier) has changed. Again, if P is greater than 1 it reflects efficiency gain in that the hospital is closer to the VRS frontier in period $t+1$ than it was to the VRS frontier in period t; the opposite holds true for a value of P less than 1. A value of S greater than 1 implies the hospital has become more scale-efficient between the two periods.

In order to calculate equation 6.5, it is necessary to consider its four constituent distance functions. As mentioned, these distance functions which make up the Malmquist can be computed using either linear-programming type approaches such as DEA, which is the most common approach, or frontier econometric approaches such as stochastic frontier analysis. The latter, however, require specific assumptions about functional form whereas DEA does not. We therefore discuss the use of the non-parametric DEA in solving these distance functions.

The application of DEA to the Malmquist index requires the solution of four linear programming problems, corresponding to the four required distance functions, for each of the n DMUs under investigation, and in each pair of adjacent time periods t and $t+1$ (Coelli, Rao and Battese 1998). Thus, if we assume constant returns to scale, and the output orientation, the function $D^t_O(X^t, Y^t)$ for DMU$_0$ can be considered by solving the following problem for each DMU in the sample:

$$[D_O^t(X_t, Y_t)]^{-1} = \max_{\phi\lambda}\phi \qquad (6.10)$$

subject to

$$\begin{aligned}
-\phi y_{0t} + Y_t\lambda &\geq 0 \\
x_{0t} - X_t\lambda &\geq 0 \\
\lambda &\geq 0
\end{aligned}$$

where x_{0t} and y_{0t} are the vectors of inputs and outputs, respectively, associated with DMU_0 and λ is a flexible vector of weights to be applied to the matrices X_t and Y_t. The parameter N indicates the maximum proportion by which all outputs of DMU_0 can be expanded such that $(x_{0t}, y_{0t}/N)$ remains feasible, as indicated by the performance of other DMUs (X_t, Y_t).

The three remaining linear programming problems are variations of (6.10):

$$[D_O^{t+1}(X_{t+1}, Y_{t+1})]^{-1} = \max_{\phi\lambda}\phi \qquad (6.11)$$

subject to

$$\begin{aligned}
-\phi y_{0(t+1)} + Y_{t+1}\lambda &\geq 0 \\
x_{0(t+1)} - X_{t+1}\lambda &\geq 0 \\
\lambda &\geq 0
\end{aligned}$$

$$[D_O^t(X_{t+1}, Y_{t+1})]^{-1} = \max_{\phi\lambda}\phi \qquad (6.12)$$

subject to

$$\begin{aligned}
-\phi y_{0(t+1)} + Y_t\lambda &\geq 0 \\
x_{0(t+1)} - X_t\lambda &\geq 0 \\
\lambda &\geq 0
\end{aligned}$$

$$[D_O^{t+1}(X_t, Y_t)]^{-1} = \max_{\phi\lambda}\phi \qquad (6.13)$$

subject to

$$\begin{aligned}
-\phi y_{0t} + Y_{t+1}\lambda &\geq 0 \\
x_{0t} - X_{t+1}\lambda &\geq 0 \\
\lambda &\geq 0
\end{aligned}$$

In problems (6.12) and (6.13), notional efficiency calculations are made for one period, taking as a reference base the production frontier corresponding to the other period. In these cases, the value of ϕ does not necessarily have to be greater than or equal to 1, as must necessarily be the case when technical efficiency is calculated using cross-sectional data. Thus, in equation 6.12 an observation in period $t+1$ is being compared with the production frontier for the previous period. If technical progress has taken place, this observation can be located beyond the production frontier, leading to a value of Φ less than 1.

The above equations yield estimates of distance functions under the assumption of constant returns to scale. In order to decompose equation 6.9 into its component parts P and S, we solve two additional linear programming problems (for each adjacent set of production points). The variable returns to scale distance function estimates required for equation 6.9 are secured by adding to (6.10) and (6.11) the constraint:

$$\sum_n \lambda_n = 1 \qquad (6.14)$$

Thus we would calculate these two distance functions relative to a VRS technology and not a CRS technology. One then uses both the CRS and VRS estimates to calculate scale efficiency (Färe *et al.* 1994; Coelli, Rao and Battese 1998).

6.3 Considerations in using the Malmquist index

One of the key considerations in applying a Malmquist index is that longitudinal data are required for which inputs and outputs are measured consistently over time. In practice this requirement is often difficult to achieve as health care data can easily be affected by changes over time in technology, merger activity or changes in data collection methods.

Another key consideration in applying a Malmquist is that scale properties of the technology are very important. A Malmquist index may not correctly measure TFP changes when VRS is assumed (Grifell-Tatjé and Lovell 1995). While these authors argue for a new TFP index which scales the Malmquist index by an additional term which accounts for returns to scale, most authors argue that CRS should be imposed when calculating a Malmquist TFP index (Coelli, Rao and Battese 1998).

Hence the DEA efficiencies in the Malmquist index are usually computed using a constant returns to scale assumption irrespective of the actual returns to scale characterising the production technology. As we have seen, for DMUs not operating under CRS, we can decompose their productivity change so that the impact of scale can be estimated as in equation 6.9. Most applications take account of this decomposition, calculating efficiencies relative to both CRS and VRS technologies. Thus all productivity changes associated with scale are captured in the index. If the Malmquist index is computed using a constant returns to scale technology, the efficiency values are the same irrespective of whether we assume an input or an output orientation (Thanassoulis 2001). Thus input and output-oriented Malmquist indices would be equivalent. This makes the decision for the analyst somewhat more straightforward than when analysis is restricted to cross-sectional data.

6.4 Previous literature on the Malmquist index in health care

An early application of the Malmquist index approach in the health care sector, as applied to productivity changes in Swedish pharmacies, was first reported by Färe *et al.* (1992). Since then, a modest number of applications in the health care sector have emerged, including an evaluation of health care reforms in Scotland (Maniadakis, Hollingsworth and Thanassoulis 1999), studies in Finland (Linna and Häkkinen 1998), Sweden (Tambour 1997), and Austria (Sommersguter-Reichmann 2000), an assessment of productivity changes in the administration of primary health care (Giuffrida 1999), studies in Veterans Administration hospitals in the United States (Burgess and Wilson 1995), in the Spanish pharmaceutical industry (González and Gascón 2004) and for community care in English county councils (Salinas-Jiménez, Pedraja-Chaparro and Smith 2003), and an assessment of reformed payment systems for diagnostic tests in Portuguese hospitals (Dismuke and Sena 1999). The approach has been applied at various levels, from the overall health care system (Färe *et al.* 1997), to the hospital level (Maniadakis and Thanassoulis 2000), to the level of hospital department (Tambour 1997). Hollingsworth (2003) provides a review of studies applying the Malmquist index in health care.

6.5 Application to acute hospitals in England

6.5.1 *The methods and data*

The Malmquist methodology is illustrated using the same data set as described previously for acute hospitals in England and as outlined in the Appendix. Data for 171 hospitals with A&E departments were analysed for the four years 1994/95–1997/98 (Söderlund and van der Merwe 1999). As before, the primary input is total cost and we take an input orientation.

We used the availability of data in other years to impute the missing data for some outpatient and Accident and Emergency data, assuming the missing values on the outputs were the same as non-missing values in adjacent periods, if these were available. This was the case for some thirty-five hospitals.

Since the total cost variable now covers more than one year, we need to take account of inflation to make the comparison over time more appropriate for equivalent input usage. We have therefore deflated total cost by the GDP deflator with the final year set as the base year. The rest of the variables are identical to those used in chapter 5. Table 6.1 shows the means for the variables used in the Malmquist models over the four years.

Total costs increased over the four years, as did many of the activity variables. The change in sample means is illustrated in Figure 6.2.

6.5.2 *Model specifications*

Five model specifications were employed using the above-listed variables. The different specifications serve to illustrate whether the efficiency scores and ranks and total factor productivity indices remain stable when variables are removed or added in the Malmquist models. We use the same specifications as in chapter 5. These are outlined again in Table 6.2.

6.5.3 *Results*

The mean Malmquist TFP change index across the 171 hospitals for each model is presented in Table 6.3. Between 10 and 31 hospitals show either positive or no change in productivity across the five

Table 6.1. *Mean values for Malmquist model variables*

Variable	Description	1994/95	1995/96	1996/97	1997/98
TOTCOST	Total cost or revenue expenditure divided by GDP deflator (1997/98 = 100) (£m)	58.911	60.282	60.862	61.553
Main activities					
INPATIENTS	Total inpatient episodes weighted by HRG case mix index	0.042	0.041	0.042	0.043
OUTPATIENTS	Total first outpatient attendances	0.047	0.050	0.053	0.053
A&E	Total A & E attendances	0.055	0.057	0.057	0.058
Additional activities					
STUDENTS	Student whole-time teaching equivalents per inpatient spell	0.502	0.564	0.641	0.649
RESEARCH	Percentage of total revenue spent on research	1.423	1.291	1.227	1.189
Other outputs					
TRANS-IN	Transfers in to hospital per spell	0.014	0.015	0.021	0.022
1–TRANS-OUT	1–Transfers out of hospital per spell	0.980	0.980	0.986	0.988
EMERGENCY	Emergency admissions per spell	0.351	0.357	0.356	0.363
FCE	Finished consultant episode inter-speciality transfers per spell	0.049	0.020	0.071	0.079
FU-OUTPTS	Follow-up outpatient attendances per inpatient spell	2.872	2.929	3.104	2.915

Variable	Description	1994/95	1995/96	1996/97	1997/98
EMERINDX	Standardised index of unexpected emergency admissions/total emergency admissions	0.024	0.059	0.026	0.020
EP_SPELL	Episodes per spell	1.077	1.074	1.092	1.085
P-15	Proportion of patients under 15 years of age	0.179	0.103	0.167	0.166
P-60	Proportion of patients 60 years or older	0.332	0.337	0.343	0.351
P-FEM	Proportion of female patients	0.572	0.571	0.575	0.574
Environmental adjusters					
MFF	Market forces factor – weighted average of staff, land, buildings and London weighting factors	87.528	87.595	86.495	86.495
AVBEDS	Average available beds	770	721	711	579
HEATBED	Heated volume per bed	3.244	3.289	3.201	3.689
SITES50B	Sites with more than 50 beds	2.158	2.152	1.854	1.854
ITINDX	Scope/specialisation index, information theory index	0.330	0.406	0.476	0.362
HERF15	Herfindahl concentration/ competition index, 15-mile radius	0.364	0.364	0.364	0.364

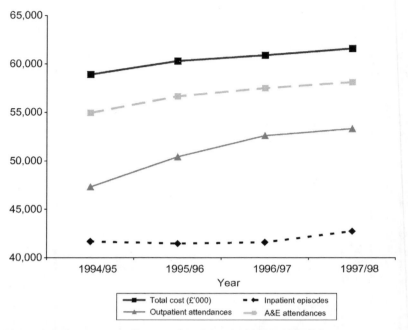

Figure 6.2. **Mean expenditure and activity, 1994/95–1997/98.**

models, whereas between 140 and 161 hospitals show productivity
decline. The TFP indices lie on average between about 0.8 and 1.3,
although in all five models the majority of hospitals show TFP decline
over time.

Figure 6.3 shows a graphic illustration of the five TFP indices over
time. Models 1 and 2 yield nearly identical results, as do the TFP
indices for Models 3 and 4. In fact, these overlay each other. This is
unsurprising as only two new variables are added from Model 1 to
Model 2 and only one variable is added from Model 3 to Model 4. The
general trend for all five indices suggests a drop in productivity between 1994/95 and 1995/96 and then an increase between 1995/96
and 1996/97 with some discrepancies between the models for the
interval 1996/97 to 1997/98. The basic Models 1 and 2 suggest a
slight increase in productivity whereas the fuller Models 3, 4 and 5
suggest a decline in productivity in the latter years of the series. These
results are not surprising since Models 1 and 2 contain only three to
five variables, whereas Models 3 to 5 contain fifteen to twenty-one
variables. The model specification therefore makes a great deal of

Table 6.2. Malmquist model specifications

Model	Variable names	Outputs included
1	INPATIENTS, OUTPATIENTS, A&E	Inpatient episodes; outpatient attendances; A&E attendances
2	As for Model 1 plus STUDENTS and RESEARCH	Inpatient episodes; outpatient attendances; A&E attendances; teaching; research
3	As for Model 2 plus TRANS-IN, TRANS-OUT, FCE, EMERINDX, P-15, P-60, P-FEM, EP_SPELL, FU-OUTPTS and EMERGENCY	Inpatient episodes; outpatient attendances; A&E attendances; teaching; research; transfers in; transfers out; inter-speciality transfers; emergency index; proportions of young, old and female patients; episodes, outpatients and emergencies per spell
4	As for Model 3 plus MFF	Inpatient episodes; outpatient attendances; A&E attendances; teaching; research; transfers in; transfers out; inter-speciality transfers; emergency index; proportions of young, old and female patients; episodes, outpatients and emergencies per spell; market forces factor
5	As for Model 4 plus AVBEDS, HEATBED, SITES50B, ITINDX, and HERF15	All outputs and environmental adjusters

Table 6.3. Malmquist TFP results

	Model 1	Model 2	Model 3	Model 4	Model 5
Mean	0.948	0.948	0.963	0.963	0.937
Std dev.	0.040	0.041	0.059	0.059	0.051
Min.	0.851	0.820	0.810	0.810	0.795
Max.	1.190	1.186	1.350	1.347	1.125
>=1	10	10	31	31	15
<1	161	161	140	140	156

difference to the TFP index and it is important for the analyst to engage in a thorough sensitivity analysis and have a clear rationale for the appropriate model specification.

As in chapter 5, we can assess the consistency of the five models by looking at the correlation coefficients of the TFP scores across the five specifications. As highlighted by Figure 6.3, the agreement is extremely high between Models 1 and 2 and between Models 3 and 4 respectively. In fact, there is very little to distinguish Model 3 from Model 4 which differs only by the MFF variable. Table 6.4 shows that the correlation between Models 4 and 5 is also relatively high. The rest of the correlations are very low.

We can decompose any Malmquist index into its constituent parts. Figure 6.4 illustrates the Malmquist index for Model 2 divided into efficiency change (relative to a CRS technology from equation 6.7), technical change (the shift in technology from equation 6.8), scale efficiency change (S from equation 6.9), overall TFP change (M in equation 6.6), and pure efficiency change (relative to a VRS technology) (P from equation 6.9). The Malmquist TFP (M) shows a decline between the first two years, followed by a slight growth between 1995/96 and 1996/97 and again between 1996/97 and 1997/98. This overall TFP movement seems to be driven to a large extent by a similar pattern for technical change T (the frontier shifting). From 1995/96 onwards the results from this model suggest consistently strong technological progress in the hospital industry. More modest changes are evident for technical efficiency change (E), pure efficiency change (P) (both following similar paths except in the final year) and scale efficiency change (s) which seems to show a relatively stable growth pattern up to 1996/97 followed by a steeper fall.

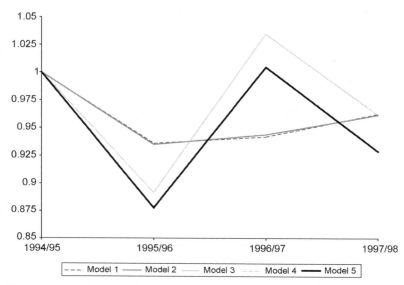

Figure 6.3. Malmquist TFP indices.

Table 6.4. Correlations between Malmquist TFP scores

	Model 1	Model 2	Model 3	Model 4	Model 5
Model 1	1				
Model 2	0.8966*	1			
Model 3	0.2920	0.4062	1		
Model 4	0.2928	0.4072	1.0000*	1	
Model 5	0.2675	0.3746	0.8604*	0.8610*	1

Note:
* Significant at 0.01 level.

Overall, there appears to have been substantial change among this sample of hospitals in the form of new production technologies. Of course, the approach assumes a contemporaneous association between changes in technology and productivity growth which may not hold in reality, particularly if there are lags between investment in new technologies and realising the benefits from those investments.

Measuring scale effects accurately in the hospital sector may also be impeded by the fact that merger activity and the reconfiguration of

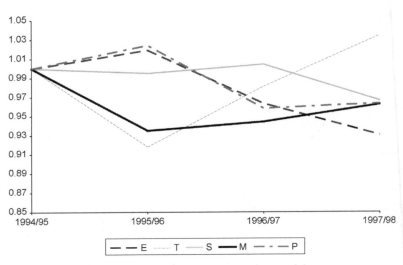

Figure 6.4. Decomposition of Malmquist index for Model 2.

hospitals can impact on the efficient scale of operation. Governments often intervene in health care markets to try to achieve economies by merging hospitals, and this was certainly the case in the sample of hospitals analysed here.

Finally, the case study illustrates inconsistencies in Malmquist indices across specifications. We thus examine whether hospitals change their efficiency scores and rankings within a model specification across time. In other words, are hospitals ranked differently in the 'league table' from one period to the next? Table 6.5 illustrates some cases for a small sample of hospitals for Model 2 with respect to the VRS technology.

Table 6.5 shows that Hospital A remains efficient over all four years. Hospitals B and C also maintain consistently high rankings over time. Hospitals D and E are also consistent over time, but are both relatively less efficient. For Hospitals F to J, there appears to be less consistency in efficiency scores and rankings over time. This may appear somewhat surprising, since we are examining the same individual hospital within the same model specification. For Hospital F the highest efficiency rating is in Year 1 with ranking declining subsequently. For Hospital G Year 2's rating is higher than the other three years. For Hospitals H and I, Year 3 seems to be different, and for Hospital J the ranking in Year 4 is higher.

Table 6.5. *Individual hospital scores and rankings for each year for Model 2*

Hospital	Year 1 Score	Year 1 Rank	Year 2 Score	Year 2 Rank	Year 3 Score	Year 3 Rank	Year 4 Score	Year 4 Rank
A	1.000	1	1.000	1	1.000	1	1.000	1
B	0.979	29	0.972	32	0.937	38	0.937	35
C	0.991	23	0.949	38	0.959	32	0.929	38
D	0.626	164	0.591	169	0.598	165	0.600	161
E	0.513	171	0.527	171	0.466	171	0.436	171
F	1.000	1	0.674	162	0.597	167	0.610	159
G	0.869	64	1.000	1	0.753	113	0.769	83
H	0.883	55	0.916	51	1.000	1	0.714	113
I	0.849	78	0.888	66	1.000	1	0.698	120
J	0.701	147	0.813	107	0.789	95	1.000	1

It is clear that the efficiency scores and the relative rankings for certain hospitals are not consistent over time. In order to examine how these changes in efficiency scores and rankings come about, we explore in more detail the data underlying Model 2 for Hospital I (see Table 6.6). Recall that Model 2 includes the three activities, inpatients (INPATIENTS), outpatients (OUTPATIENTS) and A&E (A&E), as well as teaching (STUDENTS) and research (RESEARCH). We highlight in bold the sample means for each variable over time.

If we look at Year 3 (the year in which we have the jump in ranking for Hospital I onto the efficiency frontier), we can see a large increase in outpatient activity relative to the other years and the sample mean. In Year 4, outpatient activity reverts back to previous levels. This suggests the possibility of measurement error, to which DEA is particularly vulnerable. While it is clear that this is probably measurement error in this example, it may be less easy to detect in other instances. It is clear from these examples that this may not be an isolated case and a difficult question for the analyst may be how to identify and deal with this. One approach might be to remove obvious cases of measurement error by replacing them with the moving average, or to assume them constant with another year. But these *ad hoc* decisions need to be traded off against the risk of spuriously replacing 'correct' data, and

Table 6.6. Data for Model 2 of Malmquist specification for Hospital I

Year	TOTCOST	INPATIENTS	OUTPATIENTS	A&E	STUDENTS	RESEARCH
1	71.802	0.068	0.067	0.079	0.130	1.020
Mean	**58.911**	**0.042**	**0.047**	**0.055**	**0.502**	**1.423**
2	78.519	0.067	0.073	0.083	0.160	0.950
Mean	**60.282**	**0.041**	**0.050**	**0.057**	**0.564**	**1.291**
3	83.962	0.067	0.150	0.083	0.188	0.915
Mean	**60.862**	**0.042**	**0.053**	**0.057**	**0.641**	**1.227**
4	88.969	0.065	0.074	0.078	0.217	0.879
Mean	**61.553**	**0.043**	**0.053**	**0.058**	**0.649**	**1.189**

losing one of the main elements of DEA, which is the fact that it is based on outlier observations. Notwithstanding these considerations, this example illustrates how DEA and the Malmquist index can be used as a data exploratory device. Apparent data anomalies may then be used by health planners in discussions with individual hospitals on ways to improve performance in specific areas, the possible reasons for poor performance, and, of course, ways to improve data collection.

6.6 Conclusions

This chapter has outlined the main features of a Malmquist model to assess productivity change using panel data and non-parametric DEA techniques.

There are clearly severe limitations with the illustrative example employed in the case study. Aspects of hospital output which are omitted in these models, such as unmeasured case mix, severity and quality of care, could have a profound impact on the interpretation of the results. Higher volume might be secured merely by compromising on quality. Quality variables such as waiting times, patient satisfaction measures, or those relating to patient outcomes such as successful operations, morbidity and mortality rates, might be considered important elements to include in these types of productivity analyses.

Data aside, the methodology has some unique strengths and weaknesses. The Malmquist index does not require price information, making it especially suited to the health care setting where these data are seldom available. Other advantages include the fact that no assumption about functional form is required. Having said that, the measures focus on technical efficiency and ignore the issue of allocative efficiency, which may be an important consideration in some contexts. There have been developments towards a cost Malmquist index when factor prices are available (Thanassoulis 2001).

The Malmquist index requires no behavioural assumptions about cost minimisation or revenue maximisation and can be decomposed into both technical change and technical efficiency change. The models therefore offer valuable insights into productivity change in an industry. At a macro level, the approach is able to provide useful insights into overall productivity trends. However, results are sensitive to model specification, require careful interpretation and should never be used as the sole source of policy guidance or to pass definitive judgement on individual organisations. The results are often unstable, and while data deficiencies in the given data set may be partly responsible, the volatility of individual DMUs over time may be exacerbated by the boundary technique DEA which promotes the DMU to the frontier in some years but not in others. One way to obtain an estimate of the degree of uncertainty which exists around efficiency estimates is to apply bootstrapping procedures or statistical methods of uncertainty analysis (see sub-section 5.3.5). However, if the Malmquist approach is viewed as an important but essentially exploratory form of data analysis, it can have much to commend it in situations where the alternative would be an absence of analytic insight.

7 | *A comparison of SFA and DEA*

7.1 Introduction

THE previous four chapters have examined stochastic frontier analysis and data envelopment analysis in detail. We have described the methodologies and touched on the main strengths and limitations of each. In this chapter we compare the two techniques. First, we consider why they might produce different estimates of organisational efficiency. We then outline the other key dimensions on which the techniques differ. This is followed by an empirical comparison, using some of the cross-sectional data analysed in the previous chapters. We conclude by making recommendations as to how best to interpret organisational efficiency estimates according to their sensitivity to analytical approach and modelling assumptions.

7.2 Why SFA and DEA produce different efficiency estimates

Many studies find that the results of applying SFA and DEA lack consistency, even when exactly the same variables and data are used. There are two main reasons for discrepancies in the efficiency estimates derived from the two broad analytical approaches:

- differences in how the techniques establish and shape the efficiency frontier;
- differences in how the techniques determine how far individual observations lie from the frontier.

Given that the true frontier is unobservable, the question arises as to how best it should be approximated. Is the economic theory pertaining to the analysis of efficiency sufficiently well-established to outweigh the appeal of simply relying on best practice as revealed by the data to hand?

SFA appeals to economic theory when considering the shape of the frontier and statistical criteria might be used to differentiate the appropriateness of alternative functional relationships for particular data sets. The theoretical underpinnings of SFA are derived mainly from an extension of the theory of the firm, and the suitability of this theory as a basis for efficiency analysis remains to be established. The analytical models designed to analyse firm behaviour fit within the standard economic paradigm, where interest lies in extracting sample average parameter estimates. These might, for instance, provide insight on the marginal contributions of labour and capital to output. SFA models, in contrast, are formulated primarily to extract individual estimates of efficiency from the 'unexplained' part of the model. This means that statistical tests designed to examine standard econometric models are incorrectly focused for determining the appropriateness of SFA models. We shall discuss this issue in more detail in the next chapter.

Advocates of DEA would argue that the problems of providing a prior specification of functional form can be avoided by applying the non-parametric technique. Here the frontier is defined solely by the data: the outermost observations, given the scale of operation, are defined as efficient. As such, the frontier is positioned and shaped by the data, not by theoretical considerations. Consequently, DEA is highly flexible, the frontier moulding itself to the data.

Thus, if the results of DEA and (say) a logarithmic stochastic frontier correspond, it could be concluded that the frontier truly displays logarithmic properties for the data analysed. Where the results deviate, this may be because the monotonic assumptions of the parametric function are too restrictive, and DEA is able to account for segments of the frontier where a smooth relationship is not apparent in the data. For those who approach efficiency measurement from an empirical rather than a theoretical standpoint, the flexibility of functional form offered by DEA would seem an attractive feature of the technique. The drawback, however, is that the location of the DEA frontier is sensitive to observations that may have unusual types, levels or combinations of inputs and outputs. These will have a scarcity of adjacent reference observations or 'peers', perhaps resulting in sections of the 'frontier' being unreliably estimated and inappropriately positioned (Resti 1997).

While DEA might be thought to win over the SFA method in terms of the flexibility with which it determines the frontier, this benefit is offset by how the technique interprets any distance from the frontier. There are two key differences between DEA and SFA.

First, DEA assumes correct model specification and that all data are observed without error. SFA allows for the possibility of modelling and measurement error. Consequently, if the two methods yield an identical frontier, SFA efficiency estimates are likely to be higher than those produced by DEA. If measurement error is thought to be present, then SFA may be the more appropriate technique. In some circumstances, it may be possible to sustain an argument that there is no measurement error. Indeed, Kooreman argued, in applying DEA to the nursing home setting, that 'since the survey forms have been filled out by the administrative staff of the nursing homes, who may be assumed to be well-informed about their home, measurement errors are likely to be small' (Kooreman 1994). This assumption may have less foundation in larger or more complex organisational contexts (such as hospitals), and may be further undermined if those responsible for data collection change their reporting behaviour in the knowledge that the information they provide is to be used for the purpose of efficiency assessment or reimbursement.

Second, DEA uses a selective amount of data to estimate individual efficiency scores. DEA generates efficiency scores for each organisation by comparing it only to peers that produce a comparable mix of outputs. This has two implications. First, if an output is unique to an organisation, the organisation will have no peers with which to make a comparison, irrespective of the fact that it may produce other outputs in common. An absence of peers results in the automatic assignation of full efficiency to the organisation under consideration. Second, when assigning an inefficiency score to an observation lying away from the frontier, only its peers are considered, with information pertaining to the remainder of the sample discarded.

In contrast, SFA appeals to the full sample information when estimating relative efficiency. In addition to making greater use of the available data, this facet of the estimation procedure will make individual efficiency estimates more robust to the presence of outlier observations and atypical input/output combinations.

Table 7.1. Comparison of SFA and DEA

	SFA	DEA
Assumption about functional form	Strong*	None
Distinguish random error from efficiency variation	Yes	No
Test for inclusion of variables	Imperfectly	No
Allow for exogenous factors	Yes	Yes
Allow for multiple outputs	Not readily	Yes
Provides information on 'peer' organisations	Not automatically	Yes
Vulnerable to outliers	Moderately*	Yes
Problems of multicollinearity	Yes*	No
Problems of endogeneity	Yes*	Yes
Problems of heteroscedasticity	Yes*	No
Vulnerable to small sample size	Yes	Moderately

Note:
* The assumption or problem is testable.
Source:
Adapted from Giuffrida and Gravelle (2001).

7.3 Other differences between SFA and DEA

SFA and DEA differ on a range of other dimensions, which may influence the analyst's choice of which technique to apply. Table 7.1 compares the techniques along some of these dimensions.

While SFA requires assumptions to be made about the functional form and the error distribution, the validity of some of these assumptions is testable. These tests may not always produce definitive guidance. If it is not possible to differentiate among competing functional forms on statistical grounds, and individual estimates are sensitive to the functional form applied, it would be inadvisable to draw firm conclusions about their relative efficiency. However, at least SFA can be subject to a testing process to eliminate some possible formulations. In contrast, there are no standard tests to guide model construction in the DEA framework (Pedraja-Chaparro, Salinas-Jiménez and Smith 1999).

To some extent, standard econometric tests might be applied to guide the decision about which explanatory variables to include in the SFA model. However, this is not straightforward, given that most of these tests rely on ascertaining what effect inclusion of an additional variable has on the characteristics of the unexplained (error) component of the model. As mentioned, in SFA, unlike standard econometric applications, the error itself is the major focus of interest, thus undermining the usual testing procedures. More critically, DEA has no way of testing whether particular variables make a significant contribution to the model and should be included or not. We shall return to the issue of how to judge model construction in chapter 8.

One of the key strengths of DEA over SFA is that it can readily model multiple-output production processes. SFA is ill-suited to the consideration of multiple outputs, but two methods of handling the problem have been developed. The first is to estimate a cost function rather than a production function, using duality theory to argue that the two are equivalent. However, duality holds only if cost-minimising behaviour can be assumed, which is unlikely to be the case given that the purpose of the exercise is to identify departures from cost minimisation. The second approach is to condition one of the outputs on the others in some way (see sub-section 3.2.1 for a discussion of this) (Coelli and Perelman 1996; Paul, Johnston and Frengley 2000). As with DEA, this approach imposes an implicit set of weights on the outputs. In the SFA context, the output weights correspond to sample average values and, again, this may not be appropriate when sub-optimal behaviour is thought prevalent.

Both methods may be susceptible to the influence of outliers and small sample sizes. DEA is more vulnerable to outliers, because of its inherent process of 'placing each DMU in the best possible light'. As such, DMUs with unusual production processes can easily be promoted to the efficiency frontier. Because SFA estimates are derived from full sample information, the technique is less prone to outlier influence. Of course, it may be that 'outliers' are the very organisations that are most inefficient, so excluding them on the basis of statistical criteria may undermine the exercise altogether.

Small sample sizes do not prevent the application of DEA, but as with all parametric estimation processes, SFA estimates are likely to be more imprecise the smaller the sample size (Banker, Gadh and Gorr 1993).

In the next section we turn to our own case study to explore the consistency of efficiency estimates derived from applying SFA and DEA to acute hospitals in England.

7.4 Comparison of different methodologies

7.4.1 The methods and data

We illustrate the comparison between the two techniques using a cross-sectional data set, as described in chapters 3 and 5 for 171 acute hospitals in the English NHS in 1997/98. The summary statistics for the data set are shown in Table 7.2. A more detailed discussion of the data set is in the Appendix.

7.4.2 Model specifications

There are two major specification decisions that are likely to have a bearing on the results:

1. the choice of functional form, error distribution and returns to scale; and
2. the model specification, notably which explanatory variables are included.

We first specify a baseline model (Model 1) in which total cost is used as the dependent variable in SFA and as the input in DEA. This model includes three activities of hospitals as the SFA explanatory variables and DEA outputs, these being inpatients, outpatients and A&E attendances.

When applying SFA, Model 1 assumes a linear functional form and a half-normal distribution for the error term. These assumptions are subject to sensitivity analysis, by comparing the results with those obtained when a log-log functional form is applied and when a truncated normal distribution is assumed for the error distribution.

Model 1 is estimated by DEA under variable returns to scale assuming an input orientation. As some of the variables in the data set are ratios, the BCC formulation is applied (Banker, Charnes and Cooper 1984) as the baseline model. The sensitivity of these results is examined by comparison with efficiency estimates obtained under the assumption of constant returns to scale.

We then compare the baseline Model 1 with results obtained by varying the number of explanatory or output variables. Two, more comprehensive models are specified, as shown in Table 7.3. Model 2

Table 7.2. Model variables, 1997/98

Variable	Description	Mean	Std Dev.	Min.	Max.
TOTCOST	Total cost or total revenue expenditure (£m)	61.553	28.637	15.533	182.184
Main activities					
INPATIENTS	Total inpatient episodes weighted by HRG case mix index	0.043	0.020	0.003	0.107
OUTPATIENTS	Total first outpatient attendances	0.053	0.026	0.004	0.147
A&E	Total A & E attendances	0.058	0.024	0.002	0.165
Additional activities					
STUDENTS	Student whole-time teaching equivalents per inpatient spell	0.649	1.218	0.000	6.329
RESEARCH	Percentage of total revenue spent on research	1.189	2.356	0.002	15.430
Other outputs					
FCE	Finished consultant episode inter-speciality transfers per spell	0.079	0.049	0.000	0.302
EP_SPELL	Episodes per spell	1.085	0.385	0.463	5.844
TRANS-IN	Transfers in to hospital per spell	0.022	0.017	0.000	0.175
1−TRANS-OUT	1−Transfers out of hospital per spell	0.988	0.018	0.868	1.000
EMERGENCY	Emergency admissions per spell	0.363	0.062	0.133	0.582

Table 7.2. (continued)

Variable	Description	Mean	Std Dev.	Min.	Max.
FU-OUTPTS	Follow-up outpatient attendances per inpatient spell	2.915	0.881	1.270	8.053
EMERINDX	Standardised index of unexpected emergency admissions/total emergency admissions	0.020	0.014	0.005	0.098
P-15	Proportion of patients under 15 years of age	0.166	0.113	0.000	0.950
P-60	Proportion of patients 60 years or older	0.351	0.078	0.000	0.610
P-FEM	Proportion of female patients	0.574	0.053	0.363	0.999
Environmental adjusters					
MFF	Market forces factor – weighted average of staff, land, buildings and London weighting factors	86.495	9.341	75.817	131.217
HERF15	Herfindahl concentration/competition index, 15–mile radius	0.364	0.308	0.040	1.000
AVBEDS	Average available beds	579	190	56	998
HEATBED	Heated volume per bed	3.689	1.164	1.749	8.209
SITES50B	Sites with more than 50 beds	1.854	1.021	1	8
ITINDX	Scope/specialisation index, information theory index	0.362	0.425	0.089	3.344

Table 7.3. Model specifications

Model	Variable names	Outputs included
1	INPATIENTS, OUTPATIENTS, A&E	Inpatient episodes, outpatient attendances, A&E attendances
2	As for model 1 plus STUDENTS, RESEARCH	Inpatient episodes, outpatient attendances, A&E attendances, teaching, research
3	As for model 2 plus TRANS-IN, TRANS-OUT, FCE, EMERINDX, P-15, P-60, P-FEM, EP_SPELL, FU-OUTPTS, EMERGENCY, MFF, AVBEDS, HEATBED, SITES50B, ITINDX, HERF15	All outputs and environmental adjusters

adds teaching and research activity. Model 3 includes all available output variables and environmental adjusters.

7.4.3 Results

Sensitivity to functional form, error distribution and returns to scale
Table 7.4 gives the efficiency scores for Model 1 under the various specification assumptions. We test the sensitivity of the efficiency estimates to our choice of the distributional assumption of the error term in SFA and to our choice of returns to scale in DEA.

In general the average efficiency levels for DEA are lower than for SFA. This is to be expected, since under SFA the error term is partitioned into inefficiency and error, whereas under DEA the entire shortfall is deemed inefficiency. On the whole the efficiency scores for the truncated and half-normal specifications under SFA are quite similar. The log-log SFA model produces a higher estimate of average efficiency and lower variance. This reflects the normalisation of the error that follows logarithmic transformation. As expected the efficiency scores under DEA VRS are higher than under CRS, because the VRS more tightly envelops the data, with more DMUs being placed on the frontier.

Table 7.4. Model 1 efficiency scores

	SFA efficiency scores			DEA efficiency scores	
	Truncated	Half-normal	Log-log	CRS	VRS
Mean	0.838	0.797	0.919	0.669	0.744
Std dev.	0.104	0.119	0.052	0.123	0.136
Min.	0.192	0.124	0.535	0.356	0.419
Max.	0.981	0.977	0.988	1.000	1.000
Efficient DMUs				4	14

Table 7.5. Correlations of SFA and DEA efficiency scores for Model 1

	Truncated	Half-normal	Log-log	CRS	VRS
Truncated	1				
Half-normal	0.9753	1			
Log-log	0.8410	0.7230	1		
CRS	0.6808	0.5936	0.7341	1	
VRS	0.5247	0.4402	0.5668	0.7706	1

Table 7.5 shows the correlations between the various efficiency scores for the variants of the baseline model. As might be expected there is a reasonable amount of internal consistency within each of the two analytical techniques. However, the estimates derived from the two DEA models are more weakly correlated with those from the three SFA models.

In Table 7.6 we examine the efficiency scores and ranks for a few hospitals to illustrate what happens to them under the different specification assumptions within a particular model. Hospitals A and B remain consistently efficient across all specifications, whilst Hospitals C, D and E remain consistently inefficient across all specifications. The estimated efficiency of Hospitals F to J is sensitive to specification choice. For Hospitals F and G there is consistency within the DEA models and with the log-log model in SFA, but not with the two linear SFA models. For Hospitals H to J there is little agreement within DEA,

Table 7.6. Individual hospital scores and rankings for Model 1

Hospital	Truncated		Half-normal		Log-log		CRS		VRS	
	Score	Rank	Score	Rank	Score	Rank	Score	Rank	Score	Rank
A	0.981	1	0.977	1	0.988	1	1.000	1	1.000	1
B	0.992	5	0.984	5	0.993	2	1.000	1	1.000	1
C	0.195	171	0.127	171	0.542	171	0.356	171	0.436	169
D	0.595	168	0.591	167	0.799	169	0.405	170	0.419	171
E	0.680	161	0.688	152	0.822	166	0.463	159	0.583	153
F	0.866	93	0.798	103	0.978	16	1.000	1	1.000	1
G	0.811	128	0.720	140	0.974	20	0.805	19	0.919	25
H	0.602	167	0.409	169	0.953	63	0.571	137	1.000	1
I	0.960	16	0.950	14	0.941	90	0.624	111	0.895	27
J	0.894	77	0.887	48	0.908	130	0.548	148	0.833	40

Table 7.7. Descriptive statistics for SFA and DEA efficiency scores

	SFA efficiency scores			DEA efficiency scores		
	Model 1	Model 2	Model 3	Model 1	Model 2	Model 3
Mean	0.797	0.847	0.882	0.744	0.787	0.988
Std dev.	0.119	0.094	0.096	0.136	0.137	0.038
Min.	0.124	0.164	0.282	0.419	0.437	0.769
Max.	0.977	0.979	0.984	1.000	1.000	1.000
Efficient DMUs				14	27	150

most likely because scale effects have an important influence on activities for these hospitals. This suggests that organisational estimates of efficiency can be sensitive to modelling choices other than those concerning the selection of explanatory or output variables.

Sensitivity to model specification – the choice of explanatory variables
We now examine what happens when we make comparisons across different model specifications by progressively expanding the set of explanatory or output variables in the SFA and DEA models, as shown in Table 7.7. The three SFA models apply a linear functional form and half-normal distribution for the error; the DEA models are estimated under variable returns to scale.

Table 7.7 provides summary statistics of the efficiency scores for each of the three specifications estimated by the two techniques. As would be expected, mean efficiency increases as more variables are added. For the DEA models, this is explained mainly by more hospitals being placed on the frontier – as more variables are considered, there is a greater chance that a previously 'inefficient' hospital will dominate on the added dimension and thus be considered 'efficient'. In the most fully specified model (Model 3), 150 hospitals are on the frontier, leaving only 21 inefficient hospitals, compared to 157 in Model 1.

The increase in average efficiency as the SFA models become more fully specified comes about because progressively more of the previously 'unexplained' composite error is now being captured by the addition of new explanatory variables.

Table 7.8. *Individual hospital scores and rankings under various specifications*

	DEA-1		DEA-2		DEA-3	
Hospital	Score	Rank	Score	Rank	Score	Rank
A	1.000	1	1.000	1	1.000	1
B	1.000	1	1.000	1	1.000	1
C	0.621	144	0.626	154	0.847	169
D	0.620	145	1.000	1	1.000	1
E	1.000	1	1.000	1	1.000	1
F	0.662	124	1.000	1	1.000	1
G	0.904	26	1.000	1	1.000	1
H	0.583	153	1.000	1	1.000	1
I	0.729	83	0.732	104	1.000	1
J	1.000	1	1.000	1	1.000	1

	SFA-1		SFA-2		SFA-3	
Hospital	Score	Rank	Score	Rank	Score	Rank
A	0.967	4	0.979	1	0.977	5
B	0.973	2	0.979	2	0.974	6
C	0.693	146	0.756	153	0.761	161
D	0.736	129	0.964	7	0.978	4
E	0.725	134	0.887	56	0.878	111
F	0.777	104	0.945	14	0.940	41
G	0.738	127	0.877	70	0.804	150
H	0.672	152	0.917	35	0.956	18
I	0.474	168	0.603	169	0.285	170
J	0.399	169	0.539	170	0.698	166

There appear to be some major anomalies for individual hospitals, with estimated efficiency being sensitive to how the models are specified. This is highlighted in Table 7.8 which illustrates the change in efficiency scores and rankings across the two techniques for a select few hospitals.

Hospitals A and B, for instance, remain at the top of the 'league table', irrespective of the technique applied to measure their efficiency, while Hospital C is consistently ranked near the bottom. However, for a vast array of hospitals in between, scores and rankings can jump quite dramatically. Hospital D for instance, is penalised in the most parsimonous model (Model 1) but is ranked more highly by the other models. This probably reflects the omission of teaching and research, which are important outputs for this hospital. Hospital E is consistently efficient under DEA, but is sensitive to the specification choices under SFA. Similar movements in scores and ranks are notable for several other hospitals. In particular, Hospital J is consistently efficient under DEA but generally considered inefficient under SFA. This may happen because DEA assigns high weights to output dimensions where inefficient hospitals are doing badly, in order to maximise the hospitals' efficiency score and 'put them in the best light'.

7.5 Conclusions

The case study illustrates the two important sets of choices which need to be made in the SFA and DEA models and which may have a large impact on the results, namely the choice of functional form, error distribution and returns to scale, and the choice of model specification or explanatory variables to be included. Our sensitivity analysis has not been extensive. In practice, it would be preferable to analyse a broader range of modelling assumptions.

But despite the partial nature of the sensitivity analysis, it has revealed clear inconsistencies among the different specifications and methods. Caution is therefore warranted before drawing precise interpretations of hospital efficiency scores and rankings, or placing sole reliance on a single specification. If the results had been well correlated, it might have suggested the techniques were equivalent, but in practice the correlations were fairly poor across the two techniques. Even when correlations are high, these average relationships may mask substantial movements for individual organisations. Given that the purpose of the exercise is often to derive individual, rather than merely average, effects it is unwise to rely solely on examining correlation coefficients to assess sensitivity to modelling assumptions.

Finally, irrespective of which approach is applied, good practice would be to use confidence intervals around the efficiency estimates to determine the reliability of the results and to decide whether statistical differences in efficiency are significant or simply due to sampling error (Jensen 2000). This can be done using statistical techniques for

SFA (Horrace and Schmidt 1996; Street 2003) or resampling boot-strap methods for DEA (Mooney and Duval 1993; Löthgren 1998; Hirschberg and Lloyd 2000; Barth and Staat 2005).

Ultimately, though, there is no consensus in the literature on the 'best method' for estimating the efficiency frontier. Some commentators have argued that consensus is not necessary, as long as a set of consistency conditions is met (Bauer *et al.* 1998). To the extent that there is no *a priori* reason to prefer one technique over the other, it seems prudent to analyse efficiency using a broad variety of methods to 'cross-check' the results (Stone 2002). Bauer *et al.* (1998) argue that the efficiency estimates should be consistent in their efficiency levels (with comparable means, standard deviations and other distributional properties), consistent in their rankings, consistent in their identification of best and worst performers, and consistent over time. Rarely, however, are these consistency conditions likely to be met, as is the case for the data analysed in this chapter.

In view of such inconsistency, the efficiency scores derived from SFA or DEA should not be interpreted as accurate point estimates of efficiency, and it would be inappropriate to take action solely on the basis of these estimates (Hadley and Zuckerman 1994; Newhouse 1994; Skinner 1994). Indeed, use of the techniques in isolation might create a perverse incentive for organisations to act dysfunctionally to improve their efficiency rating, such as by engaging in creative accounting, political lobbying and alteration of the input/output mix (Nunamaker 1985).

Rather, where estimates of relative efficiency are obtained, these might be used as signals about where to direct more investigative energy. For any given data set, comparison of the SFA and DEA efficiency estimates will allow organisations to be sorted into three groups. First, there will be a group where relative efficiency is sensitive to the choice of technique. It would be inadvisable to draw firm conclusions about their actual level of relative efficiency. Second, there will be organisations that appear efficient whichever technique is adopted and however the models are specified. Further analysis of the working practices of these organisations may be informative if a purpose or by-product of the exercise is to share best practice. However, because DEA assigns full efficiency to unusual observations (i.e. those which do not have peers), the method may be labelling organisations as efficient when it would be more appropriate to consider them as outliers. It may not be good practice to make policy recommendations on the basis of outlier behaviour. Finally, there will be a group of organisations that always appear inefficient, irrespective of the measurement technique employed. These might be deserving of greater scrutiny to ascertain the reasons why their performance appears to fall short of that of their counterparts.

This sorting and exploratory use of the techniques is a more appropriate response than basing regulatory policy on the analytical findings. The efficiency estimates are too sensitive to modelling choices and too imprecise to justify taking them at face value, and it is best not to expect the models to yield definitive statements about relative efficiency. In the future, the techniques may evolve to such an extent that more concrete recommendations may emanate from their application. For this to occur, a number of fundamental issues must be addressed. The next chapter considers four particularly challenging areas where further research effort is required.

8 | Unresolved issues and challenges in efficiency measurement

8.1 Introduction

I N this chapter we discuss four of the most important issues that arise when seeking to use efficiency models in the health care sector: the weights used to indicate the values of different outputs; how the efficiency models are constructed; the treatment of environmental influences on performance; and dynamic aspects of efficiency.

8.2 Output weights

There are important questions relating to the objectives encompassed by any index of efficiency, particularly when the analysis is to be used for regulatory purposes. Is it legitimate for the central policy maker to attach a uniform set of *objectives* to all organisations? If so, is it further legitimate to apply a uniform set of *weights* to these objectives? If so, how should they be chosen? If not, what is the extent of legitimate variation, and who should choose? These are fundamental issues, the answers to which determine whether or not creating a single measure of organisational performance is warranted. In our view, organisations can be ranked on efficiency only if the policy maker may legitimately (i) set objectives and (ii) attach weights to those objectives.

When comparing organizations that are charged with meeting social objectives, the set of output weights ought to reflect societal values. However, it is not a simple matter to derive such weights, particularly when organisations face multiple objectives and there is disagreement as to organisational priorities. Ultimately the selection of objectives in the public services is a job for the politicians charged with reconciling

An earlier version of this material appeared in Smith and Street (2005).

167

conflicting claims on public resources. The main role for analysts is to clarify the choices required of policy makers, to provide evidence on popular preferences, and to develop measurement instruments that most faithfully reflect the chosen objectives. Note that policy makers are effectively attaching a zero weight to any output that is excluded from the efficiency index.

In order to clarify the role of weights, consider Figure 8.1, the economist's traditional production possibility frontier *FF* for an organisation producing two outputs y_1 and y_2, reflecting two societal objectives. Two sets of preferences are illustrated by indifference curves I_1I_1 and I_2I_2, giving rise to different preferred points of production. The slopes of these curves at the points of tangency with *FF* reflect the relative valuations of the two objectives. In this case, Individual 1 places a higher relative valuation on objective y_1 than Individual 2. In general, there will be no agreement on what constitutes the preferred mix of outputs.

The use of the linear performance index implicit in efficiency analysis suggests that resolution of the trade-off problem should be guided by maximising a linear function of the two outcome measures, which are combined into a single composite indicator. The parallel lines in Figure 8.2 indicate different values of a chosen composite indicator, with scores increasing towards the top right-hand corner. Choice of the point P^* on the possibility frontier would be optimal in this example, giving a composite score indicated by the line C_1C_1. Given

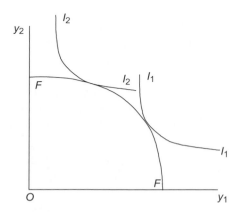

Figure 8.1. The production possibility frontier: different preferences lead to different weights.

the weights used in the composite indicator, choice of any other point on the frontier would be considered inferior (allocatively inefficient).

In practice, few organisations will be precisely on the possibility frontier. Rather, each will exhibit some level of technical inefficiency, which leads to observed outputs lying within the area indicated by the efficient frontier. In Figure 8.2, the point X indicates a realised level of performance in one organisation. According to the composite indicator, this secures a level of overall efficiency indicated by the line C_2C_2, reflecting the fact that (i) the chosen mix of outputs diverges from the 'optimal' and (ii) performance lies within the frontier. The measure of organisational efficiency can be represented by the ratio of the composite scores indicated by lines C_2C_2 and C_1C_1, the extent to which performance falls short of the maximum attainable and desired, this being the product of technical and allocative efficiency. This argument is readily extended to S outputs.

If we are unable to apply a uniform set of weights, there may nevertheless be circumstances in which all will agree that some organisations perform better than others. Figure 8.3 illustrates five organisations with identical expenditure levels and environmental circumstances. Under most assumptions about preferences, Organisation A is unambiguously inferior to Organisation D in the sense of being technically inefficient. Furthermore, Organisation B is inferior to a linear combination of organisations D and E, represented by the point B^*. However, the

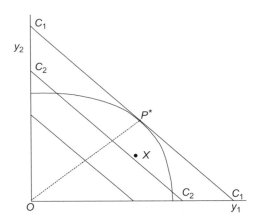

Figure 8.2. Composite scores indicated by the lines C_1C_1 *and* C_2C_2.

ranking of the Organisations C, D and E lying on the observed frontier depends on the relative weights we choose to apply to outputs y_1 and y_2. This cannot be achieved without introducing a composite indicator that reflects preferences for the two objectives.

In principle, the set of weights to be used in an efficiency index could be derived from a range of sources, such as economic studies of willingness to pay or conjoint analysis. An example (albeit the subject of fierce criticism) was the survey undertaken by the World Health Organization to infer the relative importance of health system outputs (Williams 2001). However, rather than being externally agreed upon, in most efficiency analysis studies the weights are generated as a by-product of the statistical estimation process. Indeed, some see this as an attractive feature of the methods (Cooper, Seiford and Tone 2000).

Within the parametric paradigm, it is not a trivial matter to take account of multiple outputs. Approaches include the creation of a single index of outputs, estimation of a cost function rather than a production function, or the use of distance functions (Shephard 1970; Coelli and Perelman 2000; Löthgren 2000). Irrespective of the approach, the estimated magnitude of the weight for each output usually corresponds to the value implicit in the sample mean cost of producing an additional unit of output s. Using a linear model, the weight β_s attached to output s indicates the value of an additional unit of that output, which remains constant for all levels of attainment of y_s. If a

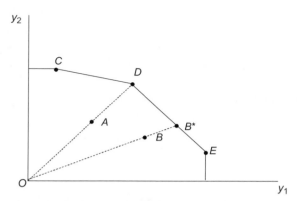

Figure 8.3. Observed performance of five systems with identical expenditure and environment.

logarithmic model is used, β_s indicates the percentage increase in composite attainment implied by a one percent increase in y_s. Hence the parametric approach is conservative in the sense that it implies that the existing expenditure choices of organisations (on average) reflect the values placed by society on the outputs. If this is not true, the estimated weights will not be appropriate.

As discussed in sub-section 5.3.3, in conventional DEA the weights, U_s, are allowed to vary freely, so that each organisation is evaluated in the best possible light. Indeed one quite frequently finds in unconstrained DEA that the highest efficiency score for an organisation can be secured simply by assigning a zero weight to one or more outputs on which it performs poorly. There has therefore been some attention to rules for restricting the flexibility of weight variations (Allen *et al.* 1997), but the efforts to date have been poorly informed by economic theory, and mainly confined to technical considerations (Pedraja-Chaparro, Salinas-Jimènez and Smith1997). The lack of a single set of weights implies that it is never appropriate to rank DEA efficiency scores in a conventional 'league table' format.

The assumptions underlying the derivation of weights in DEA and SFA are crucial to the judgements on efficiency they offer. It is, of course, possible that the weights emerging from statistical studies correspond to political preferences. However, we are not aware of any studies that have sought to verify this. At the very least, we would suggest that there is a need for careful dialogue between policy makers and analysts to ensure that the methods used reflect policy requirements.

8.3 Modelling the production process

Having decided upon what objectives are to be considered, and their relative importance, the next problem concerns how to model the process by which these may be achieved and the constraints that limit levels of attainment. That is, in the context of Figure 8.1, how is the production possibility frontier to be formalised? The focus of interest differs depending on whether one adopts a research perspective or a managerial perspective.

The research interest in productivity models is predominantly in the structure and determinants of the production process rather than specific efficiency estimates for individual organisations. Countless research questions present themselves. For example: What is the marginal productivity of a factor of production? How do returns to scale vary? What influence do external environmental factors have on efficiency? What is the aggregate level of inefficiency in the sector? These are all important questions with potentially important policy implications. However, they all fit into the traditional empirical research model in that they seek to identify aggregate (or sample average) patterns within the data. Modelling is usually a means to the end of securing a more satisfactory aggregate model with which to address the research questions.

In contrast, the managerial or policy interest is in the estimate of efficiency for individual organisations. This estimate is derived from the residual or organisation-specific effect, and the model parameters are no longer the main interest. This switch of attention turns the statistical model on its head. We believe that this may require a fundamental rethink in modelling methodology.

Traditional statistical methodology seeks to develop an empirical model that satisfies particular acceptability criteria, such as consistency (as the sample size increases, does the estimate of interest converge to its 'true' value?); unbiasedness (is the expected error in the estimate zero?); efficiency (is the sampling variance of the estimate as small as possible?); robustness (is the estimate robust to potential model misspecification, missing information and measurement error?); and parsimony (is the model as simple as possible?). Although analysts frequently use heuristics (such as the 95 per cent significance criterion), the implications of technical choices for model estimation are generally well understood, so that an informed observer can understand the degree of certainty with which inferences can be made.

However, there is no guarantee that a statistical model that satisfies such traditional modelling criteria is necessarily fit for the purpose of inferring the efficiencies of individual organisations. To take just a simple example, there might exist a small number of ambulance authorities that suffer a cost disadvantage in their emergency function. In developing an empirical model, the analyst might acknowledge this possibility and test a measure of rurality as a potential independent variable, perhaps using a conventional rule such as the 95 per cent significance hurdle. The rurality variable may not pass this test, and will be excluded so as to yield a more parsimonious model that passes misspecification tests. In conventional modelling terms, the variable is excluded from the preferred model on the grounds that it is immaterial.

However, it may be highly material for the small number of ambulance authorities whose residuals (and therefore efficiency estimates) are adversely affected by its exclusion. Therefore the model may be fit for its research purpose, but not for its managerial purpose.

Conversely, one could pay no attention to the parsimony criterion and indiscriminately include all potential explanatory variables in the productivity model. In the extreme, this might result in modelling the performance of all observations without error, leading to the conclusion that all are equally efficient. If, in reality, there is some variation in efficiency, the inability to detect it arises because some of the explanatory variables are correlated with efficiency. One therefore needs a very clear idea of the production process and the constraints upon that process if one is to model individual efficiency satisfactorily.

As with all modelling, the ideal is that technical choices should be informed by the costs of incorrect inference. In all likelihood, every organisation exhibits a level of inefficiency with respect to a true production frontier that is unobservable. The managerial concern is in the extent to which the chosen model misrepresents this true efficiency. An underestimate of individual efficiency (analogous to a Type 1 error) may result in a number of mistaken managerial actions, such as setting financial penalties, replacement of local management, demanding infeasible improvement targets, or closure of the operation. An overestimate of efficiency (Type II error) may result in complacency or mistaken designation of an organisation as a beacon of excellence. Errors of either sign can arise from model misspecification (omitted variables, functional form) or measurement errors. In principle, productivity modelling methodology should reflect such considerations, rather than relying exclusively on the statistician's traditional rule of thumb.

An obvious response to uncertainty about how best to represent the underlying set of production possibilities or technological constraints is to conduct sensitivity analysis. In DEA, this may involve changes to the scaling assumptions and bootstrapping estimates to assess statistical significance (Simar and Wilson 2004). In SFA, statistical techniques allow different functional forms, different distributions of inefficiency and the calculation of confidence intervals around inefficiency estimates (Street 2003).

Clearly such analysis is good statistical practice (Goldstein and Spiegelhalter 1996). However, the extent to which results are robust to these choices depends on the complexity of the underlying production process. In industries with a relatively simple production technology, it can be expected that results are not highly sensitive to defensible variations in technical choices. For instance, estimates of the efficiency of companies providing water and sewerage services in the UK appear robust in the face of sensitivity analysis (Office of Water Services 1999). In contrast, and as typified by the example in chapter 7, different models applied to health sector organisations rarely yield definitive or consistent conclusions. Quite modest changes in the choice of analytic technique and model specification lead to major changes in inference about efficiency, reflecting the great complexity of health care and the importance of idiosyncratic (unexplained) influences on performance (Harris 1977).

8.4 Environmental constraints

In addition to difficulties in specifying the production process, efficiency measurement of health care organisations is further complicated by the need to take account of influences on performance that lie outside organisational control. Numerous classes of factors may influence measured levels of organisational attainment. These include:

- differences in the characteristics of citizens being served;
- the external environment – for example, geography, culture and economic conditions;
- the activities of other related agencies, both within and outside the health sector;
- the quality of resources being used, including the capital stock;
- different accounting treatments;
- data errors;
- random (or idiosyncratic) fluctuation;
- different organisational priorities;
- differences in efficiency.

In the short run, many of these factors are outside the control of the organisations under scrutiny. These are commonly labelled 'environmental' variables. In the longer term, a broader set of factors is potentially under the control of the organisations, but the extent and nature of this control will vary depending on the context. So, for example, the short-run efficiency of a hospital should be judged in the light of the capital configuration that it has available. Yet, in the longer run, one might expect the hospital to reconfigure its capital resources when this is likely to lead (say) to lower unit costs.

In whatever way the uncontrollable environment is defined, it is usually the case that some organisations operate in more adverse environments than others, in the sense that external circumstances make achievement of a given level of attainment more difficult. This means that – for a given level of expenditure – the production possibility frontiers of different organisations will not be identical. The frontiers for organisations operating in difficult environments will lie inside those of more favourably endowed organisations, and the environmental influences on organisational outputs should therefore be incorporated into statistical models of efficiency.

In some circumstances, as mentioned in section 2.6, it may be possible to simplify the 'environmental' problem if organisations (such as health authorities or primary care trusts) have already been compensated financially for environmental circumstances through a funding formula. A funding formula seeks to enable organisations to deliver some 'standard' level of service, given environmental factors. So, if the funding formula is doing its job properly, there is no need to incorporate such factors into the productivity model. Indeed, all that may be needed is to examine the extent to which the standards have been secured. In short, one may need to examine only effectiveness, and not incorporate inputs (either resources or environment) into the model at all. However, in practice, most funding formulae compensate only imperfectly for environmental factors (Smith, Rice and Carr-Hill 2001).

There is an active debate about how to incorporate environmental factors into DEA (Fried *et al.* 2002). As discussed in sub-section 5.3.6, one option is to include an environmental variable as one of the inputs in the production model. In DEA, this means that organisations will be compared only with organisations operating in identical or more adverse environments. Those operating in the most adverse environments will automatically be deemed 100 per cent efficient. Another possibility is to estimate the model without environmental variables, and incorporate them only in a second-stage analysis, which seeks to explain efficiency scores as a statistical function of environment. This is problematic given that the dependent variable (the efficiency scores) will comprise a set of serially correlated values (Simar and Wilson 2004). As yet there is no generally accepted methodology for how to account for environmental variables in DEA models or how to test whether an environmental variable is a 'significant' uncontrollable influence on production possibilities.

With respect to SFA, when undertaking analysis from a regulatory perspective, a necessary condition is that all variables included as regressors are indicators of environmental factors beyond organisational control (Giuffrida, Gravelle and Sutton 2000). Again, this contrasts with the traditional approach to statistical model-building, where the aim is to select a set of explanatory variables that best explain variation in the dependent variable. It is quite likely that many potential explanatory variables are indicators of both environmental effects (which we would wish to include in the model) and policy or efficiency effects (which we would wish to exclude from the model). Most statistical modelling of efficiency relies on traditional variable selection devices to test whether an environmental variable should be included in the model. However, statistical modelling in these circumstances usually requires a great deal of knowledge of the context of the problem and an element of judgement as to which variables to include. Formal model selection devices are of limited use, and there is unlikely to be consensus as to the most appropriate choice of model.

The model selection problem is compounded when using SFA, because the analyst must make a joint decision regarding the variables to include and the model's error structure. Recall that unexplained variation from predicted output is decomposed into two parts: symmetric random error and one-sided inefficiency. Suppose, therefore, that we wish to test an environmental variable for inclusion in a SFA model. It will be a candidate for inclusion if it 'explains' a material proportion of the overall residual and therefore exhibits what is conventionally termed a statistically significant model coefficient. However, the attribution of a statistically significant effect to the additional explanatory variable may be for one or both of the following reasons:

1. It explains some of the random error. This implies that the original model suffered from omitted-variable or functional-form misspecification.
2. It explains some of the inefficiency error. This implies that the variable is correlated with the original estimates of inefficiency.

Whether the new variable should be included depends on whether it is judged to measure an unavoidable hindrance to reaching the estimated frontier (in which case it would be included) or some potentially controllable characteristic of inefficient organisations (in which case it would be omitted). There is no scientific guide to making this judgement. It can be made only with reference to the context of the specific production process under scrutiny.

8.5 Dynamic effects

One of the most problematic issues in productivity analysis is the treatment of dynamic effects. Generally, organisations operate within an historical context, drawing on past inheritances and making investments toward future performance. This implies that the production process should be modelled in a dynamic fashion, in which contemporary performance is to some extent dependent on previous investment, and contemporary inputs are to some extent invested for future outputs. This concept was introduced in sub-section 2.5.2.

The correct production model for examining current performance should include among its inputs the endowment bequeathed to current management by previous organisational efforts. This is a fiercely complex issue, as many such organisational endowments defy satisfactory measurement. For example, current performance of public health efforts to improve morbidity rates among the population may reflect previous efforts in disease prevention. In some senses these previous efforts can be considered an uncontrollable 'environmental' influence on current managerial performance. Yet, in general, we have no concrete way of quantifying this potentially important input, and most studies ignore such factors.

Equally, some elements of current effort may be directed towards future attainment. For example, investment in health promotion activities may not yield discernible achievements until years after the activities have been completed. Again, in principle, we should include such endowments as an output from the current period. In practice, they are extremely difficult to capture in efficiency assessments, especially as the investment effort may itself contain an element of inefficiency.

The implication for efficiency analysis is that any cross-sectional assessment of contemporary attainment should in principle accommodate the inherited endowment of previous actions, and the endowment left for future management. Färe and Grosskopf (1996) develop a dynamic programming framework that seeks to recognise inheritances and endowments in the context of DEA models, and demonstrate the enormous complexity of the issues involved. In applying SFA it is becoming feasible to model dynamic effects using panel data techniques (Bond 2002). However, such modelling is likely to remain a challenging endeavour, even given adequate data and estimation methods, and its usefulness for efficiency measurement has yet to be assessed.

8.6 Conclusions

In this chapter we have raised four issues that require further consideration before the techniques of efficiency analysis can be fit for the purpose of regulation. Statements about relative organisational efficiency cannot be made unless the organisations being compared pursue a common set of prioritised objectives. The appropriateness of the analytical model cannot be evaluated using standard testing procedures, and the evaluative task is more demanding the more complex the production process and the more heterogeneous the environmental constraints each organisation faces. The historical context in which organisations are located can rarely be fully appreciated by the analyst, and this lack of knowledge places constraints on model construction and interpretation.

The techniques of efficiency analysis described in the earlier chapters require further development before they can adequately deal with these issues. Moreover, alternative approaches exist that may offer greater flexibility in model construction and novel insights into organisational performance. We turn to these in the next chapter.

9 | Some alternative approaches to measuring performance

9.1 Introduction

I N the preceding chapters we have raised a number of concerns about the use of both parametric and non-parametric methods to draw conclusions about the relative efficiency of health care organisations. Many of these concerns relate to the fundamental problem of trying to derive a composite measure of organisational performance in contexts where multiple objectives are pursued or multiple outputs produced. Other concerns relate to the difficulty of formulating a coherent model of the production process and of ascertaining what constitute the environmental constraints that each organisation faces.

In this chapter we consider some alternative approaches to analysing the performance of health care organisations that seek to address some of these issues. We must emphasise that these approaches are experimental, and address only some of the concerns raised in the preceding chapters. However, they do illustrate that, depending on the purpose of the analysis, the potential exists to use a wider range of analytic tools than traditionally recommended in the efficiency literature.

The techniques discussed in this chapter address two distinct issues: the hierarchical form into which most health systems are organised, and the pursuit of multiple objectives when there is little consensus as to their relative priority. To this end, in section 9.2 we describe how multilevel modelling can be used to gain insights into the impact of different hierarchical levels on specific aspects of performance. Section 9.3 then examines the potential for using seemingly unrelated regressions to model simultaneously a set of multiple performance measures. In section 9.4 we indicate how these techniques can be integrated into a multivariate, multilevel model of performance.

The material in this chapter draws on three published papers: Hauck, Rice and Smith (2003); Martin and Smith (2005); and Hauck and Street (2005).

9.2 Multilevel modelling

All health systems are organised hierarchically. Individual physicians operate within clinical teams, which in turn may be based in departments, within hospitals, within administrative areas. A key policy question that therefore arises is: to what level of the hierarchy are variations in health system objectives attributable? Traditionally, although many commentators make the distinction between macro-, meso- and micro-level aspects of the health system, few analytic studies seek to model these distinct levels explicitly. Most efficiency analysis (including the examples in the preceding chapters) is undertaken at the meso level of hospital or administrative authority.

However, statisticians have developed multilevel (or hierarchical) models to reflect explicitly the multilevel nature of organisational structures. These have been deployed extensively in the education sector (Hill and Goldstein 1998), and there have been a number of applications in health care (Rice and Jones 1997). The question this chapter addresses is the extent to which multilevel models could be used to shed new light on organisational performance. The statistical models used to address the hierarchical structure are variations on the familiar regression-based theme. However, the error term is decomposed into parts attributable to each level of the hierarchy. For example, if the dependent variable is some measure of patient outcome arising from hospital treatment, a simple two-level model yields estimates of the 'hospital effect' on patient outcomes (after adjusting for any independent measures of patient need) and the residual 'individual effect'. The insight of this section is that the estimate of the hospital effect might be used as the basis of an organisational performance indicator, and that failure to exploit the multilevel nature of the data can lead to erroneous conclusions about organisational performance.

To illustrate, consider first the application of traditional meso-level analysis to the three hospitals shown in Figure 9.1. Suppose the measure of outcome for each of the three hospitals comprises a summary of the outcomes experienced by all patients treated in the hospital, for example the mortality rate. A conventional regression model, with the hospital as the unit of observation, might take the following form:

$$\bar{y}_j = \beta_0 x_0 + \boldsymbol{\beta}\bar{\mathbf{x}}_j + \bar{u}_j \qquad (9.1)$$

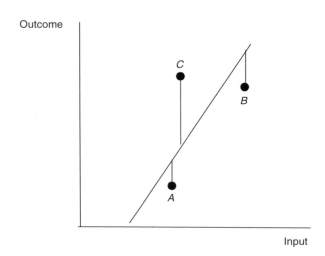

Figure 9.1. Performance ranking using aggregate organisational data.

Where $\bar{y}_j$ are the average outcomes experienced by patients treated in hospital j; $\beta_0 x_0$ is a constant term and $\beta \bar{x}_j$ is a vector of hospital-level variables thought to explain patient outcomes over and above the influence of the hospital, such as the average severity of the condition suffered. The error term $\bar{u}_j$ is assumed to have zero mean and constant variance, and can be interpreted as the vertical departure from the mean regression line of the jth hospital. If this line is assumed to reflect the *expected* level of hospital performance, these residuals can be used as the basis for performance comparison (as in a corrected ordinary least squares method (COLS)). The hospitals would therefore be ranked C,A,B.

However, the average outcomes used in Figure 9.1 are derived from individual patient data. The objective of multilevel methods is to exploit these individual-level data to best effect. Figure 9.2 shows, as lower-case letters, the individual-level data on which the aggregates in Figure 9.1 are based, indicating the hospital in which the patient was treated. The multilevel methods identify the relationship between input and outcome observed within hospitals (in this case constrained to have equal slope) as indicated by the broken lines in Figure 9.2. The hospital effect can now be interpreted as the vertical axis intercept of each hospital slope, yielding a revised ranking of C,B,A.

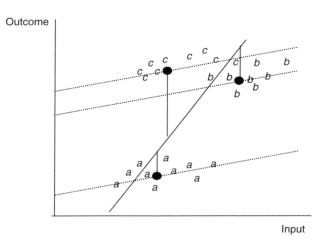

Figure 9.2. Changes in performance ranking based on hierarchical structure.

In multilevel modelling the error term is therefore decomposed into parts attributable to each level of the hierarchy. For example, if the dependent variable is some measure of *individual* patient outcome arising from hospital treatment, a simple two-level model can be specified as follows:

$$y_{ij} = \beta_0 x_0 + \boldsymbol{\beta} \mathbf{x}_{ij} + u_j + e_{ij} \tag{9.2}$$

where y_{ij} is the outcome for patient i in hospital j, i and j indicating the two levels. Estimation will yield:

- parameter estimates, β_0 and $\boldsymbol{\beta}$, for the constant and for the vector of independent variables in the model;
- an estimate, u_j, of the 'hospital effect' on patient outcomes; and
- the residual 'individual effect' e_{ij}.

The parameter β_0 can be interpreted as the level of performance in the hospital with average values across the independent variables. The terms u_j and e_{ij} are error components such that u_j is the random error for the jth hospital and e_{ij} is the random error for the ith patient in the jth hospital. These error components are assumed to have zero mean and constant variances (σ_u^2, σ_e^2). Small estimated values of u_j represent hospitals with close-to-average performance in securing patient outcomes, after controlling for the set of independent factors included in the model.

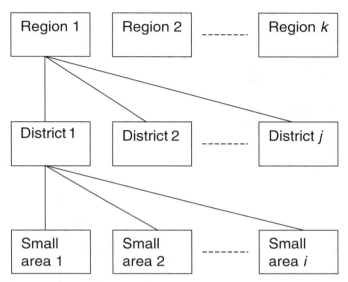

Figure 9.3. Hierarchical data structure.

We illustrate this using a model of the performance of the English health system in 1991, when health care was organised hierarchically, as shown in Figure 9.3. At the top of the hierarchy were the regional health authorities, which were responsible for financing and supervising the performance of lower-level organisations, but had little responsibility for direct patient care. Nested within the regions were 186 district health authorities, the organisations charged with planning and delivering hospital care and public health, each of which covered a population of about 250,000. Individual-level data were not available. However, data were available for 4,985 small areas, with populations of around 10,000. These were merely geographical constructs, defined for electoral purposes, but without any organisational identity so far as health services were concerned. These small areas form the lowest level in our hierarchy.

We had available data for various dimensions of health system performance and for the socio-demographic characteristics of the populations of the small areas. For this illustration we select the performance measure 'waiting time for routine surgery', measured as the ratio of actual waiting time (in days) to that which would be expected given the age and gender of the patient and the hospital speciality to

Table 9.1. Socio-demographic data used in needs index

Standardised mortality ratio for ages 0–74
Standardised limiting long-standing illness ratio for ages 0–74
Proportion of pensionable age living alone
Proportion of economically active unemployed
Proportion of dependants in single-carer households

which they had been referred. This standardised waiting time is our measure of performance, y.

Waiting times might be influenced by factors over and above the adjustments made in the standardisation procedure. We control for some of these by including an index, x_1, of the health needs of the population in each small area. This needs index was developed for the geographical allocation of National Health Service (NHS) acute sector revenues. The index comprises various socio-demographic variables that have been shown to be associated with the utilisation of acute health care, as summarised in Table 9.1. It was used as the principal basis of the geographic funding formula used in the English NHS for ten years from 1995, and was therefore generally thought to be a good general measure of the relative health care needs of geographic populations, given contemporary data limitations.

We model three sources of geographical variation in waiting times: differences in population characteristics, captured by the needs index; systematic differences in the way regions and districts formulate and implement health care policies; and random fluctuations. We therefore specify a three-level random intercept model as follows:

$$y_{ijk} = \beta_0 x_0 + \beta_1 x_{1ijk} + v_{0k} + u_{0jk} + e_{0ijk} \tag{9.3}$$

where y_{ijk} represents performance indicator y in the ith small area within the jth district within the kth region, x_0 is a constant and x_{1ijk} represents the needs index x_1 in the ith small area. The parameters β_0 and β_1 can be interpreted as the mean intercept and the mean slope across all small areas in all districts in all regions. The terms v_{0k}, u_{0jk} and e_{0ijk} are error components such that v_{0k} is the random error for the kth region, u_{0jk} is the random error for the jth district within the kth region and e_{0ijk} is the random error for the ith small area within the jth district within the kth region. All are assumed to have zero mean and constant variance $(\sigma_v^2, \sigma_u^2, \sigma_e^2)$. We can interpret v_{0k} as the parallel departure from the mean regression line $(\beta_0 x_0 + \beta_1 x_{1ijk})$ of the kth region, and u_{0jk} as the jth-district departure from the kth region in which the jth district is nested. Small estimated values of v_{0k} and u_{0jk} represent regions and districts close to average performance whilst large estimated values of v_{0k} and u_{0jk} represent regions and districts that deviate markedly from average performance. Interest lies in estimating the parameters β_0, β_1, σ_v^2, σ_u^2 and σ_e^2.

The analysis of the residual variances provides information on the extent of variability in performance at different hierarchical levels. The proportion of variance attributed to districts and regions can be interpreted as a quantitative indicator of the degree to which health authorities may be able to influence the observed performance measure. In order to obtain a quantitative measure of the proportion attributed to the regional level in comparison to that for the district and small-area levels we define the intra-class correlation coefficient for regions:

$$\rho_v = \sigma_v^2 (\sigma_v^2 + \sigma_u^2 + \sigma_e^2)^{-1} \tag{9.4}$$

with $0 < \rho_v < 1$. The closer ρ_v lies to 1 the larger the extent to which the variance in the performance indicator (conditional on the needs indicator) is attributable to the regional health authority level. Similarly, the proportion attributed to the district level is given by:

$$\rho_u = \sigma_u^2 (\sigma_v^2 + \sigma_u^2 + \sigma_e^2)^{-1} \tag{9.5}$$

again with $0 < \rho_u < 1$. Hence, larger values of ρ_v and ρ_u provide evidence of large variations in performance across regions and districts. This is interpreted as being indicative of marked differences in performance that may be amenable to health authority interventions.

Table 9.2 shows the estimates from model (9.3) for the waiting time performance indicator, indicating the intercept and slope coefficients and their standard errors, the variances attributable to regional, district and small-area levels and their standard errors, and the intra-class correlation coefficients ρ_v and ρ_u as given by (9.4) and (9.5). As expected, the estimates of the slope coefficient are positive and significant at the 5% level. The intra-class correlation coefficients indicate that 15% of the variation in performance is attributable to regions and 61% to districts. Both figures are significant at the 5%

Table 9.2. Three-level random intercept model to explain proportion of variability in performance indicators attributable to regional and district health authorities

Parameter	Description	Coefficient	Standard error
β_0	Coefficient of the intercept	0.988	0.025
β_1	Slope coefficient on need	0.030	0.003
σ_v^2	Variance of the region effects	0.006	0.003
σ_u^2	Variance of the district effects	0.025	0.003
σ_e^2	Variance of the small-area effects	0.010	0.000
ρ_v	Proportion of conditional variance attributable to regional health authorities	0.15	
ρ_u	Proportion of conditional variance attributable to district health authorities	0.61	

level, but they suggest that there is considerable variation across districts within one region, and that greater influence on waiting time performance is therefore more likely to exist at the district level.

In considering these results, it is important to bear in mind that they may be due to factors other than variation in health authorities' effectiveness. Other than variations in performance, the health authority effects may be picking up factors such as:

- variations in data collection methods;
- differences in funding levels;
- differences in the actions of other geographically defined agencies, such as local government.

More generally, as deployed here, the multilevel model cannot explain *why* the proportions of variation attributed to region, district and small-area levels differs. However, further work might explore this, for example by examining the characteristics of health authorities that explain variations in performance.

However, notwithstanding these caveats, results such as these can offer regulators useful information on the relative performance of organisations (and individual practitioners) operating within a hierarchy when a single performance measure is under scrutiny. The methods can contribute towards a more analytically satisfactory approach to performance measurement than the crude use of aggregate data. These particular results confirm that variations in measures of access (waiting time) are to a high degree attributable to health authorities. Other models (not reported here) suggest a much smaller influence of health authorities on measures of population health (such as mortality rates). Thus the multilevel methods can also help indicate the domains of health care where there is most potential for securing improvements. Future research might examine in more detail the appropriate organisational level at which to focus performance management efforts. Most importantly from our perspective, in some circumstances the methods might form the basis for a more analytically satisfactory approach to performance measurement than the use of aggregate regression methods.

9.3 Generalised statistical modelling

This book has focused mainly on composite indicators of health care performance. However, the dominant interest of many public service managers is in indicators of performance in specific service areas, rather than such aggregate measures of organisational performance. This motivates interest in modelling individual indicators of performance, along the lines suggested above. However, there may exist important relationships between individual performance measures that are lost if this is pursued solely through the piecemeal development of univariate regression models of performance. In this section, we show how a suite of performance indicators might be modelled simultaneously, using the methods of seemingly unrelated regressions.

To understand the potential importance of simultaneous modelling, we first consider a very general production process with just two indicators of organisational performance, as illustrated in Figure 9.4. If all organisations are operating in identical environments, and using identical inputs, the frontier of feasible production could be illustrated by a single curve such as FF. Then all observations will lie on or inside this frontier. However, if – as will usually be the case – organisations vary in environment or resources used, the frontier will shift. For example, the frontier F_2 might indicate a revised frontier for a set of organisations operating in a more adverse environment. A reduction

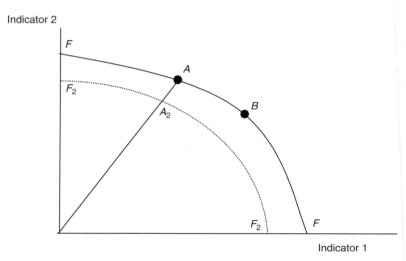

Figure 9.4. The production possibility frontier with two performance indicators.

in resources might operate in the same way, implying (say) that the feasible mix of performance achieved by an organisation at point A might be reduced to point A_2 if such a reduction were implemented.

Under this view, variations in the observed performance of two organisations might arise from a range of sources: environmental factors, resource levels, efficiency, substitution and data quality. We consider these five sources in turn.

1. The organisations might be operating in different environments, leading to variations in the feasible levels of performance. For example, different public health organisations might be operating in very different social and economic circumstances. Such influences on performance are often the most poorly understood and poorly measured aspect of the production process in health care. As environmental circumstances improve, so we would expect to observe improvements in all performance measures (albeit to varying extents). Therefore, such variations will in general give rise to a positive correlation between individual performance measures.

2. The organisations might be devoting different levels of resource input to the services under scrutiny. Variations in resources act in a similar way to variations in environmental factors in altering the capacity of the organisation to secure good performance, but are often

better understood and measured. Improvements in resources potentially increase the capacity for performance in all dimensions, and so should also give rise to a positive correlation between performance measures.

3. The efficiency of organisations might differ. Conventional productivity models seek to focus attention on variations in overall efficiency, yet run into difficulty because it is impossible to distinguish between organisational effects caused by unmeasured resource or environmental variations and those caused by efficiency variations. Again, efficiency should be positively correlated with performance in all dimensions, thereby contributing to a positive correlation between performance measures.

4. If organisations are fully efficient, improved performance on one indicator can be secured only at the expense of a worse performance on others, as the organisation moves round the efficient frontier. For example, in Figure 9.4, an efficient organisation A can improve performance on indicator 1 only by reducing attainment on indicator 2 (moving, say, to point B). In contrast with (1) to (3) above, this substitution effect implies a negative correlation between performance measures.

5. Imperfections in data quality are inherent to all health care. These might affect relative measured performance in a variety of ways. For example, if the performance measures are of the form 'attainment per head of population', then an overestimate of population would adversely affect performance in all domains, leading to a positive correlation between performance measures. If, on the other hand, the performance measures are expressed (say) in the form 'attainment in domain x per employee in domain x', then an imprecise allocation of employees between the different domains of performance might lead to a negative correlation between performance measures. Data imperfections, therefore, could contribute either positively or negatively to correlation measures.

There are therefore numerous reasons why performance on one indicator might be correlated, positively or negatively, with performance on another. Of course, if we could identify and measure the factors listed under (1) to (5) above, we could model performance on any one indicator with some confidence. Indeed, in many circumstances we have available a limited set of covariates with which we can adjust performance measures. For example, there usually exist measures that can serve to adjust performance measures to account for differences in physical or financial inputs. However, these measures are often crude and imprecise, and – in the case of environmental factors – highly contested. And, of course, when organisations pursue multiple objectives, there is, by definition, no straightforward measure of organisational efficiency.

We therefore seek to move beyond the piecemeal modelling of individual performance indicators and explicitly model covariance between indicators, without placing impossible demands on measurement instruments or modelling methodology. The fundamental insight is that in many circumstances individual regression models of performance, or more precisely the error terms from each regression, will be linked. For example, there might be some unobservable or poorly measured variable that has been omitted from the regressor set. The most obvious missing variable is, of course, inefficiency itself. We believe that simultaneous modelling of performance measures is potentially important because:

- it economises on the need for detailed modelling of individual performance measures;
- it economises on the need to measure factors that affect performance across all performance measures, such as environmental factors;
- it can reduce the very large confidence intervals observed in single equation models and caused in part by omitted or poorly measured explanatory variables;
- the more sensitive modelling of interactions may lead to different inferences about the level of an organisation's performance on specific indicators.

In short, the deployment of a more integrated model of multiple performance indicators can secure marked reductions in standard errors, and accordingly more secure performance rankings, without recourse to additional data or the highly questionable aggregation of performance indicators implicit in traditional productivity models.

The essence of the seemingly unrelated regression (SUR) approach is to model such covariances by incorporating a latent variable, which can be thought of as an implicit unmeasured 'organisational' effect on performance across all indicators. It can be defined as any influence on overall organisational performance, whether or not it is within the direct control of the organisation. Each of the five factors discussed above might contribute to the organisational effect, which therefore comprises an assortment of these influences on measured performance.

If separate performance indicators are related to each other in some way, the use of ordinary least squares (OLS) to estimate separately each regression is inefficient because it fails to utilise the information about the correlations among the indicators. Consequently, although ordinary least squares remains a consistent estimator, it no longer offers the most efficient estimates of the standard errors. To avoid this loss of information, the SUR estimator can be employed (Zellner 1962). The SUR procedure is formally known as joint generalised least squares estimation and is a method of estimating systems of regressions in which the parameters for all equations are determined in a single procedure (Greene 2000).

Formally, in the context of I performance indicators, the system of equations can be written in the following form (Zellner 1962):

$$y_{ik} = \beta_{0i} + x_{1ik}\beta_{1i} + e_{ik} \quad i = 1, 2, \ldots, I; \quad k = 1, 2, \ldots, K \quad (9.6)$$

where i now indicates each performance indicator rather than each patient or each electoral ward. Hence y_{ik} is the performance indicator for the ith objective for the kth organisation, β_{0i} is a coefficient, x_{1ik} is a $1 \times q_i$ vector of q_i regressors specific to the objective i, β_{1i} is a $q_i \times 1$ vector of coefficients, and e_{ik} is an error with $E(e_{ik}) = 0$. By stacking the k organisations above each other, the SUR model for the set of I indicators may be written as:

$$y_i = \beta_{0i} + X_{1i}\beta_{1i} + e_i \quad i = 1, 2, \ldots, I \quad (9.7)$$

or:

$$\begin{bmatrix} y_1 \\ y_2 \\ \ldots \\ y_I \end{bmatrix} = \begin{bmatrix} \beta_{01} \\ \beta_{02} \\ \ldots \\ \beta_{0I} \end{bmatrix} + \begin{bmatrix} X_{11} & 0 & \ldots & 0 \\ 0 & X_{12} & \ldots & 0 \\ & & \ldots & \\ 0 & 0 & \ldots & X_{1I} \end{bmatrix} \begin{bmatrix} \beta_{11} \\ \beta_{12} \\ \ldots \\ \beta_{1I} \end{bmatrix} + \begin{bmatrix} e_1 \\ e_2 \\ \ldots \\ e_I \end{bmatrix}$$

$$(9.8)$$

where y_i, β_{0i} and e_i are $k \times 1$ vectors, X_{1i} is a $k \times q_i$ matrix, and β_{1i} is a $q_i \times 1$ vector.

If the performance of an organisation k on two performance indicators i and p is related by unobservable factors, then e_{ik} would be correlated with e_{pk} for $i \neq p$. By estimating a SUR model, we allow for such correlation. This implies that:

$$E(e_{ik}e_{ph}') = \sigma_{ip}, \quad \text{if } k = h, \text{and } 0 \text{ otherwise,} \qquad (9.9)$$

where k and h denote two different organisations.

SUR estimation transforms the errors so that they all have the same variance and are uncorrelated. Estimation is a multistage process in which each equation is first estimated by OLS. The residuals from each of these estimations are then used to evaluate the error variances both for each equation and across equations. The errors are then transformed so that they all have the same variance and are uncorrelated – in other words, the SUR estimator 'purges' the errors of their cross-equation correlation. The explanatory variables are then subject to the same transformation. The rationale for this is that, if the unobservable factor driving the correlated errors is also correlated with other variables in the model, then the purging transformation should be applied to the estimated coefficient on these other variables. Finally, OLS estimation is applied to these transformed variables.

9.3.1 *Illustrative example*

To illustrate the principles involved with SUR estimation, we employ a data set for 135 acute hospitals within the NHS in England, and attempt to model three important aspects of performance, measured by the following indicators:

- a measure of clinical quality (the readmission rate; defined as the proportion of people discharged from hospital who are subsequently readmitted as emergencies in connection with the same episode of care);
- a measure of inpatient access to health care (the mean waiting time in days for admission for non-emergency surgery); and
- a measure of hospital efficiency (average length of stay).

A wide range of factors might explain variation in observed achievement for indicators. These explanatory factors can be divided into five broad groups: measures of supply volume, quality indicators, demand shifters, case mix indicators, and other supply shifters. There are three measures of supply volume (two for outpatients and one for inpatients) and eleven quality indicators. There are five demand shifters and three of these variables are based on measures of competing resources (general practitioner availability, a Herfindahl index of hospital competition, and the local availability of private hospital beds). There are six indicators of surgical complexity (or resource intensity) and three further variables that affect a hospital's supply capability.

We first employed stepwise methods to develop OLS models of each of the three performance indicators, as shown in equations 1, 3 and 5 of Table 9.3. How these models were developed is a matter that deserves further discussion, but it is not strictly relevant to this exposition of SUR methods. Further details are given elsewhere (Martin and Smith 2005). Ramsey's reset test revealed no evidence of misspecification in any of the three OLS equations, and the variables included are intuitively plausible. However, notwithstanding the extensive data set available for this analysis, many of the variables are only poorly measured, and we do not have measures of some potentially important influences on measured performance, such as the local demand for emergency treatment.

Table 9.4 shows the correlation matrix for the residuals from the three estimated OLS equations. Note that the three sets of residuals are all positively correlated. Although a test of the independence of the three sets of residuals cannot reject the null hypothesis of independence, a test of the independence of the residuals from the readmission rate and length of stay equations alone leads to the rejection of the null at the 5 per cent level ($\chi^2(1) = 5.766$, $p = 0.0163$). This implies that these two sets of residuals are significantly positively correlated and that there is some unobserved factor that boosts both the readmission rate and length of stay but which has not been included in the model. As noted above, this effect might arise from a mixture of influences.

We therefore re-estimated all three regressions using the SUR estimator, which utilises the information present in the cross-regression error correlations. The results from this re-estimation are presented as equations 2, 4 and 6 in Table 9.3. Although there are changes to most of the parameter (coefficient and standard error) estimates, these changes are modest, in part reflecting the relatively low correlations between the OLS error terms and because OLS remains a consistent estimator. However, in another study we have found correlations of the order of 0.64 between the errors of separately estimated OLS equations of the demand for and supply of elective surgery (Martin and Smith 2003). The SUR estimation has a correspondingly

Table 9.3. *OLS and SUR results for three performance indicators*

Dependent variable	Readmission rate		Waiting time		Length of stay	
Estimation technique	OLS	SUR	OLS	SUR	OLS	SUR
Equation	1	2	3	4	5	6
AHP_VACANCY_RATE					0.0355 (0.0127)	0.0349 (0.0119)
NURSE_VACANCY_RATE	1.3496 (0.2197)	1.2975 (0.2139)	0.0430 (0.0195)	0.0446 (0.0192)		
NEED_FOR_HEALTH_CARE			−0.4949 (0.2208)	−0.4923 (0.2174)	−0.7672 (0.1469)	−0.7630 (0.1398)
GP_AVAILABILITY			−0.5031 (0.2896)	−0.5095 (0.2845)		
HERFINDAHL15	0.0443 (0.0187)	0.0399 (0.0182)			−0.0621 (0.0128)	−0.0621 (0.0122)
PRIVATE_BEDS	0.0474 (0.0285)	0.0379 (0.0275)				
TRANSFERS_IN					−0.0773 (0.0208)	−0.0714 (0.0195)
PROP_ADMISS_60+					0.2291 (0.0614)	0.2285 (0.0576)
HRG_INDEX	0.3456 (0.1226)	0.3560 (0.1202)			0.6883 (0.1130)	0.6731 (0.1074)

Dependent variable	Readmission rate		Waiting time		Length of stay	
Estimation technique	OLS	SUR	OLS	SUR	OLS	SUR
Equation	1	2	3	4	5	6
RESEARCH_SPEND					0.0144	0.0146
					(0.0060)	(0.0056)
OCCUPANCY_RATE					0.6681	0.6992
					(0.1471)	(0.1380)
BEDS_PER_HEAD					0.5168	0.5261
					(0.0511)	(0.0479)
Adj. R^2	0.331	n/a	0.083	n/a	0.736	n/a
Ramsey test: F	1.07	n/a	1.07	n/a	1.31	n/a

Notes:

Estimated standard errors are in parentheses.

Variable descriptions

AHP_VACANCY_RATE	Allied health professionals vacancy rate (three-month vacancies expressed as a percentage of three-month medical workforce census vacancies plus staff in post), 1999–2001
NURSE_VACANCY_RATE	Qualified nursing, midwifery and health visitors vacancy rate (three-month vacancies expressed as a percentage of three-month medical workforce census vacancies plus staff in post), 1999–2001
NEED_FOR_HEALTH_CARE	Need for health care of the hospital's catchment population (the so-called 'York index')

Table 9.3. (continued)

GP_AVAILABILITY	Number of whole-time-equivalent GPs per head of population, 1999
HERFINDAHL15	Index of local NHS competition (=1 if there are no other acute providers within a fifteen-mile radius, 1995/96 data)
PRIVATE_BEDS	Availability of local private beds relative to NHS beds, 1999
TRANSFERS_IN	Proportion of spells that involve a transfer in from another hospital, 1994–1997
PROP_ADMISS_60+	Proportion of patient admissions aged over 60, 1994–2000
HRG_INDEX	Index of case mix complexity, 1994–1997
RESEARCH_SPEND	Proportion of total revenue spent on research, 1994–1997
OCCUPANCY_RATE	Bed occupancy rate, 1996–2000 (=occupied beds divided by available beds)
BEDS_PER_HEAD	Average daily number of available beds divided by population served by Trust, 1994–2000

Table 9.4. Correlations of OLS residuals

	Readmission rate	Waiting time	Length of stay
Readmission rate	1.0000		
Waiting time	0.0212	1.0000	
Length of stay	0.2067	0.0918	1.0000

Note:
Breusch-Pagan test of independence of residuals: $\chi^2(3) = 6.964$, probability = 0.0731.

larger impact on parameter estimates and standard errors, leading to important changes in policy inferences. For example, the elasticity of demand for routine surgery with respect to waiting time changes from -0.189 to -0.035, suggesting that the increase in demand caused by a fall in waiting times is considerably smaller than previous studies have claimed (Martin and Smith 2003).

SUR estimation reduces the coefficient on the need for health care variable (a measure of social disadvantage) from 1.3496 to 1.2975 between equations 1 and 2. One plausible interpretation of this might be that need and overall inefficiency levels are positively correlated (hospitals serving disadvantaged areas have lower levels of efficiency). Therefore, when the SUR estimator replaces OLS, the SUR transformation purges the need variable of its correlation with inefficiency and the resulting SUR coefficient reflects a pure need effect on readmissions, rather than a combined need and inefficiency effect.

9.4 Seemingly unrelated regression (SUR) in a multilevel context

The multilevel framework can be extended to consider multiple outcomes simply by recognising that, for the data analysed in this chapter, the performance indicators themselves are clustered, in this context within small areas (Gilthorpe and Cunningham 2000; Yang *et al.* 2002). This is a SUR model in a multilevel context.

By considering the performance indicators as the lowest tier in the data hierarchy, the possibility of within-small-area and within-health-authority correlation among indicators can be assessed. Thus the multivariate multilevel model (MVML model) is conceptualised as a three-level multilevel model, in which the set of I performance indicators (level 1) are clustered within J small areas (level 2), which are themselves clustered within K health authorities (level 3). The MVML model can be written as:

$$y_{ijk} = \beta_{0i} + x_{1ijk}\beta_{1i} + u_{0ik} + e_{0ijk} \quad i = 1, 2, \ldots, I;$$
$$j = 1, 2, \ldots, J; \quad k = 1, 2, \ldots, K \tag{9.10}$$

Thus, y_{ijk} is the ith performance indicator for the jth small area clustered within the kth health authority. The other parameters are analogous to their counterparts in the aggregate OLS and multilevel (ML) models, except that we now consider an additional level i.

The error terms u_{0ik} and e_{0ijk} are both assumed to be normally distributed with zero mean and constant variance $(\sigma_{u,i}^2, \sigma_{e,i}^2)$. e_{0ijk} represents the random error for performance indicator i in the jth small area, and we assume $E(e_{0ijk}e_{0igh}') = 0$ for a performance indicator i, two small areas j and g, and two health authorities k and h. u_{0ik} captures the health authority effect. The covariance for the ith and pth performance indicators within a health authority k is given by:

$$\text{cov}(u_{0ik}, u_{0pk}) = \sigma_{u,ip} \tag{9.11}$$

These estimates of covariance can be used to calculate the degree of correlation r_{ip} between performance indicators i and p:

$$r_{ip} = \frac{\sigma_{u,ip}}{\sqrt{\sigma_{u,i}^2 + \sigma_{u,p}^2}} \tag{9.12}$$

If the correlation is positive, it implies that a health authority that has better than average performance for indicator i also has above average performance for indicator p. A negative correlation implies that above average performance for the one indicator coincides with poorer performance for the other. This correlation is interpreted as being due to unobservable influences on performance, such as the managerial competency of the health authority or the shared influence of environmental conditions over and above those factors that we have controlled for. Consistent with the ML models, we estimate the intra-class correlation coefficient as

$$ICC_{MVML} = \sigma_{u_{0ik}}^2 (\sigma_{u_{0ik}}^2 + \sigma_{e_{0ijk}}^2)^{-1}, \quad 0 < ICC_{MVML} < 1 \tag{9.13}$$

If there are correlations among performance indicators, the residuals from the ML models, u_{0k}, and the residuals from the MVML model, u_{0ik}, may differ for the same performance indicator i. A likelihood ratio test can be used to determine whether the correlations among residuals are jointly zero or not. The ML models are the restricted models because they impose the assumption that there are zero correlations between the residuals. The test statistic is given as:

$$\lambda = 2\left(LLF_{MVML} - \left(\sum_{i=1}^{I} LLF_{ML} \right) \right), \qquad i = 1, \ldots, I \qquad (9.14)$$

where LLF_{MVML} is the log-likelihood function for the multivariate multilevel model, and LLF_{ML} is the log-likelihood function for a multilevel model applied to a single performance indicator. Asymptotically, λ has a chi-square distribution. A significant test statistic indicates that estimation as a MVML model is preferable to separate estimation of a set of ML models, and implies the presence of correlation among performance indicators. (Note that the test cannot be used to identify the particular performance indicators among which the correlation exists).

9.4.1 *Illustrative example*

We illustrate the application of SUR techniques in a multilevel framework by returning to the example introduced in the first part of this chapter. Here we analyse district performance across thirteen performance indicators, including waiting times. These indicators are listed in Table 9.5. The data are structured as shown in Figure 9.5, with performance indicators clustered within small areas, which are nested in districts. To simplify the exposition in this section, however, we ignore the clustering of districts within regions.

The likelihood ratio test comparing the ML and MVML models clearly rejects the null hypothesis of jointly zero correlations among the residuals ($\lambda_{df=78} = 9,495$, $p < 0.000$). This indicates that the MVML model improves inference by allowing explicitly for correlations among the performance indicators. The correlation coefficients for the health authority effects across the various indicators are presented in Table 9.6. Coefficients with an asterisk are significant at the 5 per cent level.

Table 9.5. Performance indicators and socio-economic variables

Performance indicators and variable descriptions

Health outcome

SMR064   Standardised mortality ratio for ages 0–64
Ratio of observed deaths from all causes in an area to the expected equivalent given the local age/sex profile and national averages

SMR6574   Standardised mortality ratio for ages 65–74
Ratio of observed deaths from all causes in an area to the expected equivalent given the local age/sex profile and national averages

SIR074   Limiting long-standing illness for ages 0–74
Ratio of observed number of people reporting limiting illness in an area to the expected equivalent given the local age/sex profile and national averages

Clinical quality

EMOLD   Emergency admissions of elderly people
Ratio of the rate of over-65 emergency admissions originating from an area to the expected given the age, sex and speciality of a patient and national averages

DEATHS   Deaths following hospital surgery
Ratio of thirty-day perioperative mortality after elective and non-elective surgery to the expected equivalent given the age, sex and case severity of a patient

Access

WTSURG   Waiting time for routine surgery
Ratio of actual waiting time in days for routine surgery to the expected equivalent given the age, sex and speciality of a patient and national averages

WTRADIO   Waiting time for radiotherapy
Ratio of actual waiting time in days for radiotherapy to the expected equivalent given the age, sex and speciality of a patient and national averages

WTLONG   Percentage of those on waiting list waiting for twelve months or more
Proportion of elective surgery admissions waiting for more than one year standardised for patient characteristics

GPACCS   Accessibility to general practitioners (GPs)
Indicator of relative accessibility given the supply of GPs, the distance to surgeries and the competition from local populations

Performance indicators and variable descriptions

ELECTEPS	Number of elective surgery episodes
	Ratio of standard surgery procedures originating from an area to the expected equivalent given the age, sex and speciality of a patient
Efficiency	
DCRATE	Day case rate
	Proportion of elective episodes in routine surgery treated as day cases standardised for patient characteristics
MATCOST	Maternity costs
	Ratio of speciality-specific fixed and variable costs for episodes to the expected equivalent given national averages
PSYCOST	Psychiatry costs
	Ratio of speciality-specific fixed and variable costs for episodes to the expected equivalent given the age and sex of a patient and national averages

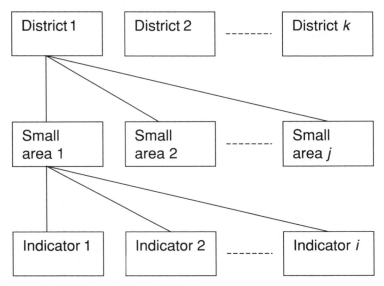

Figure 9.5. Multivariate hierarchical data structure.

Table 9.6. *Correlation of health authority effects from the multivariate multilevel model*

	SM-R064	SM-R6574	SIR074	EMO-LD	DEAT-HS	WTSU-RG	WTRA-DIO	WTL-ONG	GPAC-CS	ELEC-TEPS	DCRA-TE	MAT-COST
SMR6574	0.73*											
SIR074	0.62*	0.91*										
EMOLD	0.00	0.15*	0.05									
DEATHS	0.17*	0.30*	0.26*	0.41*								
WTSURG	−0.16*	−0.22*	−0.20*	−0.13*	−0.03							
WTRADIO	0.00	0.00	0.16	0.00	0.00	−0.10						
WTLONG	−0.12	−0.25*	−0.21*	−0.13	−0.07	0.95*	−0.13					
GPACCS	0.26	0.47*	0.48*	0.21*	0.21*	0.10	0.00	0.05				
ELECTEPS	−0.15	−0.32*	−0.25*	−0.13	−0.13	0.32*	−0.07	0.34*	−0.07			
DCRATE	0.00	−0.18	−0.12	0.00	0.00	0.40*	−0.26	0.38*	0.00	0.35*		
MATCOST	0.10	0.00	0.10	0.02	−0.04	0.14	0.26*	0.12	0.07	−0.16*	−0.15	
PSYCOST	0.16	0.15	0.27*	0.09	−0.20*	0.13	0.14*	0.11	0.28*	−0.09	−0.05	0.21*

Note:
* Significant at 0.05 level.

We find statistically significant positive correlations among the health outcome indicators, SMR064, SMR6574 and SIR074. These correlations imply that in an area with above-average mortality rates for ages 0–64, mortality rates for ages 65–74 and rates of chronic illness are above average also. There is a statistically significant positive correlation ($r_{ip} = 0.41$) between the two clinical quality indicators, DEATHS and EMOLD, implying that areas with a higher proportion of emergency admissions also report more deaths following hospital surgery. There is an almost perfect correlation between WTSURG and WTLONG ($r_{ip} = 0.95$), suggesting that one of these indicators is redundant.

These two measures of waiting time have a significant negative correlation with the health outcome measures (from $r_{ip} = -0.25$ to $r_{ip} = -0.16$), which might be indicative of trade-offs between these broad types of objectives: efforts directed at reducing waiting times may have adverse consequences for these measures of health outcome. There is also a negative correlation between health outcomes and the number of elective episodes ($r_{ip} = -0.32$), which means that, in health authorities with higher rates of illness and mortality, more elective procedures are undertaken. In contrast, there is a significant positive correlation between the health measures and the indicator measuring accessibility to GPs ($r_{ip} = 0.47$ and $r_{ip} = 0.48$). This suggests that in areas with above average illness and mortality rates people experience greater difficulties in accessing GP services.

The choice of analytical approach is likely to have an impact on the estimates of relative performance for particular districts. The sensitivity of the relative performance of each district to these decisions can be illustrated graphically. Figure 9.6 plots the district effect estimated by the OLS, ML and SUR mulitivariate multilevel (MVML) models for the waiting times performance indicator. The district effect for the aggregate OLS model, $\bar{u}_k$, is plotted on the diagonal from the 'bottom left corner' (best performance) to the 'top right corner' (worst performance) of each figure. The district effects deriving from the ML (u_{0k}) and MVML (u_{0ik}) models are indicated respectively by a diamond and triangle. The vertical lines connecting these points depict the range in values for each individual district, with longer lines indicating greater sensitivity in individual values to the choice of model specification. As can be seen, there is considerable volatility across the entire series, with the relative ranking of each district varying according

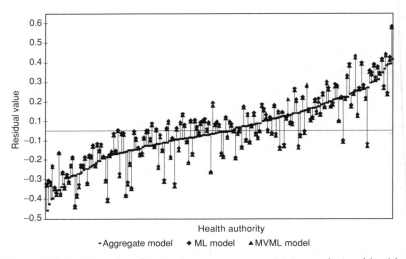

Figure 9.6. Waiting time for routine surgery – sensitivity analysis of health authority effects.

to whether OLS, ML or MVML techniques are used to analyse performance.

9.5 Conclusions

This chapter has argued that there exist a number of promising directions for future research into efficiency analysis that involve radical departures from the traditional parametric and non-parametric methods described earlier in the book. We have concentrated on the statistical procedures needed to develop multilevel and SUR models of performance, emphasising that model development is not motivated by the desire to create a single composite measure of overall organisational 'efficiency'. We would not claim that the multilevel and SUR methods described here are necessarily useful in all circumstances, or that they address all of the weaknesses of traditional methods. However, they can cast new light on organisational performance, and should certainly be considered whenever data and analytic capacity permit.

The multilevel methods described here have been well developed in other sectors (notably education). With rapid advances in the availability of good-quality patient-level data, the scope for deploying multilevel methods in health care has increased markedly (Rice and Jones 1997). Hitherto, most applications have been concerned with securing improved model parameter estimates. However, there is no reason why the methods should not be used to make inferences about performance at different levels in the hierarchy. We have found quite marked changes in inference as a consequence of moving from traditional to multilevel regression methods, so we believe their use should be considered if feasible.

The SUR approach moves beyond piecemeal modelling of measures of performance in public service organisations. SUR methods address two drawbacks to the conventional analytic approach. First, the traditional emphasis on developing a single index of performance requires that objectives are weighted in some way so that they can be aggregated. The relative value to be placed on the objectives of organisations working in the health sector is often a political issue requiring explicit consideration, rather than being subsumed as part of the technical process. By analysing objectives separately – but allowing for the possibility that they might be correlated – SUR avoids the necessity of weighting them.

Second, from a managerial perspective it will often be more useful to focus on individual performance measures in order to identify where the greatest scope for improvement lies. Yet analysis of individual performance indicators is often hampered by poor understanding of the exogenous factors that affect performance and poor measurement of those factors. The SUR methods outlined above represent a promising technology for reducing the importance of this problem by exploiting information arising from a series of regression models of organisational performance.

We most emphatically do not claim that multilevel or SUR methods – either individual or in tandem – offer a complete panacea for the problem of analysing public service performance. Rather, they offer further promising tools for gaining insights into the determinants of performance and identifying the level of attainment of individual organisations, to be set alongside the more conventional areas of efficiency analysis described earlier. No analytic approach can on its own answer the questions posed by politicians, regulators, managers, service users and the general public. However, used carefully in conjunction, they offer great potential for enhancing our understanding of health care performance.

10 | Conclusions

10.1 Introduction

THE pursuit of increased efficiency in the health care system is a major preoccupation of most developed countries. It is likely, if anything, to become more urgent as the pressures of technological innovation, an aging population and increased public expectations combine to drive up expenditure on health care still further. Moreover, it is clear that there is only limited scope for relying on conventional markets to deliver many aspects of health care. Therefore, some sort of regulatory mechanism is needed to ensure that providers are delivering health care in line with payer requirements, whether that payer is an individual patient, an insurance fund, a local government or the more general taxpayer. We would argue that quantitative analysis of the sort described in this book is an essential prerequisite of any proper regulation in the health care domain.

We have claimed that the ultimate aim of such analysis should be to assess the cost-effectiveness of a health care organisation, measured as the ratio of its valued outcomes to the resources it consumes. Few would argue with this goal in principle. Indeed, it is quite straightforward to estimate cost-effectiveness if certain conditions hold:

- there is consensus on the goals of the organisation;
- all outputs and inputs can be measured;
- the outputs can be readily valued and combined into a single measure of effectiveness;
- the organisation relies only on its own inputs to secure those outputs, and not on joint work with other organisations;
- it is straightforward to account for any environmental difficulties the organisation experiences in securing its results.

In practice, of course, these conditions do not hold. Indeed, it is the routine breach of these conditions that is such a striking characteristic

207

of much health care, and that results in the complex regulatory problem.

We believe that the techniques described in this book offer important support for the regulatory function. The volume of data available to assess health care performance has increased considerably, as health care organisations have been obliged to submit standardised electronic information, whether for performance monitoring or billing purposes. In future, even more detailed, timely and accurate information is likely to be produced, facilitated by continually improving technological capabilities and innovations such as the electronic health record. The traditional problem of inadequate, unreliable, delayed and inconsistent data is therefore being replaced by one of data overload, and a need to synthesise the information into meaningful regulatory messages. The methods of efficiency analysis described in this book have great potential to satisfy this need. In particular, we feel they make two unique and important contributions: offering information on the weights attached to health care outputs, and assessing the causes of unexplained variation in performance. We discuss these in turn.

10.2 Output weights

In principle, it is possible to envisage various experimental or survey methods that could secure information on the valuations attached to health care outputs. For example, the World Health Organization (2000) undertook a survey of key informants to estimate the relative valuation placed on five health system outputs. Various other techniques are available to infer popular valuations (Ryan *et al.* 2001). However, these methods require careful methodological development, may require very large samples, are the subject of fierce debate, and can reveal very large variations in individual preferences.

In contrast, the methods of efficiency analysis offer information on weights as a natural by-product of the analytic process. In the case of parametric analysis, the weights are the estimated coefficients on the various outputs. They indicate the value – at the margin – of an additional unit of output. In general, the estimation procedures used imply that the sample average valuation of the output determines the appropriate weight to use. This assumes that – on average – organizations apply the socially optimal priority to each output. In a non-market setting, this assumption is open to challenge. However, regulators will often feel that, in the absence of clearer guidance from policy makers, it is a reasonably neutral assumption. We would merely note that the use of parametric output coefficients is conservative, as it reflects current practice, and that it may therefore not always accurately reflect current policy priorities.

DEA adopts a completely different approach to output weights. In its simplest form, it permits complete flexibility in the weights adopted by each organisation, and therefore allows each organisation to be assessed with an entirely different set of weights. It simply requires that, given its choice of output weights, the organisation must be assessed against all other organisations, using that same set of weights. DEA then searches for the set of weights that cast the organisation in the best possible light. It therefore offers conservative judgements on its level of inefficiency, because that set of weights may not conform to the regulator's chosen priorities.

We have discussed the treatment of weights in more detail in chapter 8. We conclude that there is a pressing need to ensure that – whatever method is used – the technical analysis should be assessed in the light of the regulator's policy priorities. There is no single satisfactory approach to the treatment of output weights. Rather, the regulator needs always to consider explicitly how weights should be set, and to ensure that technical analysis is consistent with that choice. The methods described here can be used to inform but not determine the choice of weights.

10.3 Partitioning unexplained variation

Once a set of output weights has been chosen, it is a straightforward matter to construct a ratio of outputs to inputs (expressed as costs). This simple cost-effectiveness ratio may then be used to rank organisations, and there is no need for analytic techniques. However, a widespread concern in health care is the extent to which such rankings ignore external influences on performance, such as differences in patient characteristics, differences in geography, differences in input prices, and other factors outside the direct control of the organisation. A fundamental role of efficiency analysis is to offer a range of technologies for handling this complication.

The simplest approach to handling an environmental factor in both parametric and non-parametric methods is to enter it as an additional uncontrollable input into the model specification. This effectively 'excuses' any unexplained variation in performance correlated with the factor, and therefore results in increased estimates of efficiency among those organisations suffering especially adverse circumstances associated with the environmental factor.

Although having the merit of simplicity, such direct methods suffer from both methodological and practical difficulties, and a variety of multistage analytic techniques have been developed to accommodate environmental factors. These remain the subject of academic debate, and the analyst often has a delicate job of balancing the demands of methodological rigour and practical usefulness. Moreover, most methods assume that the environmental variables can be measured, and that their potential impact on performance is uncontested. In practice this is often not the case. The analyst often has available only proxy measures of the environment (for example, measures of population morbidity might be approximated by measures of mortality).

Variations in measured performance can be due to many factors: differences in the citizens being served; the external environment – for example, geography, economic circumstances, other agencies, culture; the quality of resources being used; different accounting treatments; data errors; random fluctuation; different organisational priorities; and differences in efficiency. There are often heated professional debates about which factors are legitimate uncontrollable influences on performance and which are within the control of management. Efficiency analysis can only partially contribute to these debates. There will always be room for argument over whether the apparent correlation between a putative explanatory factor and inefficiency is because it genuinely indicates an inhibition to better performance, or merely reflects a tendency of organisations with certain characteristics to perform poorly. Moreover, much depends on the purpose of the analysis. In the short run, very little may be controllable by the health care organisation, whilst in the longer term factors such as capital stock can be reconfigured. The regulator therefore needs to have a clear idea of the required scope of the analysis.

Stochastic frontier methods seek to address the problem of uncontrollable influences on performance by partitioning the variance into an efficiency element and a random element. This may appear to obviate the need to measure all potential environmental factors, as they may be captured in the random element. However, as chapters 3, 4 and 8 discuss, this makes strong assumptions about the nature of the omitted environmental variables, and requires apparently arbitrary judgements about the nature of the one-sided error term. We believe that this is a fundamental weakness of SFA that requires further methodological examination.

In chapter 9 we introduced an alternative approach to modelling multiple outputs when environmental factors are unknown or unmeasurable, using the methods of seemingly unrelated regression. As discussed, this method is experimental and also has its limitations. In particular, it focuses on the performance of individual outputs rather than offering a global measure of inefficiency. However, we argue that this may in some circumstances be more useful than seeking out the global measures that have been the traditional focus of efficiency analysis.

10.4 Unresolved technical issues

Given twenty-five years of concerted endeavour by a large research community, it may seem surprising to claim that there remain some fundamental methodological challenges for the theory and practice of efficiency analysis. Yet throughout this book we have found it necessary to highlight unresolved difficulties that the analyst must address in order to develop a satisfactory model.

In chapter 3 we suggested that the most singular difference between efficiency analysis and conventional analytic techniques is the switch in emphasis from the model coefficients to the unexplained residual. To a greater or lesser extent, the residual is interpreted as an indication of inefficiency. We do not believe that conventional model-building methods are appropriate given this changed focus. In particular, serious consequences might arise for individual organisations and the broader health system if inefficiency is incorrectly estimated. Costs of incorrect inference include:

- unrealistic targets for some organisations;
- focusing on incorrect 'beacon' organisations;
- unwarranted complacency in some organisations;
- faulty judgements about levels of inefficiency in the entire sector.

These costs take the form of faulty regulation and are very different to the costs of the Type I and Type II errors that are considered in conventional statistical analysis. In our view, the emphasis on individual residuals may therefore require fundamental re-examination of the principles of empirical model-building.

We have also referred to some other unresolved generic challenges for efficiency analysis where we feel existing methodology is deficient. As well as the problem of how to incorporate environmental variables into the analysis, we have raised concerns about the treatment of uncertainty and the development of dynamic models.

Uncertainty takes two broad forms: data uncertainty and model uncertainty. The first arises from variability in the underlying data and is well understood. Examining data uncertainty can be challenging in the context of efficiency analysis but it is nevertheless feasible using approaches such as Monte Carlo simulation. Model uncertainty is much less well understood but arises from the possibility that the underlying model may have been mis-specified. Even though it is probably the dominant form of uncertainty in efficiency analysis, it is unusual to see any formal treatment of model uncertainty, other than some sort of sensitivity analysis in the form of a presentation of results from a suite of model specifications.

Many health care settings have important dynamic characteristics that make cross-sectional analysis inappropriate. For example, outcomes from preventative programmes are often the results of years of endeavour on the part of health authorities. As discussed in chapter 2, panel data are beginning to emerge that make modelling of such processes feasible. Chapters 4 and 6 describe in detail current approaches to modelling such data. However, at this stage the development of truly dynamic efficiency models is in its infancy.

In addition to these generic issues, there are some challenges that are specific to the two broad approaches to efficiency measurement discussed in the book. Parametric methods have many strengths, most notably the need to appeal to economic theory in making specification decisions and exploitation of the full information set when deriving organisational estimates of inefficiency. However, parametric techniques require quite constraining assumptions relating to functional form, and even modest complexity can require an unfeasibly large sample size. Moreover, the most serious concern relating to SFA is the issue treated at length in chapter 8: model specification in SFA is a joint consideration relating to the choice of explanatory variables and the choice of one-sided error structure. The one-sided error could be capturing inefficiency, but it could also be capturing omitted environmental variables. Conversely, the one-sided error could be affected by incorporation in the model of variables wrongly specified as environmental. At present there is no way – other than an appeal to expert judgement – of determining whether the choice of explanatory variables and error structure is correct.

DEA gives rise to many model-building challenges for which there is little analytic guidance. These include:

- how to choose inputs and outputs in the absence of any model selection criteria;
- how much weight flexibility to permit;
- how to model and calculate uncertainty and to test for the robustness of results;
- whether data sparsity leads to biased efficiency estimates for some organisations;
- how to incorporate environmental factors (one-stage or multistage methods);
- how to test for model mis-specification.

There is some literature addressing these issues, but there remains a challenging research agenda to offer the analyst a more secure model-building methodology. In the meantime, the user should be alert to the arbitrary manner in which DEA models must often be developed.

10.5 For policy makers and regulators

This book has been aimed more at technical analysts than policy makers. However, we have highlighted some important messages for policy makers. First, efficiency modelling methodology is highly contested and still at a developmental stage. Efficiency results are dependent on numerous technical judgements for which there is often little guidance on best practice. Many of these judgements are properly political rather than technical issues (such as the choice of outputs), suggesting the need for a careful dialogue between analysts and policy makers. A central challenge is often to secure the appropriate involvement of policy makers in the model-building process.

From a regulatory perspective, it may often be the case that a very much simpler methodology than SFA or DEA is appropriate, perhaps in the form of a simple cost-effectiveness ratio. Also, there may be circumstances when analytic methods other than SFA/DEA, such as those outlined in chapter 9, may be appropriate. As suggested above, the major contributions of efficiency methods to the regulatory function are to manage large data sets, to adjust for exogenous influences on performance and to partition the unexplained variation in performance into inefficiency and other factors. However, their limitations are such that they should never be the only criterion for measuring organisational performance. Instead, they should be used in conjunction with other instruments, such as more detailed scrutiny of health care organisations, perhaps in the form of inspection.

In deploying and interpreting efficiency models, regulators may need to apply a range of criteria for model selection in addition to the conventional technical criteria. These might include practicality, parsimony, freedom from bias, plausibility, acceptability and freedom from perverse incentives. The extensiveness of these considerations indicates the complexity of the real-world regulatory problem when compared with the textbook considerations discussed in this book.

In short, we believe that efficiency models can make a valuable contribution to any health care regulatory regime. Whilst, in order to ensure that they are used appropriately, we have dwelt on their limitations, they nevertheless offer powerful insights into organisational performance. We have been struck by how rarely they appear to have been used in real-world (as opposed to academic) health care settings. Whilst they can only ever inform and never determine regulatory judgements, they must surely become part of the analytic armoury of any competent regulator.

Appendix
Data description

Table A.1 gives a description of the data set used in the case studies in chapters 3 to 7 of this book. The data set includes four years of data for the period 1994/95–1997/98 and covers acute NHS hospital trusts in England. The variables are described in more detail below.

Table A.1. Descriptions of variables in data set

Variable	Description
TOTCOST	Total cost or total revenue expenditure
INPATIENTS	Total inpatient episodes weighted by HRG case mix index
OUTPATIENTS	Total first outpatient attendances
A&E	Total A & E attendances
STUDENTS	Student whole-time teaching equivalents per inpatient spell
RESEARCH	Percentage of total revenue spent on research
FCE	Finished consultant episode inter-speciality transfers per spell
EP_SPELL	Episodes per spell
TRANS-IN	Transfers in to hospital per spell
TRANS-OUT	Transfers out of hospital per spell
EMERGENCY	Emergency admissions per spell
FU-OUTPTS	Follow-up outpatient attendances per inpatient spell
EMERINDX	Standardised index of unexpected emergency admissions/total emergency admissions
P-15	Proportion of patients under 15 years of age

Table A.1. (continued)

Variable	Description
P-60	Proportion of patients 60 years or older
P-FEM	Proportion of female patients
MFF	Market forces factor – weighted average of staff, land, buildings and London weighting factors
HERF15	Herfindahl concentration/ competition index, 15-mile radius
AVBEDS	Average available beds
HEATBED	Heated volume per bed
SITES50B	Sites with more than 50 beds
ITINDX	Scope/specialization index, information theory index

TOTCOST measures total revenue expenditure and where the data are used in a multiperiod context, the expenditure has been deflated by the GDP deflator. Hospitals produce inpatient episodes of care (INPATIENTS) which are weighted by a healthcare resource group (HRG) case mix measure which groups patient activity into resource-homogeneous categories (Benton *et al.* 1998). In order to estimate a case mix index for a hospital, all episodes are allocated to a healthcare resource group and weighted according to the expected cost of that HRG (Street and Dawson 2002). The average cost weight for all cases treated over a year forms the scalar case mix index for each hospital. The national average case weight was set to equal 100, and case mix indices above 100 thus represent hospitals that have treated a more complex than average mix of cases. This index was then used to adjust inpatient episodes.

Additional activities include total first outpatient attendances (OUTPATIENTS) and A&E attendances (A&E). Teaching activity is picked up through medical student whole-time teaching equivalents per inpatient spell (STUDENTS). Teaching and research (RE-SEARCH) activities constitute important secondary outputs of NHS hospitals.

Measurement of the volume of inpatient care performed by NHS acute hospitals has been through the finished consultant episode (FCE) which measures the length of time a patient is under the care of a single consultant. During a single hospital admission, however, multiple FCEs might occur as a result of transfers within hospitals or between consultants. The inpatient spell, or set of episodes constituting a single admission, thus serves as a slightly higher level of aggregation of inpatient activity. Spells requiring inter-speciality transfers are likely to be more complex than those which can be fully treated by a single consultant or within a single speciality. Given the adjustment for episodes per spell (EP_SPELL), FCE captures the additional effect of inter-speciality transfers over and above the average multiple FCE.

Large fluctuations in levels of emergency admissions imply that more fixed capacity has to be retained for a given average level of activity. EMERGENCY measures the proportion of spells that involve an emergency admission. EMERINDX is a standardised index of unexpected emergency admissions divided by total emergencies and captures unpredictable demand patterns.

The basic unit of outpatient activity is assumed to consist of first, rather than follow-up, outpatient attendances. Many outpatient attendances occur because patients require follow-up for some time following the first attendance. Since such follow-up attendances constitute genuine additional health care output, FU-OUTPTS measures non-primary follow-up outpatient attendances per inpatient spell.

HRGs may inadequately represent the health care requirements of patients, so this is captured by additional variables. P-15 measures whether hospitals expend more resources on younger patients, diagnosis and other factors being equal (Söderlund *et al.* 1995). Elderly patients (P-60) are likely to have more complex care needs, and these may not be captured entirely by HRGs, which have only limited age sensitivity. P-FEM captures any gender-specific differences in health care requirements and costs.

Market prices for inputs including land, buildings and labour differ between hospitals because of their geographic location (MFF). Arguably this represents an unavoidable environmental influence on the ability of hospitals to deploy inputs efficiently.

Average bed numbers (AVBEDS) may be considered fixed in the short run. While hospital managers do have some control over the size and capacity of their institution, it is expected that there will be some reluctance radically to alter capacity. Decreasing hospital capacity might be particularly difficult because of public opposition and implied job loss.

Heated volume per bed (HEATBED) captures potential inefficiencies in how hospital buildings are used to create treatment capacity (represented by beds). A large amount of heated volume per bed is assumed to represent less efficient use of capital.

Single-speciality hospitals are likely to draw patients from further afield, and have greater short-term variation in demand for services because of the lack of cross-speciality compensation effects. Economies of specialisation, in contrast, might occur where relatively under-utilised, specialised fixed resources are centralised in one institution, rather than spread over many. This can be examined through the inclusion of an information theory index (ITINDX) which calculates the degree to which the proportions of different case types (HRGs) in a hospital differ from the national average proportions of case types. The formula used for derivation of the information theory index is given by Farley (Farley 1989; Farley and Hogan 1990). An increased IT index indicates a relatively more specialised hospital (i.e. one with a narrower scope of activities). General hospitals typically have an IT index of between 0.2 and 0.5, whereas this may increase to 2.5 in a highly specialised, single-discipline, hospital.

Hospitals that are located on a number of sites, rather than concentrated in one location, are likely to suffer from duplication of some capital and staff inputs, as well as incurring communication and management difficulties, thus increasing costs. The number of major sites with more than fifty beds (SITES50B) was chosen to exclude sites that were simply isolated accommodation or chronic care or outpatient facilities.

References

Aigner, D., Lovell, C. A. K. and Schmidt, P. 1977. 'Formulation and estimation of stochastic frontier production function models'. *Journal of Econometrics* 6: 21–37.

Ali, A. I. and Seiford, L. M. 1993. 'The mathematical programming approach to efficiency analysis', in H. O Fried, C. A. K. Lovell and S. S. Schmidt (eds.), *The Measurement of Productive Efficiency*. Oxford: Oxford University Press, pp. 120–59.

Allen, R., Athanassopoulos, A., Dyson, R. G. and Thanassoulis, E. 1997. 'Weight restrictions and value judgements in data envelopment analysis: evolution, development and future directions'. *Annals of Operations Research* 73: 13–34.

Anand, S., Ammar, W., Evans, T., Hasegawa, T., Kissimova-Skarbek, K., Langer, A., Lucas, A. O., Makubalo, L., Marandi, A., Meyer, G., Podger, A., Smith, P. C. and Wibulpolprasert, S. 2002. *Report of the Scientific Peer Review Group on Health Systems Performance Assessment*. Geneva: World Health Organization.

Atkinson, T. 2005. *Atkinson Review: Final Report. Measurement of Government Output and Productivity for the National Accounts*. Basingstoke: Palgrave Macmillan.

Audit Commission and Department of Health 1999. *NHS Trust Profiles Handbook – 1997/98*. London: Audit Commission.

Baltagi, B. H. 2005. *Econometric Analysis of Panel Data*, 3rd edn. Chichester: Wiley.

Banker, R. D. and Morey, R. C. 1986. 'Efficiency analysis for exogenously fixed inputs and outputs'. *Operations Research* 34: 513–21.

Banker, R. D., Charnes, A. and Cooper, W. W. 1984. 'Some models for estimating technical and scale inefficiencies in data envelopment analysis'. *Management Science* 30: 1078–92.

Banker, R. D., Conrad, R. F. and Strauss, R. P. 1986. 'A comparative application of data envelopment analysis and translog methods: an illustrative study of hospital production'. *Management Science* 32: 30–44.

Banker, R. D., Gadh, V. M. and Gorr, W. L. 1993. 'A Monte Carlo comparison of two production frontier estimation methods: corrected ordinary least squares and data envelopment analysis'. *European Journal of Operational Research* 67: 332–43.

Banker, R. D., Charnes, A., Cooper, W., Swarts, J. and Thomas, D. 1989. 'An introduction to data envelopment analysis with some models and their uses'. *Research in Governmental and Non-Profit Accounting* 5: 125–63.

Barth, W. and Staat, M. 2005. 'Environmental variables and relative efficiency of bank branches: A DEA-bootstrap approach'. *International Journal of Business Performance Management* 7: 228–40.

Bates, J. M., Baines, D. and Whynes, D. K. 1996. 'Measuring the efficiency of prescribing by general practitioners'. *Journal of the Operational Research Society* 47: 1443–51.

1998. 'Assessing efficiency in general practice: an application of data envelopment analysis'. *Health Services Management Research* 11: 103–8.

Battese, G. E. and Coelli, T. 1988. 'Prediction of firm-level technical efficiencies with a generalized frontier production function and panel data'. *Journal of Econometrics* 38: 387–99.

1992. 'Frontier production functions, technical efficiency and panel data: with application to paddy farmers in India'. *Journal of Productivity Analysis* 3: 153–69.

Bauer, P. W., Berger, A. N., Ferrier, G. D. and Humphrey, D. B. 1998. 'Consistency conditions for regulatory analysis of financial institutions: a comparison of frontier efficiency methods'. *Journal of Economics and Business* 50: 85–114.

Benton, P. L., Anthony, P., Evans, H., Light, S. M., Mountney, L. M. and Sanderson, H. F. 1998. 'The development of Healthcare Resource Groups version 3'. *Journal of Public Health Medicine* 20: 351–8.

Bessent, A., Bessent, W., Elam, J. and Clark, T. 1988. 'Efficiency frontier determination by constrained facet analysis'. *Operations Research* 36: 785–96.

Bhattacharya, A., Lovell, C. A. K. and Sahay, P. 1997. 'The impact of liberalization on the productive efficiency of Indian commercial banks'. *European Journal of Operational Research* 98: 332–47.

Blank, J. L. T. and Valdmanis, V. 2005. 'A modified three-stage data envelopment analysis: The Netherlands'. *European Journal of Health Economics* 6: 65–71.

Bond, S. 2002. 'Dynamic panel data models: a guide to micro data methods and practice'. *Portuguese Economic Journal* 1: 141–62.

Bowlin, W. F., Charnes, A., Cooper, W. and Sherman, H. D. 1985. 'Data envelopment analysis and regression approaches to efficiency estimation and evaluation'. *Annals of Operations Research* 2: 113–38.

Breyer, F. 1987. 'The specification of a hospital cost function'. *Journal of Health Economics* 6: 147–57.

Burgess, D. F. 1975. 'Duality theory and pitfalls in the specification of technologies'. *Journal of Econometrics* 3: 105–21.

Burgess, J. F. and Wilson, P. W. 1995. 'Decomposing hospital productivity changes, 1985–1988: a nonparametric Malmquist approach'. *Journal of Productivity Analysis* 6: 343–63.

Casu, B., Girardone, C. and Molyneux, P. 2004. 'Productivity change in European banking: a comparison of parametric and non-parametric approaches'. *Journal of Banking and Finance* 28: 2521–40.

Caves, D. W., Christensen, L. R. and Diewert, W. E. 1982. 'The economic theory of index numbers and the measurement of input, output and productivity'. *Econometrica* 50: 1393–414.

Charnes, A., Cooper, W. W. and Rhodes, E. 1978. 'Measuring the efficiency of decision making units'. *European Journal of Operational Research* 2: 429–44.

 1981. 'Evaluating program and managerial efficiency: an application of Data Envelopment Analysis to program follow through'. *Management Science* 27: 668–97.

Charnes, A., Cooper, W. W., Lewin, A. Y. and Seiford, L. M. (eds.) 1994. *Data Envelopment Analysis: Theory, Methodology, and Application.* Boston: Kluwer Academic Publishers.

Charnes, A., Cooper, W. W., Wei, Q. L. and Huang, Z. 1989. 'Cone ratio data envelopment analysis and multi-objective programming'. *International Journal of Systems Science* 20: 1099–118.

Chilingerian, J. A. 1994. 'Exploring why some physicians' hospital practices are more efficient: taking DEA inside the hospital', in Charnes, A., Cooper, W. W., Lewin, A. Y. and Seiford, L. M. (eds.), *Data Envelopment Analysis: Theory, Methodology and Application.* Boston: Kluwer Academic Publishers, pp. 167–94.

Christensen, L. R. and Greene, W. H. 1976. 'Economies of scale in US electric power generation'. *Journal of Political Economy* 84: 655–76.

Christensen, L. R., Jorgenson, D. W. and Lau, L. J. 1973. 'Transcendental logarithmic production functions'. *Review of Economics and Statistics* 55: 28–45.

Coase, R. H. 1937. 'The nature of the firm'. *Economica* 4: 386–405.

Coelli, T. 1996a. 'A guide to FRONTIER version 4.1: a computer program for stochastic frontier production and cost function estimation'. Working Paper 96/07, Centre for Efficiency and Productivity Analysis, University of New England, Armidale, NSW.

1996b. 'A guide to DEAP version 2.1: a data envelopment analysis (computer) program'. Working Paper 96/08, Centre for Efficiency and Productivity Analysis, University of New England, Armidale, NSW.

1998. 'A multi-stage methodology for the solution of orientated DEA models'. *Operations Research Letters* 23: 143–49.

Coelli, T. and Perelman, S. 1996. 'Efficiency measurement, multiple-output technologies and distance functions: with application to European railways'. Discussion Paper 96/05, CREPP, University of Liege.

2000. 'Technical efficiency of European railways: a distance function approach'. *Applied Economics* 32: 1967–76.

Coelli, T., Rao, D. and Battese, G. 1998. *An Introduction to Efficiency and Productivity Analysis*. Boston: Kluwer Academic Publishers.

Cook, R. D. and Weisberg, S. 1982. *Residuals and Influence in Regression*. London: Chapman and Hall.

Cooper, W. W., Seiford, L. M. and Tone, K. 2000. *Data Envelopment Analysis: A Comprehensive Text with Models, Applications, References and DEA-solver Software*. Boston: Kluwer Academic Publishers.

Cornwell, C., Schmidt, P. and Sickles, R. C. 1990. 'Production frontiers with cross-sectional and time-series variation in efficiency levels'. *Journal of Econometrics* 46: 185–200.

Coulter, A., and Magee, H. 2003. *The European Patient of the Future*. Maidenhead, Berkshire: Open University Press.

Davidson, R. and MacKinnon, J. G. 1985. 'Testing linear and loglinear regressions against Box–Cox alternatives'. *Canadian Journal of Economics* 18: 499–517.

Dismuke, C. and Sena, V. 1999. 'Has DRG payment influenced the technical efficiency and productivity of diagnostic technologies in Portuguese public hospitals?' *Health Care Management Science* 2: 107–16.

Doyle, J. and Green, R. 1994. 'Efficiency and cross-efficiency in DEA: derivations, meanings and uses'. *Journal of the Operational Research Society* 45: 567–78.

EuroQol Group 1990. 'EuroQol – a new facility for the measurement of health-related quality of life'. *Health Policy* 16: 199–208.

Everitt, B., Landau, S. and Leese, M. 2001. *Cluster Analysis*. London: Arnold.

Färe, R. and Grosskopf, S. 1996. *Intertemporal Production Frontiers: With Dynamic DEA*. Boston: Kluwer Academic Publishers.

Färe, R., Grosskopf, S., Lindgren, B. and Poullier, J. P. 1997. 'Productivity growth in health care delivery'. *Medical Care* 35: 354–66.

Färe, R., Grosskopf, S., Lindgren, B. and Roos, P. 1992. 'Productivity changes in Swedish pharmacies 1980–1989: a non-parametric Malmquist approach'. *Journal of Productivity Analysis* 3: 85–101.

Färe, R., Grosskopf, S., Norris, M. and Zhang, Z. 1994. 'Productivity growth, technical progress and efficiency changes in industrialised countries'. *American Economic Review* 84: 66–83.

Farley, D. E. 1989. 'Measuring case mix specialization and the concentration of diagnoses in hospitals using information theory'. *Journal of Health Economics* 8: 185–207.

Farley, D. E. and Hogan, C. 1990. 'Case-mix specialization in the market for hospital services'. *Health Services Research* 25: 757–83.

Farrell, M. J. 1957. 'The measurement of productive efficiency'. *Journal of the Royal Statistical Society*, Series A, 120: 253–90.

Farsi, M., Filippini, M. and Kuenzle, M. 2003. 'Unobserved heterogeneity in stochastic frontier models: a comparative analysis'. Working Paper 03–11, Department of Economics, University of Lugano.

Feldstein, M. S. 1967. *Economic Analysis for Health Service Efficiency: Econometric Studies of the British National Health Service*. Amsterdam: North-Holland.

Fernández, C., Koop, G. and Steel, M. 2000. 'A Bayesian analysis of multiple-output production frontiers'. *Journal of Econometrics* 98: 47–79.

Ferrier, G. D. and Lovell, C. A. K. 1990. 'Measuring cost efficiency in banking: econometric and linear programming evidence'. *Journal of Econometrics* 46: 229–45.

Ferrier, G. D. and Valdmanis, V. 1996. 'Rural hospital performance and its correlates'. *Journal of Productivity Analysis* 7: 63–80.

Fisher, I. 1922. *The Making of Index Numbers*. Boston: Houghton Mifflin.

Folland, S. T. and Hofler, R. A. 2001. 'How reliable are hospital efficiency estimates? Exploiting the dual to homothetic production'. *Health Economics* 10: 683–98.

Fried, H. O., Lovell, C. A. K. and Schmidt, S. S. (eds.) 1993. *The Measurement of Productive Efficiency*. Oxford: Oxford University Press.

Fried, H. O., Lovell, C. A. K. and vanden Eeckaut, P. 1993. 'Evaluating the performance of U.S. credit unions'. *Journal of Banking and Finance* 17: 251–65.

Fried, H. O., Schmidt, S. S. and Yaisawarng, S. 1999. 'Incorporating the operating environment into a nonparametric measure of technical efficiency'. *Journal of Productivity Analysis* 12: 249–67.

Fried, H. O., Lovell, C. A. K., Schmidt, S. S. and Yaisawarng, S. 2002. 'Accounting for environmental effects and statistical noise in data envelopment analysis'. *Journal of Productivity Analysis* 17: 157–74.

Gerdtham, U. G., Rehnberg, C. and Tambour, M. 1999. 'The impact of internal markets on health care efficiency: evidence from health care reforms in Sweden'. *Applied Economics* 31: 935–45.

Gilthorpe, M. S. and Cunningham, S. J. 2000. 'The application of multi-level, multivariate modelling to orthodontic research data'. *Community Dental Health* 17: 236–42.

Giuffrida, A. 1999. 'Productivity and efficiency changes in primary care: a Malmquist index approach'. *Health Care Management Science* 2: 11–26.

Giuffrida, A. and Gravelle, H. 2001. 'Measuring performance in primary care: econometric analysis and DEA'. *Applied Economics* 33: 163–75.

Giuffrida, A., Gravelle, H. and Sutton, M. 2000. 'Efficiency and adminis-trative costs in primary care'. *Journal of Health Economics* 19: 983–1006.

Goldstein, H. and Spiegelhalter, D. J. 1996. 'League tables and their limita-tions: statistical issues in comparisons of institutional performance'. *Journal of the Royal Statistical Society*, series A, 159: 385–443.

González, E. and Gascón, F. 2004. 'Sources of productivity growth in the Spanish pharmaceutical industry 1994–2000'. *Research Policy* 33: 735–45.

Greene, W. H. 1990. 'A gamma-distributed stochastic frontier model'. *Journal of Econometrics* 46: 141–63.

   1993. 'The econometric approach to efficiency analysis', in Fried, H. O., Lovell, C. A. K. and Schmidt, S. S. (eds.), *The Measurement of Productive Efficiency*. Oxford: Oxford University Press, pp. 68–119.

   1995. *Limdep Version 7.0 User's Manual*. Castle Hill, NSW: Econometric Software, Inc.

   2000. *Econometric Analysis*. Upper Saddle River, N. J.: Prentice-Hall.

   2002. *Limdep Version 8.0 Econometric Modelling Guide*. Plainview, N.Y.: Econometric Software, Inc.

   2004. 'Distinguishing between heterogeneity and inefficiency: stochastic frontier analysis of the World Health Organization's panel data on national health care systems'. *Health Economics* 13: 959–80.

   2005. 'Reconsidering heterogeneity in panel data estimators of the stochastic frontier model'. *Journal of Econometrics* 126: 269–303.

Grifell-Tatjé, E. and Lovell, C. A. K. 1995. 'A note on the Malmquist productivity index'. *Economics Letters* 47: 169–75.

Grosskopf, S. and Valdmanis, V. 1987. 'Measuring hospital performance: a non-parametric approach'. *Journal of Health Economics* 6: 89–107.

Hadley, J. and Zuckerman, S. 1994. 'The role of efficiency measurement in hospital rate setting'. *Journal of Health Economics* 13: 335–40.

Harris, J. E. 1977. 'The internal organisation of hospitals: some economic implications'. *Bell Journal of Economics* 8: 467–82.

Hauck, K. and Street, A. 2005. 'Performance assessment in the context of multiple objectives: a multivariate multilevel approach', Centre for Health Economics, University of York, Mimeo.

Hauck, K., Rice, N. and Smith, P. 2003. 'The influence of health care organisations on indicators of health system performance'. *Journal of Health Services Research and Policy* 8: 68–74.

Hausman, J. 1978. 'Specification tests in econometrics'. *Econometrica* 46: 1251–71.

Hill, P. W. and Goldstein, H. 1998. 'Multilevel modelling of educational data with cross classification and missing identification for units'. *Journal of Educational and Behavioural Statistics* 23: 117–28.

Hirschberg, J. G. and Lloyd, P. J. 2000. 'An application of post-DEA bootstrap regression analysis to the spillover of the technology of foreign-invested enterprises in China'. Paper 732, Department of Economics, University of Melbourne.

Hollingsworth, B. 2003. 'Non-parametric and parametric applications measuring efficiency in health care'. *Health Care Management Science* 6: 203–18.

Hollingsworth, B. and Parkin, D. 2001. 'The efficiency of the delivery of neonatal care in the UK'. *Journal of Public Health Medicine* 23: 47–50.

Hollingsworth, B. and Smith, P. C. 2003. 'The use of ratios in data envelopment analysis'. *Applied Economics Letters* 10: 733–5.

Horrace, W. C. and Schmidt, P. 1996. 'Confidence statements for efficiency estimates from stochastic frontier models'. *Journal of Productivity Analysis* 7: 257–82.

Hough, J. R. 1985. 'A note on economies of scale in schools'. *Applied Economics* 17: 143–4.

Iezzoni, L. I. 2003. *Risk Adjustment for Measuring Healthcare Outcomes*, 3rd edn. Baltimore: Health Administration Press.

Intriligator, M. D. 1978. *Econometric Models, Techniques and Applications*. Englewood Cliffs, N. J.: Prentice-Hall.

Jensen, U. 2000. 'Is it efficient to analyse efficiency rankings?' *Empirical Economics* 25: 189–208.

Jondrow, J., Lovell, C. A. K., Materov, I. S. and Schmidt, P. 1982. 'On the estimation of technical inefficiency in the stochastic frontier production function model.' *Journal of Econometrics* 19: 233–8.

Koopmans, T. C. 1951. 'An analysis of production as an efficient combination of activities', in Koopmans, T. C. (ed.), *Activity Analysis of Production and Allocation*. Monograph No. 13, New York: Wiley.

Kooreman, P. 1994. 'Nursing home care in The Netherlands: a nonparametric efficiency analysis'. *Journal of Health Economics* 13: 301–16.

Kuh, E. and Meyer, J. R. 1955. 'Correlation and regression estimates when the data are ratios'. *Econometrica* 23: 400–16.

Kumbhakar, S. C. 1990. 'Production frontiers, panel data, and time-varying technical efficiency'. *Journal of Econometrics* 46: 201–11.

Kumbhakar, S. C. and Lovell, C. A. K. 2000. *Stochastic Frontier Analysis*. Cambridge: Cambridge University Press.

Laspeyres, E. 1871. 'Die Berechnug einer mittleren Waaren-preissteigerung'. *Jahrbücherfür Nationalökonomie und Statistik* 16: 296–314.

Lee, Y. H. and Schmidt, P. 1993. 'A production function model with flexible temporal variation in technical efficiency', in Fried, H. O., Lovell, C. A. K. and Schmidt, S. S. (eds.), *The Measurement of Productive Efficiency*. New York: Oxford University Press, pp. 237–55.

Lewis, H. F. and Sexton, T. R. 2004. 'Data envelopment analysis with reverse inputs and outputs'. *Journal of Productivity Analysis* 21: 113–32.

Linna, M. 1998. 'Measuring hospital cost efficiency with panel data models'. *Health Economics* 7: 415–27.

Linna, M. and Häkkinen, U. 1998. 'Determinants of cost efficiency of Finnish hospitals: a comparison of DEA and SFA'. Systems Analysis Laboratory Research Report A78, Helsinki University of Technology.

Löthgren, M. 1998. 'How to bootstrap DEA estimators: a Monte Carlo comparison'. Working Paper Series in Economics and Finance 223, Stockholm School of Economics.

2000. 'Specification and estimation of stochastic multiple-output production and technical inefficiency'. *Applied Economics* 32: 1533–40.

Lovell, C. A. K. 2000. 'Measuring efficiency in the public sector', in Blank, J. L. T. (ed.), *Public Provision and Performance: Contributions from Efficiency and Productivity Measurement*. The Hague: North-Holland.

Lozano-Vivas, A., Pastor, J. T. and Pastor, J. M. 2002. 'An efficiency comparison of European banking systems operating under different environmental conditions'. *Journal of Productivity Analysis* 18: 59–77.

Maddala, G. S. 1988. *Introduction to Econometrics*. London: Collier Macmillan.

Malmquist, S. 1953. 'Index numbers and indifference surfaces'. *Trabajos de Estatistica* 4: 209–42.

Maniadakis, N. and Thanassoulis, E. 2000. 'Assessing productivity changes in UK hospitals reflecting technology and input prices'. *Applied Economics* 32: 1575–89.

Maniadakis, N., Hollingsworth, B. and Thanassoulis, E. 1999. 'The impact of the internal market on hospital efficiency, productivity and service quality'. *Health Care Management Science* 2: 75–85.

Martin, S. and Smith, P. C. 2003. 'Using panel methods to model waiting times for NHS surgery'. *Journal of the Royal Statistical Society*, Series A, 166: 369–87.

2005. 'Multiple public service performance indicators: towards an integrated statistical approach'. *Journal of Public Administration, Research and Theory* 15: 599–613.

McKinnish, T. G. 2000. 'Model sensitivity in panel data analysis: some caveats about the interpretation of fixed effects and differences estimators'. Unpublished manuscript, Department of Economics, University of Colorado, Boulder. Available at http://spot.colorado.edu/~mckinnis/fe053100.pdf (accessed February 2006).

Mooney, C. Z. and Duval, R. D. 1993. *Bootstrapping: A Nonparametric Approach to Statistical Inference*. London: Sage Publications.

Newhouse, J. P. 1994. 'Frontier analysis: how useful a tool for health economics?' *Journal of Health Economics* 13: 317–22.

Nishimizu, M. and Page, J. M. 1982. 'Total factor productivity growth, technical progress and technical efficiency change: dimensions of productivity change in Yugoslavia, 1965–78'. *Economic Journal* 92: 920–36.

Nunamaker, T. R. 1985. 'Using data envelopment analysis to measure the efficiency of non-profit organizations: a critical evaluation'. *Management and Decision Economics* 6: 50–8.

Office of Water Services 1999. *Future Water and Sewerage Charges 2000–05: Draft Determination*. London: OFWAT.

Ozcan, Y. A. and Cotter, J. J. 1994. 'An assessment of efficiency of area agencies on aging in Virginia through data envelopment analysis'. *The Gerontologist* 34: 363–70.

Paasche, H. 1874. 'Ueber die Presentwicklung der letzen Jahre nach den Hamburger Börsennotirungen'. *Jahrbücher für Nationalökonomie und Statistik* 23: 168–78.

Parkin, D. and Hollingsworth, B. 1997. 'Measuring production efficiency of acute hospitals in Scotland, 1991–94: validity issues in data envelopment analysis'. *Applied Economics* 29: 1425–33.

Paul, C. J. M., Johnston, W. E. and Frengley, G. A. G. 2000. 'Efficiency in New Zealand sheep and beef farming: the impacts of regulatory reform'. *Review of Economics and Statistics* 82: 325–37.

Pedraja-Chaparro, F., Salinas-Jiménez, J. and Smith, P. C. 1997. 'On the role of weight restrictions in data envelopment analysis'. *Journal of Productivity Analysis* 8: 215–30.

1999. 'On the quality of the data envelopment analysis model'. *Journal of the Operational Research Society* 50: 636–44.

Pindyck, R. S. and Rubinfeld, D. L. 1991. *Econometric Models and Economic Forecasts*. New York: McGraw-Hill.

Pitt, M. M. and Lee, L. F. 1981. 'The measurement and sources of technical efficiency in the Indonesian weaving industry'. *Journal of Development Economics* 9: 43–64.

Polachek, S. and Yoon, B. 1996. 'Panel estimates of a two-tiered earnings frontier'. *Journal of Applied Econometrics* 11: 169–78.

Puig-Junoy, J. 1998a. 'Measuring health production performance in the OECD'. *Applied Economics Letters* 5: 255–9.

    1998b. 'Technical efficiency in the clinical management of critically ill patients'. *Health Economics* 7: 263–77.

Resti, A. 1997. 'Evaluating the cost-efficiency of the Italian banking system: what can be learned from the joint application of parametric and non-parametric techniques'. *Journal of Banking and Finance* 21: 221–50.

Rice, N. and Jones, A. 1997. 'Multilevel models and health economics'. *Health Economics* 6: 561–75.

Roll, Y., Cook, W. and Golany, B. 1991. 'Controlling factor weights in data envelopment analysis'. *IEEE Transactions* 23: 2–9.

Rosko, M. D. 2001. 'Cost efficiency of US hospitals: a stochastic frontier approach'. *Health Economics* 10: 539–51.

Ryan, M., Scott, D. A., Reeves, C., Bate, A., van Teijlingen, E., Russell, E. M., Napper, M. and Robb, C. M. 2001. 'Eliciting public preferences for healthcare: a systematic review of techniques'. *Health Technology Assessment* 5(5): 1–4.

Salinas-Jiménez, J., Pedraja-Chaparro, F. and Smith, P. C. 2003. 'Evaluating the introduction of a quasi-market in community care: assessment of a Malmquist index approach'. *Socio-Economic Planning Sciences* 37: 1–13.

Scheel, H. 2001. 'Undesirable outputs in efficiency valuations'. *European Journal of Operational Research* 132: 400–10.

Schleifer, A. 1985. 'A theory of yardstick competition'. *Rand Journal of Economics* 16: 319–27.

Schmidt, P. 1985. 'Frontier production functions'. *Econometric Reviews* 4: 289–328.

Schmidt, P. and Lin, T. 1984. 'Simple tests of alternative specifications in stochastic frontier models'. *Journal of Econometrics* 24: 349–61.

Schmidt, P. and Lovell, C. A. K. 1980. 'Estimating stochastic production and cost frontiers when technical and allocative inefficiency are correlated'. *Journal of Econometrics* 13: 83–100.

Schmidt, P. and Sickles, R. C. 1984. 'Production frontiers and panel data'. *Journal of Business and Economic Studies* 2: 299–326.

Shephard, R. W. 1970. *Theory of Cost and Production Functions*. Princeton: Princeton University Press.

Simar, L. and Wilson, P. W. 2004. 'Estimation and inference in two-stage, semi-parametric models of production processes'. Discussion Paper. 0307, Institut de Statistique, Université Catholique de Louvain.

Skinner, J. 1994. 'What do stochastic frontier cost functions tell us about inefficiency?' *Journal of Health Economics* 13: 323–8.

Smith, P. C. 1997. 'Model misspecification in data envelopment analysis'. *Annals of Operations Research* 73: 233–52.

2002. *Measuring Up: Improving Health System Performance in OECD Countries*. Paris: OECD.

2003. 'Formula funding of public services: an economic analysis'. *Oxford Review of Economic Policy* 19: 301–22.

Smith, P. C. and Street, A. 2005. 'Measuring the efficiency of public services: the limits of analysis'. *Journal of the Royal Statistical Society*, Series A, 168: 401–17.

Smith, P. C., Rice, N. and Carr-Hill, R. 2001. 'Capitation funding in the public sector'. *Journal of the Royal Statistical Society*, Series A, 164: 217–41.

Smith, V. K. 1981. 'Elasticities of substitution for a regulated cost function'. *Economic Letters* 7: 215–19.

Söderlund, N. and van der Merwe, R. 1999. ' Hospital benchmarking analysis and the derivation of cost indices'. Discussion Paper 178, Centre for Health Economics, University of York.

Söderlund, N., Milne, R., Gray, A. and Raftery, J. 1995. 'Differences in hospital case mix, and the relationship between case mix and hospital costs'. *Journal of Public Health and Medicine* 17: 25–32.

Sommersguter-Reichmann, M. 2000. 'The impact of the Austrian hospital financing reform on hospital productivity: empirical evidence on efficiency and technology changes using a non-parametric input-based Malmquist approach'. *Health Care Management Science* 3: 309–21.

Stevenson, R. F. 1980. 'Likelihood functions for generalized stochastic frontier estimation'. *Journal of Econometrics* 13: 57–66.

Stone, M. 2002. 'How not to measure the efficiency of public services (and how one might)'. *Journal of the Royal Statistical Society*, Series A, 165: 405–34.

Street, A. 2003. 'How much confidence should we place in efficiency estimates?' *Health Economics* 12: 895–907.

Street, A. and Dawson, D. 2002. 'Costing hospital activity: the experience with healthcare resource groups in England'. *European Journal of Health Economics* 3: 3–9.

Tambour, M. 1997. 'The impact of health care policy initiatives on productivity'. *Health Economics* 6: 57–70.

Thanassoulis, E. 1993. 'A comparison of regression analysis and data envelopment analysis as alternative methods for performance assessments'. *Journal of the Operational Research Society* 44: 1129–44.

2001. *Introduction to the Theory and Application of Data Envelopment Analysis: A Foundation Text with Integrated Software.* Dordrecht: Kluwer Academic Publishers.

Thompson, R. G., Langemeier, L. N., Lee, C. T. and Thrall, R. M. 1990. 'The role of multiplier bounds in efficiency analysis with application to Kansas farming'. *Journal of Econometrics* 46: 93–108.

Timmer, C. P. 1971. 'Using a probabilistic frontier production function to measure technical efficiency'. *Journal of Political Economy* 79: 776–94.

Tofallis, C. 2001. 'Combining two approaches to efficiency assessment'. *Journal of the Operational Research Society* 52: 1225–31.

Torgerson, A. M., Forsund, F. R. and Kittelesen, S. A. C. 1996. 'Slack-adjusted efficiency measures and ranking of efficient units'. *Journal of Productivity Analysis* 7: 379–98.

Törnqvist, L. 1936. 'The Bank of Finland's consumption price index'. *Bank of Finland Monthly Bulletin* 10: 1–8.

Üstün, T. B., Chatterji, S., Mechbal, A. Murray, C. J. L. and WHS Collaborating Groups. 2003. 'The World Health Surveys', in Murray, C. J. L. and Evans, D. B. (eds.), *Health Systems Performance Assessment: Debates, Methods and Empiricism.* Geneva: World Health Organization.

Varian, H. R. 1978. *Microeconomic Analysis.* New York: W. W. Norton.

Vitaliano, D. F. 1987. 'On the estimation of hospital cost functions'. *Journal of Health Economics* 6: 305–18.

Wagstaff, A. 1989. 'Estimating efficiency in the hospital sector: a comparison of three statistical cost frontier models'. *Applied Economics* 21: 659–72.

Ware, J. E. and Sherbourne, C. D. 1992. 'The MOS 36-item Short Form Health Status Survey (SF-36)'. *Medical Care* 30: 473–83.

White, H. A. 1980. 'A heteroskedasticity-consistent covariance matrix estimator and a direct test for heteroskedasticity'. *Econometrica* 84: 817–30.

Williams, A. 2001. 'Science or marketing at WHO? A commentary on "World Health 2000"'. *Health Economics* 10: 93–100.

Williamson, O. E. 1973. 'Markets and hierarchies: some elementary considerations'. *American Economic Association* 63: 316–34.

Wong, Y. H. B. and Beasley, J. E. 1990. 'Restricting weight flexibility in data envelopment analysis'. *Journal of the Operational Research Society* 41: 829–35.

World Health Organization 2000. *World Health Report 2000.* Geneva: WHO.

2001. *Report of the Scientific Peer Review Group on Health Systems Performance Assessment.* Geneva: WHO.

Yang, M., Goldstein, H., Browne, W. and Woodhouse, G. 2002. 'Multi-variate multilevel analyses of examination results'. *Journal of the Royal Statistical Society*, Series A, 165: 137–46.

Zellner, A. 1962. 'An efficient method of estimating seemingly unrelated regressions and tests of aggregation bias'. *Journal of the American Statistical Association* 57: 500–79.

Zhao, Y., Guthridge, S., Magnus, A. and Vos, T. 2004. 'The burden of disease and injury in Aboriginal and non-Aboriginal populations in the Northern Territory'. *Medical Journal of Australia* 180: 498–502.

Zuckerman, S., Hadley, J. and Lezzoni, L. I. 1994. 'Measuring hospital efficiency with frontier cost functions'. *Journal of Health Economics* 13: 255–80.

Author index

233

Subject index